Thirty Thousand Years

of

Loneliness

Thirty Thousand Years

of

Loneliness

The Evolutionary Aspect

of

Being Human

Joachim R. von der Heydt

Dedicated to

Bodo von Wedel, Dr.jur.,

my granduncle,

who tried to convert an apolitical scientist,

but failed,

and

Magda von der Heydt-Coca, Dr.phil.,

my wife,

who succeeded.

CONTENTS

PROLOGUE

Sapiens is now the only species in the genus Homo, but several Homo species lived during the last million years, and not so long ago three others besides Homo sapiens still roamed the earth. But no trace of them could be found from the last 30,000 years. When Sapiens expanded across the world, the others disappeared. Should we be concerned today about our evolutionary heritage? The world has become more civilized since Genghis Khan devastated countries and wiped-out entire civilizations in the 12th century. Having science and enlightenment, we place our hopes on the progress of civilization. But a country considered one of the most civilized, Germany, produced the Holocaust. The 20th century saw 38 genocides, and the young 21st already three. The U.S. has been the idol of egalitarian democracy, but now we discover with horror that many Americans despise democracy. Outbreaks of racism and hate in a Christian society?

This book is an attempt to understand human society by looking at evolution. What made us humans special is the inheritance that evolution created since the human and chimpanzee lines diverged. Just by looking at what is typically human, we recognize many peculiar human traits of behavior that must have an inheritable component. Like the ability to balance on two legs, which requires sophisticated computations. The brain must sense the direction where the gravity vector will be pointing in the next moment and plan for a step that will bring a foot to where the vector points on the ground. To every engineer it is clear that this requires elaborate computations and there must be a structure in the brain that can do that. It would be ridiculous to think that parents can instruct their one-year-old child how to perform these computations, or that an infant is able to learn them by watching people walking.

The basic structure for these computations must be inherited. A similar argument holds for the ability to learn and use a language. Also the way we behave as parents, which is strikingly different from all the apes, is based on inherited programs. And inherited generally means, there are evolutionary roots.

The one conclusion from Darwin's theory, that the brain too is a product of evolution, and therefore mental faculties are also to some extent inheritable, has met fierce resistance. Many people reject this conclusion as "biological determinism" because inheritability has been ideologically interpreted to imply that intellectual capabilities differ between people by nature, an argument invariably used to justify racism.

But rejecting the inheritability of mental faculties as a license for racism we reject the insight that it is that very inheritance what creates racism because among the genes that enabled Homo sapiens to prevail over its competitor hominids are genes that produce aggression and the psychology of "us" and "them" which creates loyalty and patriotism but also xenophobia and racism. It instills existential fears in "us" and hate against "them."

Of course, we have also other social genes which are the basis of compassion, responsibility, sense of fairness, and moral intuition. Most of us share these traits, and they produce very strong feelings, like the love to our children and parents. But, despite their ubiquity and strength, they can be drowned out in society by those aggressive traits. The reason for this paradox, I argue, is that the mechanisms of the altruistic traits are strong only in the near-field, the family and face-to-face society, whereas the mechanisms of the aggressive competitive traits have far-field action, the ability to move crowds.

The aggressive-competitive inheritance can become a danger for democracy when the democratic institutions have flaws that enable an aggressive minority to grab power. That happened to the Weimar Republic in Germany when the polarization between extreme Left and extreme Right paralyzed the parliament, helping the Nazi party to seize power without being legitimized by a majority of votes of the people. It can happen in the U.S. because the two-party system allows an aggressive racist minority to control one of the parties.

Present political debates blame political extremism and racial prejudice on a lack of public awareness, or a biased media culture, demanding better education and public consciousness. Germany is trying to educate the public through schools and the media and by memorials about the Nazi crimes to keep the memory alive. Authors in the U.S. are decrying a lack of consciousness about the crimes of the slave society and the continuing racial discrimination, trying to awake memories and educate. I am worried that education and memories alone are not enough. That they cannot come up against the power of the 'evil genes' because the inheritable component of human behavior, even if it might be small, is always there, recreated whenever a baby is born, while education always needs to start from scratch.

Acknowledging the genetic component is not just a matter of science but has very practical consequences. The varied representation of the genes across people means that each trait has its distribution, and distributions have fringes of extreme over- and under-representation. Some people are overly aggressive, others less so, some are compassionate, others lack compassion. Sense of justice also varies between people. Democracy rests upon the assumption that most people have good moral intuition. Therefore, to make a moral state stable, it needs institutions that guarantee that laws and government honor the will of a majority of the people. Flaws of the institutions can enable a minority to create a state that ignores the will of the people. Variation of genes across people also means that not everybody is equally suited to become a police officer. Instead of luring candidates with the opportunity to defend authority and the honor of wearing the police badge, candidates should be tested and selected. And to be able to select, the community must offer attractive salaries. These are important practical implications. It is not good to ignore the inheritable component of the human mind.

I wrote this book in the hope that understanding the evolutionary roots of the human mind, including its dark side, will help us to identify the cracks in our civilization, to foresee dangerous developments and react in time. Trying to understand the biological roots of the human mind and society makes us realize that our genetic inheritance often contradicts our agreed-upon values. Nature has endowed us with the most complex organ on earth, the brain, but that does not mean we have to accept everything we are given as good. Fighting for goals like social justice, peace, and equal rights for women, is an up-hill battle. There may never be a definite victory where the enemy is not a bad tradition but an evil gene. As always, it is prudent not to underestimate the enemy.

TRYING TO UNDERSTAND

THE EVOLUTIONARY PERSPECTIVE

As a child I loved fables, not because of their morals (which were really the intent of their authors), but because in fables animals can talk. I think all children cherish the idea of talking animals. The famous children's books "The Wind in the Willows" and "Winnie the Pooh" tell stories of animals who are talking and thinking like humans; perhaps not quite like adults, but in a peculiar, enchanting way. Looking around at the other species on earth, isn't it strange how we are so different? Researchers have tried to teach animals to speak, or communicate in some way that is like speech, but not with much success. A shimmer of communication with 'the others', that's all there is. Being aware of our loneliness on this planet, we dream of intelligent beings on remote planets we might be able to communicate with.

Ever since Darwin published "The Descent of Man" we are torn between two feelings, one: biologically he is right; the other: he cannot be right because humans are so different from all other species. Not only that Homo sapiens walks and talks and uses tools and fire, which are certainly innovations of evolution that improved chance of survival, but there are other specifically human behaviors whose evolutionary values appear mysterious. Why do humans weep and laugh? Why is the beautiful sex in humans the female, whereas in other species the males wear the beautiful plumage? Why do all cultures have the institution of marriage? Why do we love our children and grandchildren and cherish our friends, but go to war and brutally kill each other?

Hominids have been thriving on earth for millions of years. Fossils indicate that 'Homo erectus'[1] emerged in Africa about two million years ago, and there is firm evidence that they have used stone tools and fire for more than a million years. As vast as this timespan may seem, two million years is short considering that simians, the monkey ancestors of apes and humans, thrived already 60 million years ago. Continental drifts divided the simian families into new- and old-world species that could not cross-bread for the last 35 million years. Nevertheless, today's new- and old-world monkeys are surprisingly similar, indicating that the ancient monkeys of that time were much like present-day monkeys. The great apes emerged about 15-20 million years ago. On that background, the appearance of Homo erectus marks the beginning of a recent development.

Apparently, Homo erectus was a success story: paleontologists speculate that several species of them lived at the same time for hundreds of millennia, one of them being our ancestors. For sure we know that four homo species still roamed the earth 60 thousand years ago, Homo sapiens and three others. And one of them, the Neanderthal, might have had language. But 30 thousand years ago, it seems, those others had all disappeared.

We do not know much about people like Homo erectus, except that they could fabricate stone tools for spear points, for butchering animals and many other purposes, and that they used fire and ate cooked food. And they lived in groups and had a society (as do the apes). While some scientists have argued that the use of fire enabled those hominids to eat cooked food which allowed them to consume more calories and, as a result, to develop larger brains, the order of causation may well have been the reverse: once brains had developed that provided the intelligence for the use of tools and the control of fire – fire that all other animals flee in panic – this was a breakthrough that set a fantastic development in motion. The new intelligence was an immediate advantage in the struggle for survival and henceforth intelligence was a factor in evolution. There was of course intelligence before, such as highly sophisticated visual and auditory processing as can be seen in present-day monkeys, but that intelligence just served the immediate requirements in foraging and escaping predators; it was only a faculty of limited value in addition to having keen senses and being able to move fast. But the use of tools for hunting and the use of fire to prepare food and scare off dangerous predators were huge advantages, creating an

---

1 The term 'Homo erectus' (from Latin *erectus* = upright) designates the first recognizable members of the genus Homo. However, ape-like species that walked upright appeared long before H erectus. More details will be given below.

enormous evolutionary pressure that must have suddenly sped up brain development. Indeed, the volume of the brains has been increasing steadily from early Homo erectus to Homo sapiens.

Years before present

6 million	Chimpanzee and human lines split
3.6 million	Footprints of bipedally walking hominids
~2 million	Homo erectus, human-like fossils
~1 million	Early migrations out of Africa
~300,000	Homo sapiens originates in Africa
~70,000	Homo sapiens appears in Eurasia
60,000	4 Homo species still share Eurasia
30,000	No other Homo species besides Sapiens

Table 1. Dates of human origin

This development of the brain is the great mystery of human existence. How is it possible that a brain that began to give its owner the ability to kindle fire and throw spears a million years ago evolved into a brain that created relativity theory and the nuclear bomb? The human brain is so incredibly powerful even compared to modern computers that the term 'artificial intelligence' seems like a joke to me. We can run, climb mountains, ride bicycles and steer jet planes; we can remember and recognize thousands of faces and interpret patterns of sound in which a human voice is drowned in the noise of an airplane. A baseball batter can hit a ball that approaches at a speed of 100 km/s, but the neurons that signal the ball's path and control his movement only signal at a pace of *milliseconds*, compared to the *nanosecond* pace of transistors in today's computers. That is, the brain is constructed of elements that are a million times slower than those of the computer. Computers can handle amounts of data that dwarf the brain's capacity by far. But still, a computer-driven car steers its owner into a truck blocking the road because the artificial intelligence interprets the truck as a piece of sky (true, computers are always alert, are not distracted and don't get tired). In dealing with the automatic functions of my car and struggling with the speech recognition of phone systems I don't feel like being immersed in artificial intelligence, but rather like surrounded by artificial morons.

Compared to the brains of other living creatures on earth, the human brain is a monster. It has come to dominate an entire planet, driving other species to extinction at a dizzying speed. Crown of creation, plague of the planet. Where does this monster come from? What is its true nature and why does it behave as it does?

This book is a plea for a rational understanding of human nature. Not that we should be rational in general. But looking at ourselves we need a rational view. We cannot solve the mounting problems of humanity without a true understanding of our nature. We cannot simply trust our constitutions, laws, and values – we need to understand. For a gardener it is not enough to water the plants according to the rule, she/he must also know where sun and shade are in the garden, and where the slopes, and understand that water flows down so that plants on a slope need more water than the same kinds of plant at the bottom. The problems we face today are big, and the problems our grandchildren will face are huge; it is uncertain if they can be solved at all, but there is no hope if we do not try to understand human nature.

How Can We Understand The Human Mind?

A rational understanding of the human mind has been attempted many times in history but was always abandoned too soon. The struggle for rational understanding reminds me of Grimm's tale "*Tischlein deck dich* (The wishing table)" in which a tailor has three sons and a beloved goat whose milk had helped to feed the family. So he asks his sons to graze their goat. First, he entrusts the precious goat to the eldest, instructing him to take care that the goat finds the best herbs. The son takes the goat out as the father told him, and after the goat had been grazing all day, he asks her if she is satisfied, upon which she replies "I'm so full, I cannot eat one leaf more"; and so the son takes her home. The father asks his son, if the goat ate well, which the son affirms, but he wants to check it himself and goes to the stable and asks the goat if she was satisfied. But the goat replies: "How could I be satisfied, I only jumped about the little creek and found not a single leaf." The father gets angry, scolds the son a liar and beats him until he runs out of the house. The same repeats with the other sons; each tries his best to satisfy the goat, the goat says, "I'm so full, I cannot eat one leaf more", but back home, she tells the father, "How could I be satisfied, I only jumped about the little creek and found not a single leaf," and the father gets angry. At the end, after having kicked out his three sons he takes the goat out himself, and when the same happens to him, he finally realizes that the goat is a liar and chases her away; he sees his mistakes and grieves. This is only the beginning of the story; the three sons finally return home to their father after completing their apprenticeships, each with a present of magical power. But so far, I think, the story resembles the history of the attempts to understand human nature. While the reports by the sons were truthful, the Zeitgeist, the "spirit of the time," rejected them.

(1)

The first son was the Enlightenment, when the idea of free rational thinking first emerged in modern history. Following the promise of science to provide a universal method of explaining the world, it seemed possible for the first time to rationally understand nature and the universe without the hypothesis of God. Both Hume and Kant argued convincingly that clarity of thought can tell us what we can know and what we cannot know. Both argued that it is possible to understand rationally not only the laws of the inanimate nature, but also our human condition: that we are endowed with *Vernunft* (reason) that enables us to see what is true and false, and what is moral and immoral. Traditional tenets like proofs for God's existence and the immortality of the soul were relegated to the realm of the irrational, imagination, and hope. Hume argued that all our knowledge is ultimately based on experience and logical reasoning, but his contemporaries were appalled by the bare logic of his arguments.

In contrast, Kant, who was certainly influenced by Hume's Treatise, argued that there is also truth beyond experience and reasoning, and he called this 'metaphysics'. He had strong arguments for a metaphysical basis of both, knowledge and ethics. In both cases, his arguments were ultimately based on the nature of the human mind which determines the conditions of perception, reasoning, and judgment. The axioms of geometry can be derived neither from experience nor from logical reasoning; we know that the shortest connection between two points is a straight line because we cannot imagine otherwise. Thus, according to Kant, our knowledge comprises more than what we learn from experience. And, similarly, our ethical judgments are not derived from experience, but are based on our innate knowledge of good and evil, and our free will to attempt the good; and any system of laws is bound by this knowledge. Importantly, Kant was not atheist. He only clarified our limits of knowledge, the border between knowing and believing.

Hume's and Kant's arguments were widely recognized by scholars at their time. But then, the voice of the goat was heard: "That is not enough, how can we be satisfied with a rational understanding? How can we understand human passion, joy, love, and art? Our desires, our insatiable longing for the ideal, the impossible, strive for eternal truth? Our sense of justice? The divine in human nature. For all this, the explanation must be God. *"Brüder über'm Sternenzelt muss ein lieber Vater wohnen* (Brothers, above the starry canopy there must dwell a loving Father)."[2] In the end, neither Hume's nor Kant's contemporaries were ready to accept a world view without *a proof* of God's existence.

Hume and Kant conceived their philosophical systems to include the sciences and psychology (Kant even made important contributions to science, such as a hypothesis about the origin of the solar system, still accepted today, that explains the peculiar fact that the orbits of the planets all lie essentially in one plane, and that they all orbit in the same sense – towards east). While both Hume and Kant presented convincing arguments that were as rational as those of science, subsequent scholars *proclaimed* their philosophies, trying to persuade rather than convince the reader. In essence they abandoned the claim of an inclusive philosophy, either excluding the natural sciences, or proposing a hierarchy in which the Geist (spirit) dominated both the thoughts and the natural phenomena. This led to a nuisance scission between '*Geisteswissenschaften*' and '*Naturwissenschaften*' ('humanities' versus 'sciences') which still dominates the academics today, especially in Germany. Now, which of the two resorts would harbor the attempts to understand the human mind? This is obviously a tricky question. First thought: the humanities of course. It's all about the *Geist*. But what about psychology? Much of Hume's and Kant's arguments were actually rooted in psychology. Kant invoked the *Vernunft*; he also carefully distinguished perception, the result of sensory input, from *Vorstellung*, the mental representation. Moreover, the 19th century saw the birth of a new discipline, 'psychophysics' (a term coined by Gustav Fechner) which explicitly resides in the sciences: one of Fechner's achievements was to demonstrate that perceived intensity can be described well by a logarithmic law. Since then, experimental psychology considers itself a science. Thus, the new scission of philosophy (new because neither the Greeks nor the thinkers of the Enlightenment would have agreed to split knowledge into two separate domains) led to a serious problem of philosophy. Understanding human nature, which is clearly the most important issue of philosophy, became, and still is, the business of two competing scholarly disciplines.

(2)

A world view without God was unthinkable for Hume's and Kant's contemporaries. But in the 19th century the Zeitgeist turned atheist, and for many scientists God was no longer an acceptable explanation for human nature. So, when Darwin's evolutionary theory was published it was quickly and widely accepted; the new theory gradually supplanted God in explaining many aspects

---

[2] From Friedrich Schiller, Ode to Joy

of human nature. This was the second son who set out to graze the goat; and indeed, he guided her to a veritable abundance of delicious herbs. The new theory provided a consistent and extremely parsimonious account of how the fantastic variety of species had evolved, including a myriad known only from fossils. It was the dawn of a new era of biology. And it also projected an entirely new and surprising picture of where the human comes from. But, again, the goat was not content: "How can I be satisfied with evolutionary roots; what is important is destiny!" The idea of evolution by selection made its impact, and soon scholars and philosophers began to expand this idea beyond biology. Can we not steer our evolution? We should be able to improve the human race! Are "we" not superior to "the others"? Evolution is competition, survival of the fittest! – It seems that Darwin's theory had opened Pandora's Box.

Although Darwin did not know how inheritance works (he was not aware of Gregor Mendel's groundbreaking discovery of the rules of heredity, and nobody knew what might be its code and the mechanism of its variation which is one cornerstone of Darwin's theory) he already speculated about inheritance of human character traits and the possibility that the high rate of proliferation of the working class might endanger the achievements of civilization (his main concern certainly being the British civilization).

Darwin's theory of evolution had an enormous impact beyond the realm of biology. Its philosophical expansion is perhaps the most disastrous error in human thinking. Not only did "The Descent of Man" meet furious resistance among religiously minded people, it also stimulated the fantasy of less religious people, leading to the Eugenics movement and its despicable results. The deliberate, officially sanctioned assassinations of victims on medical or psychological pretexts in Nazi Germany had their roots in the idea of evolution.

Darwin's biological theory was misinterpreted. It influenced even thinkers who did not understand the underlying science at all. Perhaps the most influential misunderstanding is represented by Nietzsche's philosophy. His "Zarathustra" deplores the mentality of the "last men" who live narrowly concerned with the present and do not "throw goals ahead." He preaches them the *Übermensch* (overman) as an idol, suggesting that striving for it will make humans stronger and eventually able to reach the idol. If evolution created humans, we should be able to ascend to higher levels if we only have the resolve to do it. The will has magic powers and can eventually create the *Übermensch*! (The idea of a magic change by will was obviously borrowed from Schopenhauer who argued that will is inherent, to various degrees, not only in Man, but in all things, even the inanimate, and that will is the cause of all changes.)

Coming from a deeply religious Christian-Protestant family (his father had been a Lutheran minister), Nietzsche first opted for the study of theology. But at some point he turned atheist and spent the rest of his days trying to debunk the Christian religion and decry Christian moral values. His "Zarathustra" does not present any rational arguments; ironically, in trying to derogate religion Nietzsche appeals to religious feelings, using a language that is strikingly similar to the gospels of Jesus. "Zarathustra" reads more like a poem, and not at all like a philosophical treatise.

It is obvious that Nietzsche had little understanding, if any, of biological evolution. He certainly saw the impact that Darwin's "Descent of Man" made in Germany on scientists as well as the general public. And the claim that humans had evolved from apes inspired him to postulate that they must follow this path ahead to finally become the *Übermensch*:

> What is ape to Man? A laughing stock or painful embarrassment. And Man shall be that to overman: a laughing stock or painful embarrassment. You have made your way from worm to Man, and much in you is still worm. Once you were apes, and even now, too, Man is more ape than any ape... Man is a rope, tied between beast and overman—a rope over an abyss ... what is great in Man is that he is a bridge and not an end.[3]

Specifically, Zarathustra asks Man to renounce the Christian moral imperatives which are for the weak; becoming *Übermensch* they will be free to choose their moral values: the values of the strong. It is unclear what kind of being the *Übermensch* will be and how mankind can reach that state; what is clear is that the "Zarathustra" tries to replace traditional values by values that are, in part, fundamentally evil, such as denying compassion (*Mitleid*). This is also the message of Nietzsche's collection of aphorisms "Zur Genealogie der Moral (On the Genealogy of Morality)."

Confused as Nietzsche's writings are, the "Zarathustra" had enormous influence. It is known that in the First World War young Germans serving, and dying, in the trenches on the Western Front carried this little book with them like a bible. It seemed to help these young people to see meaning in a world that had apparently lost its meaning. The cataclysmic experience at the front was the primordial moment of the 20th century.

---

[3] From Friedrich Nietzsche „Also sprach Zarathustra. Ein Buch für Alle und Keinen" Schmeitzner, Chemnitz 1883. English "Thus Spoke Zarathustra: A Book for All and For None," translation RJ Hollingdale, New York: Penguin Classics (1961).

Assigning a divine role to evolution is a dreadful error in philosophy that still permeates modern thinking. It led to a fundamental misconception of evolution, even among less religious people: because evolution created humans and the divine in human nature, evolution must have a goal and must be ultimately good. Although this thought is not always expressed explicitly, it has penetrated our view of biology and how we see our place in nature. Struck in awe by the discoveries of the wonders of life on earth, it is hard not to fall into the trap of the prejudice that, what evolution created must be good. How often do we say, when in doubt whether some behavior is good or bad, "but that is natural," how often do we justify industrial products by qualifying them as "natural," or accept environmental changes caused by human activity because similar changes also occur "naturally." On the other hand, when we see obviously evil human behavior, we reject it as inhumane, something that cannot be human nature. "Of course" rape cannot be a natural form of human behavior. When concluding a study of human aggressive behavior, a geneticist discussed her results "tongue in cheek" as evidence for the existence of genetic code for an evil human trait. I find it remarkable that she found it necessary to add "tongue in cheek."

(3)

The third son led the goat to a marvelous and most diverse grazing ground. The goat was certainly full at the end of the day, although I don't know what it actually ate of all the choices. That is, I don't know how much of the new insights the public absorbed and was ready to accept.

In the first half of the 20th century the biological sciences saw fantastic progress in several fields that bear on the question of human evolution.

First, there was the discovery that genetic mutations could be studied in the laboratory. While peas chosen by Gregor Mendel to study the laws of inheritance, the fruit fly was the species of choice to study mutations. Not only could the occurrence of spontaneous mutations be observed, it was also found that the rate of mutations could be manipulated, it was accelerated when the flies were exposed to x-rays. These studies set the stage for a frantic search for the molecular code of inheritance. In the 1940ies the search led to an unsuspected candidate, a molecule that chemists before had rated as the most boring kind of molecule found in cells because it consisted of large numbers of only four kinds of small building blocks, a seemingly monotonous accumulation like a wall constructed of bricks of four colors. But it turned out that this class of molecules, the deoxyribonucleic acid (DNA) are the scrolls on which the genetic code is written. This discovery of course led to the deciphering of the code which is well known today as 'sequencing' which results in a map called the 'genome'. One of the important results is the possibility to compare our genome, the one of Homo sapiens, with those of other primates, specifically the apes. It also became possible to compare the genomes within the human population and determine how it varies between individuals, between the major races and between populations in different parts of the world. Today everybody can obtain for a little money the information where her or his ancestors likely came from and of which races they were.

A second field of science that made progress that interests us here was paleontology. As more and more ancient bones were found and could be dated with improved methods, a detailed picture of human evolution emerged. For example, it turned out that not so long ago several human species roamed on earth, not just Homo sapiens. The first indication of this was of course the discovery of a skull in Neanderthal in the 19th century, which looked human, but was quite different from the skulls of the 'Cro-Magnon' and modern humans. For a while the possibility was discussed that the Neanderthal might be our ancestor, but when researchers found bones of two clearly different species, Neanderthal bones and bones of modern-type humans, in the same region (of Palestine) and in the same layer of sediments, it became clear that the two species of humans had lived there at the same time, and that the Neanderthal could not be our ancestor. Another important find was the discovery of paintings of animals of exquisite quality and beauty first in Altamira, and more recently in the Chauvet cave, the oldest of which date about 30 thousand years ago. These paintings are remarkable for their realistic quality of representation, depictions of animals featuring sophisticated pictorial cues such as 3-D rendering by shading near the contours and arrangement of groups of animals partially occluding one another with corresponding variation of size, the occluded figures being depicted as smaller than the occluding figures. Although of high artistic quality, the caves were probably not art galleries. Most likely they were a place of ceremonial gatherings, indicating that their visitors were in some way religious.

The discovery of the cave paintings and other pieces of art that date from the time when more than one homo species had lived simultaneously raised the question of who the artists were. Until recently research had indicated that all pieces of art found were from Homo sapiens, review papers maintaining that there was not one piece that had been attributed to Neanderthals. But that changed in 2018 when a team of researchers applied a new technique that allows dating of art painted on walls of carbonate rock.[4] The method determines the age of carbonate outcrops that form on top of the paintings. Because these precipitations are younger than the painting, their dating provides a minimum age of the paintings. They investigated three Spanish caves that contain large numbers of paintings and engravings in a vast array of forms, including hand stencils and prints, geometric shapes, and figurative representations of animals, including horses, deer, and birds. The results showed that these paintings are older than 64.8 thousand years, which predates the arrival of Homo sapiens in Iberia by at least 20 thousand years. Thus, we now know that besides Sapiens, the Neanderthal also created art and was capable of producing symbolic representations.

A third field where progress was made was the biology of animal behavior, a new science called ethology. Ethologists demonstrated that some types of animal behavior are the result of evolutionary adaptation and must therefore be inheritable. In an enlightening experiment Konrad Lorenz showed that even some complex patterns of behavior are apparently preprogrammed. After hatching, pigeons develop the ability to fly without any training or prior experience. Revolutionary was also the discovery of communication in insects by Karl von Frisch who observed that the individual bee communicates to companion bees the direction of rich resources of food by a dance-like pattern of walking in the hive. Perhaps the most miraculous phenomenon of insect inherited behavior is the migration of Monarch butterflies which, starting from their winter quarters in Mexico, travel thousands of kilometers through North America to eventually return to the same location in Mexico. The twist is that this journey takes three generations of butterflies, each including deposition of eggs and hatching of larvae that wrap themselves in cocoons and eventually metamorphose into butterflies! This three-generation journey means that their little brains (insect brains have only a few hundred thousand neurons – compared to hundreds of millions to many billions in mammalian brains) can hold navigation plans for the three different legs of flight, and somehow, they can activate the appropriate plan in each of the three consecutive generations.

Inheritance of behaviors was of course known before; in the 19th century the term 'instinct' was coined for this phenomenon. However, scholars quickly asserted that human behavior is the exception (hear the goat!) and still today one can often hear and read that humans have fewer instincts than animals, an

---

[4] D.L. Hoffmann et al., "U-Th dating of carbonate crusts reveals Neandertal origin of Iberian cave art." Science 359, 912–915, 2018.

opinion that I will try to correct later on; the opposite is probably closer to the truth.

Patterns of behavior observed in animals are often misinterpreted as learned rather than genetic, like in the example of birds beginning to fly mentioned above. I used to walk by a little lake in one of Baltimore's parks, where I can often see dozens of turtles sunbathing on logs that stick out of the water. Usually I just hear them plunge into the water because they respond with flight to the appearance of a human, like all animals in the wild. Now, what is interesting is that the young and the old turtles jump at different times. One might expect the old turtles to jump first, leading the young ones, because they have the experience. In fact it's the opposite, the young turtles plunge first, then the old ones, and some of the oldest turtles even have the nerves to stay rather than give up the warm sun. Obviously experience matters, but in the reverse: all turtles are born with a flight instinct, but when they get older, with the experience of park visitors not hunting them, the instinct weakens, it 'habituates.'

The amazing discoveries in the first half of the 20th century paved the way for a rational understanding of human nature which, however, did not take place. We can now read our genetic code, we can see in some cases how genes correlate with behavior, as in the examples of face recognition and the ability to learn to read. Paleontology discovered where our ancestors came from, how they diverged from other related humans, and when our last human relatives disappeared. We know the time spans of evolution: when Homo erectus emerged, and when Homo neanderthalensis and Homo sapiens, and we can at least imagine fairly realistically their environment and how they lived and managed to survive and thrive. We know that the human brain developed, that mutations took place that created and modified mechanisms of motivation and behavior, and intelligence, – and we know, at least roughly, the conditions of selection that drove the changes. The human brain, as we study it today, is the result of this process. All this knowledge is close to grasp, rational understanding seems around the corner, but, strangely enough, it did not happen. We are still content with the complacent subjective picture that we have of ourselves.

So, when the third son came back with the goat from those wonderful grazing grounds, the goat either lied to the father saying it was still hungry, or it had lied to the son saying it was satisfied, but in fact did not like the herbs and was frustrated and still yearning for true satisfaction. Those discoveries were made while the world was busy with two world wars and struggling with the infamous Nazi ideology that claimed that the question of good and evil was race, and that people of the "Arian race" must dominate the other people. In a naïve twist of the Darwinian idea of natural selection they proclaimed their war as the struggle for survival. In Hitler's words, if the German people could not win, they should perish.

When the world woke up from that nightmare the terrible error of expanding evolutionary theory beyond the realm of biology was finally generally recognized, albeit late. So it is understandable that ideas in the post-war era swayed in the other direction. Since racism was obviously evil, scholars concluded that one should not use the term race at all, and even that race distinctions do not really exist but are only a product of wrong education. Recently they went so far as to denounce the German *Grundgesetz* (Constitution of 1949) as politically incorrect because in article 3 it mentions race, saying that "Nobody should be disadvantaged or privileged because of their gender, their descent, their *race*, their language, their homeland and provenance, their belief, their religious or political convictions" (my translation). The critics want to correct the constitution, hoping that eliminating the word race will eliminate racism. This discussion took place as recently as 2019.

The critique of this constitution indicates a new round of confusion of ideas. The Constitution of 1949 was born in the spirit of renewal under the recent impression of the German disaster, when flaws in the previous (the 'Weimar') constitution were identified as causal to the catastrophic breakdown of the rule of law. It is in fact a great modern constitution that has so far proven to fulfill its function very well. The allergic reaction to the term 'race', one might think, is ok; after things went wrong on the previous course, steering the ship a little too much in the other direction might be appropriate. But intellectual confusions are never ok, and I think the tenet that there is no place for racism in the human mind, based on the assumption that every feat of human behavior is a product of environmental influence and education, is an error that is dangerous and makes us ill prepared for the problems we are facing today.

The American incarnation of the tailor's third son is the biologist-entomologist Edward O. Wilson. Whereas standard evolutionary theory maintains that the individual is the unit of selection, Wilson concluded from his studies of ants and other animals that kin selection can also be an important motor in evolution. In his book "Sociobiology: The New Synthesis" (1975) which he described as the "systematic study of the biological basis of all social behavior" he drew parallels between animal and human social behavior. Like the third son was surprised and disappointed by the response of the goat back in the stable, so was Wilson by the reaction of his fellow scientists who criticized him for promoting a "deterministic view of human society and human action." In the ensuing discussions he was even accused of racism, misogyny, and sympathy for eugenics.

Indeed, the second half of the 20th century saw a wave of rejection of Darwinism. Evolutionary theory was attacked on rational and irrational grounds. In fact, the wave of rejection hit science in general, calling into question its role in society. Scientists were blamed for creating the possibility to tap nuclear energy and for their naivety of believing they would be able to control the use of their achievements. Revealing the influence of ideology in human thinking, scholars disputed that any knowledge, even in science, could be objective. The result was a general turn to the irrational, towards religion and irrational philosophies. In West-Germany, the first government under the new constitution was Christian-Democrat, not Social-Democrat, despite the fact that the Christian churches had widely approved of, and supported Hitler, while Social Democrats had been persecuted and sent to concentration camps. The Zeitgeist turned to Existentialism and Neo-Marxism. Both dispute that human nature could be understood rationally based on science, or that it would even be beneficial to do so, denying traits of human social behavior that are not under the control of the mind, and affirming that any negative developments could be avoided by the right education, for example anti-authoritarian pedagogy. A new expression of the scission between humanities and sciences that had once stifled the Enlightenment.

Meanwhile, modern psychology had firmly established the existence of stereotypical brain mechanisms that are rigid, defying experience and conscious control. Much of the insight into the role of such brain mechanisms, especially in perception, came from discoveries made by the German Gestalt psychologists in the first three decades of the century who were then removed from chairs in the Universities under the Nazi regime and forced to emigrate. Ironically, in post-war Germany, their discoveries were ignored or rejected. Contrary to the evidence from psychology, ethology and brain sciences, the view that the brain is like a blank slate at birth on which experience and education would write their texts became the dominant doctrine.

To every biologist it is clear that behavioral traits result from two components, the influence of the genes and the influence of the individual experience. No biologist would question the importance of learning, especially in forming the human mind. In contrast, many people outside biology are convinced that the genes have no influence, and that environment and education do everything. These people then brand the inclusive view as "biological determinism."

Even now, half a century since the publication of "Sociobiology," rejection of the notion that genes contribute is common, although the scientific evidence is now overwhelming. Traditionally, the genetic influence was demonstrated by twin- and adoption studies. Twin studies compare how strongly behavioral parameters correlate between identical twins (which share their genes to 100%) and fraternal twins (which share only 50%), thus trying to measure the genetic component; adoption studies compare the behavioral similarity of siblings raised in the same family with the similarity of siblings raised in different families, thus trying to partial out the influence of the environment.

But recent advances in genetic science have made it possible to measure the influence of the genes directly. Across eons, mutations continuously alter a small proportion of the genes, with the result that each individual human has a slightly different set of genes (except identical twins whose genes are the same). Today it is possible to scan the entire genetic code of a person for mutations, reading out at each location the mutated piece of code; and by correlating the mutations with results from personality tests one can determine the influence of genetic information on behavioral traits.

Still, the public has taken little notice of the scientific progress, and ardent denial of the genetic component of the human mind is still widespread.

Biologists of course look at the whole picture of evolution, of which humans are a part, and relate human social behavior to animal social behavior. But for understanding the human mind, I argue, it is more important to see where humans differ from other species, even from their closest ape relatives. The two-parent family is strikingly different from the promiscuous society of chimpanzees and the dominant-male-and-harem society of gorillas. In fact, it is rare among mammals which generally task the mothers with raising the offspring, while the fathers contribute little more than their sperms.

When thinking about the evolutionary aspect of behavior I realized that many human behaviors seem to be produced by modular mechanisms that can be discerned by their patterns of associated emotions. That instinctive behaviors are linked to emotions has long been recognized by anthropologists, and, by inference, also in animals by ethologists. To see this, one only needs to observe the attempts of a one-year-old infant to stand up: the initial unrest and the urge to perform this task, and the happy smile – obvious satisfaction – after successfully executing the task. We have an urge to talk, and talking gives us pleasure, deprivation of talking makes unhappy and has been used for torture. The concomitant emotions point to the evolutionary roots of behaviors.

Human instinctive behaviors may be more complex that those of animals, but they are undoubtedly similar. I call those modular mechanisms 'engenes,' a contraction of 'engine' and 'gene,' assuming that they consist of brain mechanisms that each have their genetic basis.

But genetic basis does not mean stereotyped. Genetic information resides in a number of DNA strings, long molecules in the chromosomes that have the form of a double helix. The rungs of such a double helix are made up from two types of 'base pairs' which constitute the bits of genetic coding. The human genome consists of 6 billion rungs of base pairs, and about 99% of them are shared by all people, whereas, due to mutations, about 1% (60 million) vary across the population. Thus, the genomes differ from person to person; every baby comes to the world with a different set of engenes.

—

At this point I also need to explain what this book is not about. It is not about the question whether the character of an individual can be 'predicted' from her/his genes. Recent advances in medical genetics have made it possible to determine risks for certain heritable diseases based on the genetic code of an individual. One first correlates the mutations with the occurrence of certain diseases in a large sample of people ('genome wide association studies'). Then, one uses the resulting set of correlations to calculate for an individual person, based on her/his genome, the risk for developing any of those diseases. Thus, one first estimates how much each of the mutated code contributes on average, and then applies these estimates to an individual. The result is called the 'polygenic risk score'. To obtain reliable estimates, one needs data from hundreds of thousands of individuals, both healthy and affected by the diseases. More recently, psychologists have tried to derive 'polygenic risk scores' also for behavioral traits, where the 'risk' could be something negative, like the risk of developing a mental illness, or something positive, like intelligence. Some books would have you believe that with this method a person's achievements in school can be predicted from her/his genes (indeed, from birth; the genes do not change when a person grows up). Readers might even think that one could detect a predisposition for becoming a mass murderer.

But mental traits are only about 50% inheritable, the rest depends on individual development and experience, like upbringing, education, traumatic events, etc. As a result, predictions for an individual have limited reliability. I think there is no practical value in trying to predict Hitlers or Stalins or Maos, even if one had their full genetic codes. Rather, we must accept that behavioral traits vary between individuals not only because of their varied genes, but also because of variable realization of the genetic plan in the individual, a process that is virtually impossible to predict. Moreover, their ascent to power was only partly due to their characters, but depended also on other conditions and random incidents. Competition for the grip on power is a roulette; some are washed up by the tides of history.

In the individual, the influence of the genes is limited and predictions are uncertain; across millions, predictions are rock solid. There is no doubt about the influence on society of inheritable traits that are shared by millions of people. From the collective inheritance it is easy to see, for example, why so many people rather obey an authoritarian ruler than follow the rules of democracy. One can see why xenophobia and racism are so common all over the world.

Behavioral traits, like bodily traits, have their statistical distributions. Most people's height is about average, but some are unusually tall, others unusually small. These are the fringes of a normal distribution. The same is true of character traits like inclination towards depression, greed for power, the ability to feel compassion, or measures of intelligence. For each trait, there are people in which it is overly strong and others in which it is marginally weak. This book is not so much about the fringes as it is about the big mass in the center. The fringes are a statistical necessity, there is little one can do about them. What is important is to understand what produced the variation and what it means for the society. This book is not about the special qualities of the Hitlers, but about the qualities of the millions who follow them.

THE IRRATIONAL HUMAN MIND

There is no question that the human mind is irrational. Everybody knows these dramatic examples: people drink although they know very well it is ruining their life; people smoke knowing that it may lead to long painful illness and death; young women marry men they know have a tendency for violence; people who want more social justice elect strong leaders that trample it. Many traits of human nature do not seem to make sense. Watching a group of joking and giggling teenagers one might think that nature prepared them for a role in entertainment, not for the most serious of all possible roles in life, to procure offspring to secure the survival of their species.

Can we have a rational picture of our irrational mind? While the brain produces lots of irrational behavior, it can also be used for rational thinking, which was discovered already by the ancient Greek philosophers and rediscovered in the Enlightenment. As I will explain in more detail later, the world we see is not the physical world, but a product of our brain, and, although not based on rational thinking, it is perfectly useful for living. It enables us to plan our actions; it motivates us and gives us pleasure. As Kant noticed, we have no direct experience of 'the things themselves'; we can only perceive them through our senses. We perceive what our brain creates from the sensory input. With our modern education we may not realize that; we think the world we perceive is actually the physical world that we are taught in school. For example, taking a walk in a moonlit night the moon seems to follow us. When we were children we noticed that and were surprised; as adults we ignore it although we still perceive it the same, as the reader may verify at the next occasion. Of course, rationally we know that there is only one moon and it cannot follow everybody. We have learned the Copernican view of the universe (which is counterintuitive), accepting that the moon is actually far away and that its apparent following movement must be an illusion.

There are countless examples where intuitive contradicts rational insight, but that is not a practical problem, we live in the intuitive world, but look at it rationally when necessary. So, what I mean by 'irrational' are decisions and actions that are entirely based on intuition and emotion, without rational correction. Human behavior is mostly irrational, but it often needs to be checked and corrected by reasoning; that is the rational part. Looking at things rationally does not mean to exclude or suppress our intuitive view; it only means to append a note by reasoning. And we do this all the time.[5]

But do we want to look at ourselves rationally? We can deal with the illusions; they do not hinder us to think about the nature of the world rationally. So, why then is it so hard to think about our own nature rationally? – When thinking about the world that surrounds us, we just need to overcome our ignorance. But thinking about our own nature, we also need to overcome our prejudice and pride. Above, I recounted how human pride since the Enlightenment rejected the rational view time and again. So, the problem is not irrationality, but self-complacency. Having all kinds of irrational processing going on in our brains should not hinder us to obtain a rational picture of its nature; if we want to, we can have a rational view of our irrational mind.

---

[5] 'Irrational' is often used to mean mistaken or wrong, especially when people are arguing about someone's emotional decision, but that is a different usage. Perceptions and feelings cannot be mistaken or wrong; nobody can verify or falsify a perception or a feeling. Only rational statements can be true or false. I became aware that what I describe here as 'irrational' is part of what is known in psychology as 'System 1'. See Daniel Kahneman "Thinking, Fast and Slow", Macmillan 2011.

A common misunderstanding is that rationality abolishes the irrational, including emotions, passions, and spiritual experiences. Often a person is qualified as rational, meaning unemotional and cold. Many people think that science, trying to explain everything, will strip the world of its mysteries, leaving only the bare bones of mathematical descriptions without the flesh of emotions. I don't think so. Accepting the Copernican worldview does not make a sunset less romantic. If rational understanding abolished passion, then gynecologists would have no offspring, which, as far as I can see, is not true at all. I don't know what kind of science those people have in mind. The goal of science is not to explain everything, but to understand, and understanding here means to be able to predict the outcome of an experiment, predict the future from knowing the present situation. As every scientist knows, whenever science solves a mystery, new mysteries emerge that defy explanation by current understanding. There is no end to the mysteries, especially in brain science. It is true though, that rational thinking sometimes does conflict with our spiritual world. In my own experience it did change my religious beliefs. But that must not be so necessarily. In any case, we do not seem to have a choice; we can close our eyes, but we cannot stop thinking.

Being irrational is an important part of our character. The world that we perceive and in which we plan our actions is a genuine construction of the ancient brain; it is not the product of rational thinking. Our choices and actions are often irrational and idiosyncratic; irrational behavior is normal. But we must be aware of it. Paired with ordinary stupidity, irrational thinking can become the fertile ground on which vile leaders sow their crops. Like when people who venerate Jesus as the son of God and their savior, knowing that Jesus had a Jewish mother and therefore was undoubtedly Jewish (or a Half-Jew in their terms), and his disciples and the apostles all were Jews, when these people then believe that the Jewish race is detrimental and needs to be extinguished. The Holocaust and other genocides are not merely accidents in human history. I believe they are rooted in human nature. They are examples that strike us as exceptionally horrific. Other, less extreme examples of human behavior and social development are also worrisome, developments that have been attributed variously to accidental circumstances, historical reasons, wrong mindset, ideologies, or to the capitalist system.

Human society is based on human behavior which, of course, is rooted in human nature. I find it strange that theories of society tend to ignore the obvious, and hence deny any role of inherited traits in causing the problems human society is facing. Rather, the prevailing view is that human nature is divine and if there are problems, then negative influences of environment should be blamed, existing bad traditions, or wrong education. But we need to look in the mirror. We cannot just see the divine in Man and ignore its dark side.

Of course, we should not expect that rational understanding will solve the basic problems of human existence. Understanding the mechanisms of pain does not take the pain away. Or consider the choice of how we want to die. Most people, when asked, say that a sudden death is preferable to dying after long suffering. But when patients whose heart is failing are presented with the choice of having a pacemaker implanted or not, most of them choose the pacemaker, which takes away the sudden death option, but makes it likely that the heart increasingly fails to meet the metabolic demands of the body, leading to a protracted and physically agonizing death. Rational planning of one's own death conflicts with the fundamental innate drive to live. But such conflicts should not deter us from trying to obtain a rational view of ourselves. For one, I think, we cannot live in denial; once we learn and understand, there is no way back into the innocence of ignorance. Also, whether rational thinking can solve a problem may be uncertain, but that abstaining from rational thinking causes problems *is* certain.

Understanding human nature is a formidable task. It involves not only understanding the patterns of our behavior, and where they come from, we must also analyze our values, and where they come from, the values of family and society, of patriotism and religion. We feel strongly about good and evil, but unfortunately these feelings do not always agree with our accepted ethical laws. The people of Israel received commandments, one of which says you must not kill, but the young David promised to his King Saul to slay a hundred Philistines and brought him a hundred foreskins as proof. The people did not see that as evil. The English rejected slavery with moral disgust when pirates sold captured English seamen into slavery, but they accepted that millions of Africans were enslaved and shipped across the Atlantic like merchandise. They did not see that as evil.

I propose here to follow the path of Enlightenment and freely use the power of reasoning that was given to us, without cultural preconceptions and free of restrictions from extrinsic authorities. Compared with the situation two hundred years ago we are in a much better position given the wealth of knowledge we command. A true understanding of human nature means that we understand where those irrational traits come from. We then need to think about whether we can accept them as good or not. And that of course requires that we also understand the basis of moral judgments which, I argue, are likewise part of our human biological nature. We must understand what motivates us to act as we do, and why we feel something to be just or unjust, moral or immoral, as we do. Again, there is no principal problem in trying to understand this rationally.

But rational understanding in itself, of course, does not give us moral values. We need to choose our moral values, and this requires fundamentally irrational decisions. These are onerous decisions that no one can alleviate for us. This book is about understanding, not about the choice of values. I do not want to influence anyone's beliefs or values, but simply open eyes for how inheritable behavioral mechanisms influence society and politics.

Writing about the human mind inevitably evokes feelings of good and evil; most people feel that family values are good, racism is bad, etc. But the insight about the evolutionary origin of human behavior and values does not depend on our feelings. In science it is easy to see that truth does not depend on emotions, but writing about the human mind is difficult because it relies on the use of terms of common language that are already loaded with emotions. When I talk about 'evil genes' it is shorthand for inheritable traits that conflict with what we want to achieve. Qualifying something as 'good' or 'evil' depends on the definition of the goal, and in this book I assume the goal is to realize a free and just society as envisioned in the American Constitution.

I don't have a political agenda or recipe for happiness. This book is an essay trying to connect the dots. It's mainly based on well-known facts from biology and brain science illustrated with commonplace observations and personal anecdotes. Some parts may appear speculative. But recent findings of paleontology and paleogenetics seem to support my thoughts, and recent political developments seem to confirm my fears. To readers who find my statements objectionable I apologize. I hope they will still find my book entertaining and thought-provoking.

OUTLINE

I discuss human evolutionary inheritance in three parts: "Whence it came," "What it did," and "What can we learn." PART ONE provides the foundation for the analysis in Parts Two and Three. It consists of a brief explanation of the principles of the Darwinian theory of evolution with a collection of clarifying thoughts. The aim is to explain its most important points in a simple way that will be understandable to a broad audience.[6] Next I consider the specific

---

[6] Readers interested in the biology of evolution should turn to the work of authorities such as Edward O. Wilson; for the debate about the theory of evolution, see Ernst Mayr, "One Long Argument: Charles Darwin and the Genesis of Modern Evolutionary Thought"

conditions that drove the development of early hominid species after they split off from apes, specifically, the evolution of the human social brain. Based on the work of ethologists on the structure of instinctive behaviors of animals and what Lorenz calls the "grand parliament of the instincts" I argue that human behavior likewise is under the influence of a set of modular behavioral mechanisms that each have their genetic basis. The evolution of these 'engenes', specifically those that influence social behavior under the competitive conditions of early hominids, created the behavioral mechanisms that are the basis of human society. I show that evolutionary engenes account for a variety of human social behaviors, ranging from family life to the political and cultural spheres. A crucial point is that the strength of each engene has a statistical distribution; in a population of millions, one can thus find large numbers of individuals in which a particular engene is extremely strong and others in which it is extremely weak.

In PART TWO, I use these insights to explore some of the lowlights of recent human history that appear like inexplicable breakdowns of civilization. Looking at this history, recognizing the reproduction of the genetic factor across generations gives a pessimistic outlook. But further exploration also reveals engenes that stand like pillars supporting the edifice of a free and fair society – which gives hope.

In PART THREE, I draw conclusions that are relevant to contemporary politics and the fate of Western democracy.

Harvard University Press, 1993; Jerry A. Coyne, "Why Evolution Is True" Penguin, 2010; and Ian Tattersall, "Human Evolution" Cambridge University Press, 2022.

I.1 HOW EVOLUTION WORKS

The evolution I talk about in this book is the evolution of genetic inheritance. The term evolution is often applied broadly to all kinds of developmental processes; authors talk about cultural evolution, evolution of economic systems, evolution of democracy, evolution of music, evolution of ideas, cosmic evolution. All this has nothing to do with what I discuss here.

In a nutshell, Darwin's theory of evolution consists of two basic assumptions, natural selection, and random mutations. Mutations continuously produce random variants within each species, and natural selection preserves some of the variants and eliminates the others. While natural selection seems to make sense intuitively, the assumption that mutations are random is notoriously hard to accept. How can the complex design of an organism emerge by a random process? Or just a single organ like the eye? The eye consists of many components: the optics consisting of the corneal surface at the front and the lens inside, the ciliary muscle that allows the lens to contract so as to focus the image on the receptor surface, the retina, which in itself is a marvel of engineering. And this little camera can be rotated very fast and then held stable by three pairs of muscles corresponding to the three axes that a rigid body can rotate about. To build this perfectly functional piece of engineering obviously requires a huge number of individual decisions and adjustments that must be consistent with each other. Can this be achieved by flipping a coin for every decision? Even after millions of attempts, the chance of creating an eye would be close to zero because of the large number of decisions that need to be correct.

But the randomness of mutations, at first no more than Darwin's ingenious intuition, was confirmed beyond doubt once the molecular mechanisms of heredity were understood. The solution of the riddle was already given by Darwin himself:

Yet reason tells me, that if numerous gradations from a perfect and complex eye to one very imperfect and simple, each grade being useful to its possessor, can be shown to exist; if further, the eye does vary ever so slightly, and the variations be inherited, which is certainly the case; and if any variation or modification in the organ be ever useful to an animal under changing conditions of life, then the difficulty of believing that a perfect and complex eye could be formed by natural selection, though insuperable by our imagination, can hardly be considered real.[7]

In other words, what makes a difference is the continuous validity checking by the selection mechanisms after each new mutation. To understand this, perhaps it helps to imagine an apprentice crafting some artifact that requires, say, ten binary decisions to be made correctly. He does not know the correct answer to any of these, so he is just guessing at each step. Then, after making the ten decisions his chance of getting a useful artifact would be one in 1024 (1/2 to the 10th); that is, if he tried again and again a thousand times, he would likely have to discard the piece about a thousand times on average. However, if his master gave him feedback after each step, his chance of success would be much better, because, at each step, he has a 50 percent chance that his guess is right. He can then proceed to step two. If his first guess is wrong, he discards the piece and makes a new one. Now knowing the correct decision at step one, he can proceed to step two, and so on. If he prepares to make 11 pieces, he can be sure to finish one correct piece in the end (in the worst case, he will guess wrong in all ten decisions and discard the piece ten times). Thus, the count of pieces he must discard is only a number between 0 and 10. This is also how evolution works: natural selection is the master; mutations produce incremental variations, and each time, natural selection tests if the new variant improves fitness or not.

Vision is the most powerful of all the senses nature has created; at any point in space, the wave fronts of light carry an enormous amount of information. Being able to use some of it gives a species a huge advantage. Therefore, eyes are ubiquitous in the animal kingdom and appear quite early in evolution. According to fossils, animals with eyes appear already in the Cambrian period about 540 million years ago, long before the age of dinosaurs. Imagine the number of eyes evolution has tested since!

---

[7] Charles Darwin, "On the Origin of Species." London: John Murray, 1859. https://www.vliz.be/docs/Zeecijfers/Origin_of_Species.pdf, p 88. Accessed 15 Feb 2022

I need to emphasize here the enormity of the time spans of evolution which are truly "insuperable by our imagination." Life appeared about 4 billion years ago – four thousand times a million years. That is when evolution started. We often forget that life continued while the earth underwent dramatic changes. The migration of geese between India and Mongolia, crossing the Himalayas twice a year, was programmed in their brains millions of years ago, before the Himalayas were formed. Homo sapiens lived through periods of glaciation during which most of Europe and Northern Asia were covered by ice, and forests gave way to vast grasslands for tens of thousands of years.

Evolution is sometimes confused with the effect of breeding. Breeders can modify the features of a plant or animal species within ten generations, or even fewer. This was of course known long before Darwin, and he often referred to the similarity of natural selection to breeding. But breeding only selects from the variety of genomes that already exist in the population, whereas evolution modifies the genome. Every mutation carries a chance of creating something new. Successful evolutionary innovations may take tens of thousands of generations. Thus, the time scales are vastly different.

It's not only time what counts in evolution's gigantic test laboratory, but also the number of individuals of a species in which the mutations are tested. One can appreciate the importance of mutation testing by looking at plant biology. Plants cannot move, so a species can only spread by distributing seeds, either through the wind, or with the help of animals. But why do plants produce millions of pollens? An oak tree sends billions (numbers with 9 zeros) of pollen grains into the air every season. The pollen grains cannot make new plants; they are the male gametes that can only become seeds by merging with female gametes of the same species. So, what's the point of loading the air with clouds of pollen dust (to the dismay of people who are allergic to it)? It does not help spreading the species. But it spreads precious information: mutations to be tested in other members of the species. If the genome of the tree happens to have a new mutation it will be included in half of the billions of pollen dust particles. – Nature's information technology.

I.1.1   The Master Who Corrects the Design of the Apprentice Is
         Selection

The master who corrects the design of the apprentice is selection. The quality of vision afforded a reproductive advantage to some individuals so that their genes prevailed, leading to a gradual improvement over time. Other functions evolved by immediate elimination of individuals. The example of aversion against spiders may illustrate this. Monkeys like humans have a strong aversive reaction when seeing a spider. Many millions of years ago, perhaps during ages when our ancestor species were insectivores, they 'learned' to avoid venomous spiders. What must have happened, according to the theory, is that regularly individuals died from the byte of spiders and thus lost the chance to reproduce their genome, until some random mutation created a brain mechanism that responded to the sight of a spider and, again by random mutation, inhibited the feeding response. How crude the visual cognition mechanism might have been initially, and how subtle that inhibitory effect, over thousands of generations it produced a specific and robust aversion. It's specific because we do not react similarly to the sight of a beetle or a grasshopper, and it is so strong that some people scream and turn away when they see a spider, even if it is only a toy. A similar aversion exists for snakes; it is specific for the general shape of snakes and the way they move but does not discriminate poisonous from non-poisonous snakes; that needs to be learned by the individual. Thus, the evolution of a species is a road seamed by countless graves at every bent.

The randomness of mutations does not mean that the direction of evolution is random. Evolution is like a river: it finds its way to the ocean although the water of course does not know where the ocean is. It is as if the river has a plan with a goal. Evolution also seems like it has a plan. One can say it has a direction; each species (with some exceptions, see below) adapts continuously to its environment, and this process of course has a direction. For the river, the environment is the terrain; at any point in its course the turn it takes is given by the terrain and the force of gravity. In evolution, a species turns in the direction that is most advantageous given the environment at that point. The resulting course is anything but random; it is determined by the forces of selection exerted by the environment and by the genetic makeup of its population at that time. Selection can only select from the available options, that is, the range of genetic variants existing in the population at that time. This means that the course of evolution of each species is highly constrained. Selection preserves the genetic variants of the individuals that survive, so that the population slowly gets enriched with those variants, while other variants gradually disappear. Those that make the individual unfit to reproduce of course disappear quickly, but others that do not affect the reproductive fitness of the individual will stay in the population for a long time. This is a process of incredible complexity: The mechanism of evolution (according to this theory) implies that every species that has prevailed until today looks back at a long chain of genetic mutations that, at any point, afforded the individual fitness to reproduce.[8] Like the river which, at any point, looks back at a long chain of turns each of which satisfied the conditions of terrain and gravity. And just like every river has its unique shape, every species has its unique genome.

But evolution does not always follow this scheme. There are exceptional species that have become so powerful that they could turn the process around: instead of adapting to the given environment, they *adapted the environment* to their needs. One example that comes to mind is the beaver which dams rivers to create its habitat (the countless Beaver Dam Roads in the U.S. testify to their power). And of course – Homo sapiens. In keeping with the metaphor, there are also examples of rivers that have apparently adapted their environment, like the Colorado River which excavated a huge canyon, thereby removing an enormous mass of rock, so much that the earth, relieved from the weight of that mass, expanded, moving the surface around the canyon up by hundreds of meters.

The link to the past also explains the puzzling observation of species that look similar and behave similarly, although they are from widely separated branches of evolution, a phenomenon called "convergence". For example, the gray wolf *(Canis lupus)* and the now extinct Tasmanian wolf *(Thylacinus cynocephalus)* are both large, nocturnal fast moving predators that feed on other mammals; but the two are not closely related, the Tasmanian wolf is a marsupial, the gray wolf a placental mammal, clades that separated in the mid-Jurassic period more than 100 million years ago.[9] There are several other examples of pairs of species in the two clades that are strikingly similar, filling corresponding "niches" in the environments on different continents. At first glance, this seems like strong evidence for the influence of the environment: the similarity seems

---

[8] Of course, evolution often proceeds in a twisted path rather than a straight line. I remember, as a graduate student, I mentioned my thoughts about this evolutionary constraint in a discussion with Jerry Lettvin who happened to be a guest in the University of Zurich. Professor Lettvin vehemently disputed this idea: "You think that evolution cares about the past?" he exclaimed, and mentioned the example of a species of frogs that use their eyes to swallow prey: pressing with the lid muscles on the eyeballs they push the food down the throat.

[9] Marsupials and placentals represent two different solutions to the problem of protecting the embryo from its mother's immune system. Marsupials give birth at an early stage of development and the tiny newborns are essentially in a fetal state, but come equipped with a mechanism that enables them to cling to the hairs on the belly of the mothers and climb into the pouch where they attach to the nipples and suck. In the placental branch, evolution came up with the invention of the placenta, a tissue bag that isolates the embryo from the mother's blood stream while permitting nutrients to transfuse.

to be the result of adaptation to similar environments. In fact, it rather shows the power of the genetic constraint: they are similar because the adaptations started from a common genome. Despite the 100 million years of isolation from each other the two clades have about 80 percent of their genomes in common. A species can adapt to the environment, but only within the invisible constraint of the genome; at any stage a species can only implement a small fraction of all conceivable changes. The flying squirrel of North America and the sugar glider of Australia both have flaps of skin between the front and back legs that enable them to extend their leaps by air gliding. They could have grown wings instead like the mythological griffin, but that option was not in their genetic repertoire.

Whether it develops organs or brain structures, evolution always builds on the past. It usually works by modifying existing organs and functions, or by introducing new structures whose functions supersede those of older structures. Thus, innovations typically come about by modifying or superseding an existing genetic code. Perhaps the most bizarre example of evolutionary modification is the development of the turtle shell. Who would have guessed: the shell is a modified rib cage! Here, evolution performed the incredible task of transforming the bones inside the animal into a shell that envelopes it, leaving gaps for head and legs to move. There must have been intermediate steps in this transformation, and evolution found a way such that every step was an animal that succeeded in the struggle for survival. The topology of this magic trick remains a mystery to me.

This peculiar way of modifying previous structures to serve a new function is also characteristic of the development of brain mechanisms. For millions of years early mammals were relegated to underground life because of the powerful rein of the ferocious dinosaurs. When they emerged after the dinosaurs were wiped out (66 million years ago, by the gigantic catastrophe caused by the impact of a meteor) their vision was poor and adapted to the low-light conditions of nocturnal life. Their eyes contained mainly rods: receptors that are highly sensitive, but do not provide color vision. Only gradually a small proportion of cones were added, and only two types of cones, one that is sensitive to light of short wavelengths (S-cone) and one that is sensitive to medium to long wavelengths (M-L cone). This was all the ancestors of primates had available for color vision. At some point, in old-world primates, a mutation duplicated the M-L cone gene, resulting in two cone families whose pigments by additional mutations and selection then became slightly different over time, resulting in M cone and L cone. And that is what we inherited. Their spectral absorption curves are quite similar and largely overlapping; one peaks at a wavelength that we perceive as yellow, the other at a wavelength we perceive as greenish yellow. Incredible as it sounds, we owe the perception of the most beautiful of all colors, red, to this subtle difference between those cone sisters (and also the perception of green, of course).

A mutation can instantly modify a structure, but that a later mutation will reverse the modification is extremely unlikely. Occasionally, over millions of years, evolution comes up with a new brain structure that serves a certain function better than the existing one. When that happens, it generally does not delete the old genetic code, but simply adds additional mechanisms that inhibit or disable the old structure. A striking example is the development of mammalian visual systems. In non-mammalian vertebrates, the tectum, a midbrain structure, is the main visual processing machine, but in mammals, the more recently evolved cerebral cortex[10] serves most of the visual functions, while the role of the ancient tectum (the superior colliculi) is greatly reduced. In primates, it performs only limited visual processing for the control of eye movements. Thus, much of the visual functions of the tectum have been disabled and taken over by new visual regions of the cerebral cortex. Monkeys and humans become blind when the visual cortex is injured, so much has the visual function of the ancient structure been reduced. This unique importance of the visual cortex was painfully realized during the First World War before the steel helmet was introduced, when countless brain lesions were produced by grenade splinters. The peculiar way of evolutionary innovation has created a complex hierarchy of structures (brain stem, midbrain, forebrain and more) which makes understanding the brain difficult.

Evolution has used the innovation-by-modification strategy also for behavioral mechanisms, as pointed out by ethologists.[11] This same strategy can be found in the evolution of human behavior, where basic instincts evolved into the complex mechanisms that create society and culture, as the following chapters will show. It is often thought that complex behavioral patterns need to be learned. For example, it is commonly assumed that fledgling birds learn to fly, perhaps by trial and error, with training, or by imitating an adult bird. But in one of his ingenious experiments Konrad Lorenz showed that the flight coordination develops perfectly with age and without learning. He raised a

---

[10] The cerebral cortex is the large structure sitting like a hood on top of the brain that, in larger mammals, fills most of the cavity of the skull; and the visual cortex is the part of the cerebral cortex where neurons are activated by visual stimuli, that is, the part that processes visual information.

[11] See Konrad Lorenz, "On aggression"; Edward O. Wilson, "Sociobiology".

number of pigeons in tubes so that they could not open their wings, and then released them one after the other on different days. He observed that their first attempt to fly improved over time, and that the pigeon that was released on the last day could fly immediately and flew right to the most distant post in the yard, although it had had no chance to exercise its wings at all.

I.1.2   Experience Interacts With the Innate Blueprint of Development

In the example of the eye we considered only the innate blueprint for the development, but I argued above that the unfolding of the inherited design in the individual generally goes hand in hand with experience. It's a process that first uses the genetic information and after birth successively incorporates environmental information coming in through the senses.

The similarity of the design of our eyes and those of other primates clearly indicates that we have inherited the design from our primate ancestors. But is it completely inherited? Does experience play a role in the development of the individual? The eye can be compared to a camera, and as such, the optics at the front must focus the image on the receptor surface, the retina, which depends on the focal length of the optics. To produce a sharp image the focal length must be accurately matched to the distance between optics and retina (more precisely, between the posterior nodal point of the optics and the retina). The nervous system can focus the eye deliberately on the object of interest by deforming the lens, which is flexible (not the ones in my eyes, unfortunately, but in those of people under age 50). The range of focusing is limited to between 25 cm and infinity in the normal healthy eye, which means that, by stretching and thereby flattening the lens, the eye can change its focal length from about 21 mm to 23 mm, a narrow range of 2 mm (less than a tenth of an inch). But during childhood, when the body grows, our eyes are also growing. How does the eye of the embryo know the right size? – The answer is, it doesn't. At birth the optics are not matched to the size of the eye, so babies have blurred vision. But once they start to see, the eyes miraculously grow until the length of the eyeball exactly matches the optics so that the image of distant objects is focused when the lens is flattened, and near objects are focused when the lens is contracted. How is that possible? Experiments first carried out in chicks and later in monkeys have shown that one can stimulate the growth of the eye experimentally by defocusing the eye (for example with a drop of atropine which paralyzes the ciliary muscle so the lens cannot contract). By doing this continuously in one eye of a baby monkey while it is growing, researchers[12] found that the axial length (front to back) of the treated eye became several millimeters larger. Even without measuring, just by looking at cross sections of the two eyes one could easily see that the treated eye was much longer. The eye became myopic.

So what happened? There are neural circuits in the retina that detect when the image is more blurred than it should be, and these circuits stimulate growth to achieve the size that permits unblurred vision. The nature of the mechanism is not entirely clear. Apparently, it is local; when only half the image is blurred, say the half on the nasal side of the retina, the back of the eyeball grows more on the nasal side than the temporal side.

Primates, including humans, have excellent vision. In fact, under appropriate conditions, visual acuity reaches the 'diffraction limit', that is, the physical limit of resolution given by the wavelength of the light and the size of the pupil (a larger pupil giving higher resolution: humans have higher visual acuity than rhesus monkeys, and eagles even higher than humans![13]). Such high performance is only possible with tight control of the optical and mechanical parameters, and the image-based control of growth just described is one of them. It makes the eyes grow until the ciliary muscle can perfectly focus the image.[14]

---

[12] TN Wiesel, E Raviola (1977) Myopia and eye enlargement after neonatal lid fusion in monkeys. Nature 266(5597):66-8.

[13] R Shlaer (1972) "An Eagle's Eye: Quality of the Retinal Image." Science 176 (4037): 920-2.

[14] Unfortunately, under the conditions of modern human life this ingenious design has tragic consequences that evolution did not anticipate. Children today grow up with a lot of activity indoors where the light intensity is orders of magnitude lower than outside daylight: reading with dim illumination and watching electronic displays (the difference in lighting is grossly underestimated in perception because of its compressive characteristic – just take a smart phone display outside into the sunlight and you will see how weak it is). The prolonged activity under low light conditions stimulates the accommodation (the ciliary muscle) in the same way the blurred image does in young babies, with the result that the eyeball resumes growing in the axial dimension, causing myopia (short-sightedness). This has led to a huge epidemic of myopia in young people. In Europe, myopia is now prevalent among 42 per cent of adults aged 25 to 29 years; the percentage is similar in the U.S., and even worse in East Asia. This is tragic, not only because it condemns people to wearing strong glasses all their lives, but the overlong shape of the eyeball (which is normally rather spherical) also pulls the retina away from the back wall of the eye, eventually leading to retinal detachment and loss of vision. All these terrible consequences could be avoided simply by allowing school children sufficient outside

The growth regulation of the eye is but one example of countless ways that sensory experience modulates the execution of the genetic blueprint of development, specifically, the development of the brain.

I.1.3   Reflexive Evolution

The concept of natural selection is often summarized in the phrase "survival of the fittest", implying that selection favors mutations that better adapt a species to its environment. In fact, natural selection is more complex, including motors of selection that do not improve the fitness of a species. An obvious example is the phenomenon of sexual selection, which Darwin already described as an evolutionary mechanism contrary to the principle of survival of the fittest.

Sexual selection

> *Die Welt wird schöner von Tag zu Tag,*
> *man weiß nicht, was noch werden mag.*
>
> The world is getting more beautiful day by day,
> who knows where that might lead.
>
> Anonymous

Animals of species with sexual reproduction (which are the vast majority) have perceptual mechanisms that enable them to select mates of the opposite sex. These mechanisms must be able (1) to recognize individuals of the same species among others, and (2) to recognize and select among those an individual of the opposite sex for mating. Because mating is necessary for reproduction, these mechanisms are essential and have evolved to a high degree of perfection. To appreciate the sophistication of these mechanisms, imagine the challenge to recognize one's own kind among the many different species of birds, some of which can be quite similar in appearance. For instance, there are 41 species of warblers visiting the East coast of North America, a family of migratory birds that are all similar in size and shape and prefer similar habitats, but each species has distinct calls and patterns of coloration. The differences are often subtle, but the birds have sufficiently acute visual and auditory perception to avoid crossbreeding (which is obviously uncommon because otherwise we would not have those distinct species).

---

activity at regular intervals. See L Spillmann,. "Stopping the rise of myopia in Asia." Graefes Arch Clin Exp Ophthalmol 258(5):943-959, 2020

For the second challenge, selecting individuals of the opposite sex, a variety of cues can be used, including smell, shape, size, and color, as well as behaviors such as calls and movements. In some bird families, like the birds of paradise, males wear fantastic patterns of plumage. The existence of bird species in which the males have beautiful colored tail feathers is a puzzle of evolution: why do the females have that extravagant taste for design of form and color? And, of what use is it to the species that they should select this seemingly useless ornament?

The key to the puzzle is that both, the perceptible feature and the perceptual mechanism are genetic and thus passed on from generation to generation. As Ronald Fisher (the mathematician who invented analysis of variance) noted, a feature may have been associated by chance with general well-being, making it a useful index of survival strength, and natural selection will therefore have enhanced in females a taste for that feature, but, "even if, in the course of time, it ceases to be any index of vitality whatever, the taste for it would continue to increase in strength, if it has already become strong, because although the offspring show no general superiority in the ordinary course of life, they retain their ascendancy in sexual selection, and have, therefore, a better chance of surviving; it is only when a feature has become so harmful as to overbalance this advantage that the taste for it among the females will have reached its maximum and will begin to diminish."[15]

In other words, if a perceptual preference has emerged for one reason or the other (perhaps by chance) in one sex, sexual selection will enhance the preferred feature in the other sex, and recursively enhance the perceptual preference in the same sex. If there is a preference for a certain color in the female population of a bird species, a male bird in which the preferred color is pronounced will be at an advantage over males in which that color is less pronounced. Across generations, this will enhance expression of that color in the male population. Conversely, a female bird with a strong preference for the color will be at an advantage over other females, because, by choosing males in which the color is particularly pronounced, it selects genes that will make that color pronounced in her male offspring, putting them at an advantage over other males. Over time, this will enhance expression of the perceptual color preference in the female population.

---

[15] R A Fisher, "The evolution of sexual preference". Eugenics Review. 7 (3): 184–192, p. 187, 1915.

It is important to understand that this kind of positive feedback is a necessary consequence of the theory of evolution. It must play a role wherever genetic codes for an external feature and a corresponding perceptual preference exist. Indeed, we find that examples of positive feedback loops are ubiquitous. As Fisher noted, the loop will exaggerate the features until they become so harmful that the negative effect sets off the advantage. In the example of birds of paradise, the large colored feathers of course make the males an easy catch for their predators. Thus, in general, sexual selection will enhance the effective feature until an equilibrium is reached when the advantage in sexual selection is outweighed by the concomitant disadvantage in the environment.

Because positive feedback between expression of a feature and its perceptual preference is a necessary consequence of the mechanisms of evolution it applies to many observations in different species and there is no point in searching for other explanations in each specific case. But this does not keep scientists from suggesting their own explanations. The large antlers of male deer are a striking example of sexual selection. When they have a choice, the does tend to mate with the buck that has the bigger antlers, which over time further enlarges them, but wearing large antlers of course is a handicap when escaping predators. Thus, evolution will increase the antlers until the handicap outweighs the sexual selection advantage. Instead, it has been proposed that does select a buck with large antlers because they indicate genes that provide unusual survival fitness because the buck has managed to survive despite the handicap (handicap theory). However, it is easy to see that this cannot be the explanation because, while the offspring may gain genes that give them extra fitness, they also inherit the problem of having to run through the forest with large antlers.

The scope of reflexive evolution

Sexual selection may seem like a unique case of natural selection, but in fact other kinds of within-species selection mechanisms that do not further fitness are ubiquitous in the animal kingdom and of particular interest also for understanding human nature. I use the term *reflexive* for evolutionary mechanisms that are not driven by adaptation to the environment or competition between species, but by competition within a species. Reflexive, like the reflexive verbs, which denote actions in which the subject of the action is also its object.

Sexual evolution is an example that is obviously reflexive, but there are many other kinds of reflexive evolution. Squirrels in the park may serve as an example. Squirrels bury nuts in the ground and remember the places so that they can later retrieve the nuts when the winter comes and food gets scarce, a behavior that very likely has a genetic code. In the forest it may be a good strategy because other animals who don't know the places are unlikely to find the treasures. But in the city, where grounds suitable for digging are few, it can be lucrative for a squirrel to watch where others have been digging, or just dig randomly, to find the nuts hidden by its consorts. This behavior benefits the individual squirrel, but at the expense of the others, and with no benefit for survival of the species. Thus, where squirrels compete for food, the genes responsible for the steeling behavior will accumulate in the population. Another even more nasty example are lions, where dominant males, when taking over a female from another male, often kill her offspring from the first relationship. Clearly, lions that have the genes responsible for this behavior will spread their genome more effectively than lions that do not have them. Red fox cubs fight to establish the rank order among the siblings, and about 1/5 of them die as a result (and are eaten by their mates) before they leave the burrow. Clearly, fox cubs that have a strong drive to fight and kill siblings are more likely to procreate their genes. This behavior might alternatively be thought as a straight evolutionary mechanism, providing the stronger individuals with a better chance and thus improving the genome. So, here only a component of evolution might be reflexive. But the case of the Lion behavior is an example of purely reflexive evolution.

In short, I call *reflexive* the evolution of a behavioral pattern that expands its genetic representation within the population of a species without necessarily improving its fitness towards the environment. By "without necessarily" I mean that the expected effect on fitness can be zero. A behavior might seem to have a positive effect on fitness, e.g., one might think that Lions that kill offspring more often than average might also be larger on average, and thus the effect would be an increase in size, which would seem like a positive effect. However, because each species has generally reached its optimum size through ages of evolution, a further increase will have a negative effect. In equilibrium, the expected effect on fitness is null.

The few examples described above illustrate forms of reflexive evolution other than sexual, and because reflexive evolution always involves interaction between members of the same species, it is not surprising that these other (non-sexual) forms are characteristic of social species. One of the first books I remember was Selma Lagerlöf's "Nils Holgersson's wonderful journey across Sweden," and what impressed me most was the scary story of *Glimminge Hus*, in which a local population of black rats is attacked by an invading army of gray rats. When ethologists studied rats systematically, long after Lagerlöf wrote her fictive story, they confirmed the fierce fighting between distinct clans of rats and found that they identify themselves by smell. Generally they afflict the other rats with wounds at the belly or the back which often lead to infections and death. However, evolution has also produced a type of 'killer rat' that systematically bite the arteries of the throat, killing the opponent instantly. Researchers also observed that rats sometimes erroneously attacked their own kind and only realized their error when it was too late, because recognition by smell takes some time.

Another species of highly social animals are the meerkats of South Africa. Meerkats make systems of burrows where they live together in large groups. When the animals are outside foraging, one older adult takes the role of a sentinel, carefully watching the surrounding. They look cute with their pinscher-like faces and big eyes, especially the sentinels which sit or stand upright, looking like little human creatures. I loved to see them in zoos where they are common. So I was deeply disappointed to read what ethologists write about them. They do have a sophisticated society, including an organized defense of the clan and daycare to free mothers to go foraging, but also including infanticide and brutal wars between rivaling groups.

Like meerkats, chimps also show sudden aggressive group behavior. Chimps usually live in groups of families in harmony and mutual support; but once in a while the mood of a group rather abruptly switches to aggression against a neighboring group, culminating in brutal campaigns that leave many dead, sometimes destroying the other group entirely: a sudden outbreak of hateful behavior, if the use of human terminology here is permitted. It has been debated if observations of this kind were rather the effect of the presence for some time of the human observers and their camp (and food resources) close to the range of a chimp population. But it seems unlikely that a group of chimps would develop such specific and coordinated behavior just in that particular situation, had there not been behavioral mechanisms already in place; and recent careful studies have confirmed that such aggressions are indeed part of the normal behavior of chimps. Interestingly, the closely related species of bonobos, whose gene pool has been isolated from that of the chimps by the natural barrier of the Congo River, does not show this aggressive behavior.

As a rule, in social species that are successful, within-species competition evolves aggressive behaviors. This is the typical course of reflexive evolution which enhances the procreation of the corresponding genes in a population without improving the fitness for survival of the species. We humans too, unfortunately, look back at an evolutionary history of competition, perhaps even fiercer competition than that among chimps.

Mutations provide the material for natural selection. They create genetic diversity. And diversity is generally considered as beneficial because it enables a species to adapt to changes of the environment. Adaptation to the environment has become the standard measure to evaluate mutations. But mutations also mean innovation. Our obsession of using the yardstick of adaptive value makes us blind to this important aspect of evolution. What is the adaptive value of language? Did the emergence of language improve success in hunting? Or increase the chance of finding edible roots? Perhaps. But certainly language represented a huge advantage among groups of humans competing for the same resources, not only for coordinating actions within a group, but also for deceiving members of other groups. Thus, there must have been immense evolutionary pressure towards improvement of language skills. Measured in terms of fitness relative to other species, the advantage of language is doubtful, but for competition within the species its emergence has been a huge success. Thus, language is first and foremost a product of reflexive evolution.

As we will see, reflexive evolution has created a wide spectrum of behaviors among Homo sapiens, from loving fathers to rapists, from the heaven of music to the hell of genocide. But before we get to all this we need to look more closely at the evolution of Homo sapiens, or at least what we know about it.

I.2   WHERE WE COME FROM IS WHAT WE ARE

Human evolution is often misinterpreted as a Pythia that will tell us where we are going, as if evolution had a goal. Because we feel unique as a species and superior to all others (and the human brain certainly is) and since Homo sapiens only appeared recently, it is tempting to think that evolution must have a plan. Of course, within Darwin's theory, there cannot be a plan. It is a misinterpretation that penetrates human thinking from Hegel to Nietzsche to Teilhard de Chardin. The sobering truth is that all the facts of evolution only tell us where we come from, but not where we are going. All the species we see today are successful examples of evolution, individuals whose ancestors succeeded to create offspring over thousands and thousands of generations. But evolution is oblivious of its goal. Nothing we learn from studying fossils across millions of years and from examining modern genes and ancient genes can give us a hint of what lies ahead of us in the thousand years to come, except for that which depends on what we inherited from the past. So let's have a look at where we come from.

I.2.1   The Peculiar Way We Perceive the Past

We see the past in a peculiar way. We remember a lot of the past 5 years, and we know perhaps as much (or less) about the 50 years before that. We learn in school about the past 5 hundred years that we call the modern age, which started with the Renaissance, the exploration of the oceans and the discovery of the New World. We learn less about the 5 thousand years before that, the historical age, which began with the earliest Egyptian scriptures. What happened before that we can only infer from deposits of bones, fossils and stone tools. About 15 thousand years ago (or perhaps earlier?) humans first domesticated dogs and began to transition from hunters/gatherers to agricultural societies, 300 thousand years ago the species of Homo sapiens was born, but people called Homo erectus, who walked upright, hunted animals with spears and grilled them on fire roamed the earth already for 2 million years. When we look at past eons, perception contracts time.

I have tried to visualize this in Figure 1. At the top I plotted some of the significant steps in the way we tend to perceive them, as a smooth linear progression. In fact, I used a logarithmic time scale here. The bottom plot shows the same steps on the real time scale (I skipped here the emergence of primates some 55 million years ago, which would have required seven more pages attached on the left). On this scale, almost everything we know happened in an incredibly short period. The entire historical age shrinks to almost nothing, and the age of agriculture (~10 thousand years) lasted only 0.5 percent of the period of Homo erectus (~2 million years). The events after 'Agriculture' all pile up almost vertically, which is remarkable, an acceleration that is mysterious.

Although the top plot represents the past in the way we intuitively see the succession of events, the bottom plot with the linear time scale is relevant for understanding evolution. This is because gene mutations trickle at a constant rate in *real time*, that is, the frequency of mutations per individual and generation is roughly constant. The fact that the number of generations after the transition to agriculture (the Neolithic revolution) is only 0.5 percent of the number of generations since Homo erectus emerged means that only half a percent of what the mutation-and-selection process achieved since then likely comes from this period.[16] Thus, what distinguishes us from the earliest Homo erectus has been created nearly all during the Paleolithic.

---

[16] The rate of accumulation of mutations in the genome of a species also depends on the number of individuals; the more individuals live at a time, the more mutations occur. But

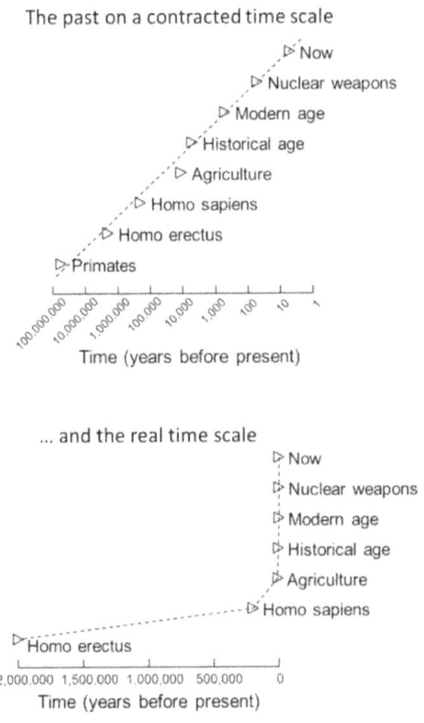

Figure 1. The peculiar way we perceive time

the world population of hominids seems to have remained relatively constant over most of the time. Recent estimates based on the diversity of the present human genome indicate a rather constant 'effective population size' for H sapiens of either 12,000 or 32,000 individuals, depending on the way the mean mutation rate is estimated. This relatively small number has been interpreted as a result of a very long history, starting ~ 2 million years ago, of small population size. See P Sjödin, AE Sjöstrand, M Jakobsson and MGB Blum, "Resequencing data provide no evidence for a human bottleneck in Africa during the penultimate glacial period" *Mol. Biol. Evol.* 29(7): 1851-60 (2012). The 'effective population size' roughly corresponds to the number of breeding individuals in the population. It is a parameter in models of population genetics that make certain simplifying assumptions. The corresponding 'census population' which is more difficult to estimate, is much larger, roughly by a factor of ten.

If we try to understand evolution, we need to appreciate the vast expanse of time of the prehistoric ages. It might seem as if life in those ancient times was dragging on in monotony, but this is just our ignorance. Previous centuries appear to us more uniform than the recent ones, but in terms of biological life, a century then was as long as a century now. People in the stone age probably experienced their days between birth and death with as much excitement as we do. There were about twelve thousand generations of Homo sapiens before us, three hundred thousand years, all densely filled with action, the struggle to survive, find mates and raise offspring, extend pastures and planting grounds, and defend possessions.

In the warm summer of 1991, hikers in the Ötztal Alps discovered, sticking out from the ice of a glacier at the height of 3200 m, what seemed to be part of a human body. It turned out to be the frozen body of a man who died 5,300 years ago and was preserved in the ice until the glacier recently receded. When I read about this discovery and its subsequent investigation at the University of Innsbruck, I was excited, not only about the description of the details how this Neolithic man was dressed, his leather shoes stuffed with moss for insulation to walk over snow and ice, and his tools, including a fire starter kit, a long bow with arrows and a copper ax. I was also moved because I knew that particular area on the border between Austria and Italy. As a student I had spent time skiing with a friend in the exclusive skiing resort of Obergurgl, but we did not have the money to use the lifts and therefore put fur under our skis and took to snow mountain climbing. One day, after spending a night in the Hochwilde Haus we passed the Tisenjoch and might have walked over 'Ötzi' (that's how Austrians lovingly call him) who was buried in the ice. So I vividly imagined how this stone age man had been passing from the valleys on the Northern side of the mountain range over to what is today South Tyrol, perhaps on a hunting trip or after visiting family, when he was caught by a sudden weather change and died from exhaustion, and was then buried in snow and ice.

But then, after ten years of examination by mummy experts, a radiologist searching for the stomach that previous examinations had not found (researchers wanted to analyze its content) took a new chest x-ray. The corpse was found in an awkward posture draped over a bolder and compressed by the ice so that the stomach had been pushed up into the lung area. But in the x-ray he also saw a shadow near the left shoulder. Scrutinizing the CT scans again he discovered a flint arrowhead that had penetrated the shoulder blade. It had been overlooked in the previous examinations. He also found the entrance hole in the skin on the back: Ötzi had been shot from behind, ambushed. Nobody knows why Ötzi was murdered; it was not robbery because the archer did not take the copper ax, a precious tool at that time, but pulled out the shaft of the arrow, apparently to leave as little trace as possible. Ötzi was not a poor hunter, as his clothing and equipment shows, he might have been an important person, and someone must have hated him. Learning about the discovery of the arrowhead changed my imagination of the lonely hiker caught by the unpredictable forces of nature and changed my idyllic view of the Neolithic in general.

History, as I remember it from my high school textbook, appears like a chain of alternating beads of war and peace. "War is the father of all things" Heraclites has been quoted, a pre-Socratic Greek philosopher, and he may be right. Wars spread innovations of technology and new political rules. The earliest historical documents tell the history of wars in the bronze age (see Plate 1, Sargon's victory stele). Large battles, it has generally been assumed, took place when powerful urban civilizations emerged, like in Mesopotamia, whereas the rural societies of Northern Europe living in homesteads scattered across the country, where the bronze age arrived only thousand years later, were thought to have been rather peaceful, except for skirmishes between local clans. But in 1996 an amateur archaeologist found a single upper arm bone sticking out of the steep riverbank of the Tolense River, a small river that meanders through an idyllic landscape in Northern Germany. A flint arrowhead was stuck in the bone. Later excavations found skeletons of more than hundred men and six horses, among war clubs, spears, swords, and knives strewn all over. The marks in the bones showed that bronze- and flint-tipped arrows were loosed at close range, piercing skulls and lodging deep into the bones of young men. The excavations showed that a stretch of 3 kilometers along the river was the site of a gruesome battle that took place 3,200 years ago. Archeologists estimate that about 800 men died of a total of 5000 involved. The Paleolithic too might not have been the paradise of hunters and gatherers that we often imagine. – So much to help our imagination in appreciating the density of events and excitement of past ages.

*Plate 1. Prisoners on King Sargon's victory stele,
circa 4300 years before present*

I.2.2   Evolution of Brain Size

Ever since Darwin proposed his theory of the origin of the species, nothing has incited more controversy than his positioning the human species among the million other species. Among the naturists of Darwin's time, and even before, the concept of a tree of evolution was well accepted, and having the human species in that tree was not perceived as a problem. Subsequent research in paleontology and genetics has cemented and expanded this concept, and ethologists have pointed out lots of parallels between animal and human behavior. But still, in my view, and certainly in the eye of the non-scientific observer, it seems hard to accept that theory because humans are so different from all the animals we know. I think despite all the scientific evidence for the theory, science must accept that humans are special, and this is not just our anthropocentric perspective. The difference is vast. Humans have language and society, literature, laws and arts and science. It is intuitively clear that all these differences are somehow related to the brain, because, as neurologists know, any of the capabilities that make us special can be compromised, often selectively, when the brain is diseased or aging.

Fossils, of course, do not tell us much about brain function, but one thing is clear: the size of the brain increased enormously during the past 3 million years. Figure 2 shows how the volume of the brain grew, as estimated from the skulls of our putative ancestors or related hominids. Paleontologists can make estimates of brain volume only in cases where at least a number of skulls have been found that apparently belong to the same period or the same stage of evolution. That is why there are only four data points, and I plotted these at the center of each stage as labeled on the right. The graph shows that, between Australopithecus and Homo sapiens, the brain volume tripled.[17] Now, brain size as such is not a measure of mental capacity or intelligence. Whales have much bigger brains than humans in volume as well as number of neurons. And also in terms of brain size relative to total body size we are not at the top, but the mouse is. What is remarkable about the growth of brain volume in the human lineage is the increase within a species over a short time span: a three-fold increase occurred over a period of only three million years. Compared to the 40 million years of primate evolution which resulted in brains of only 400 cm^3, this is extraordinarily fast. The growth of brain volume is all the more remarkable as it required a corresponding increase of the head size of babies at birth and thus a higher risk for the mother. Apparently, the benefit of larger brains outweighed the loss from higher maternal mortality.

---

[17] The measures are estimates, not precise data, and they specify absolute volumes, disregarding variations in body size; this is also the reason why I did not include the Neanderthals whose brains were even larger than that of modern humans – they were overall bigger. Also, to be fair, chimpanzees are somewhat lighter than humans; and Australopithecus afarensis was even smaller; so in relative measures their brains would be slightly larger than suggested by the figure.

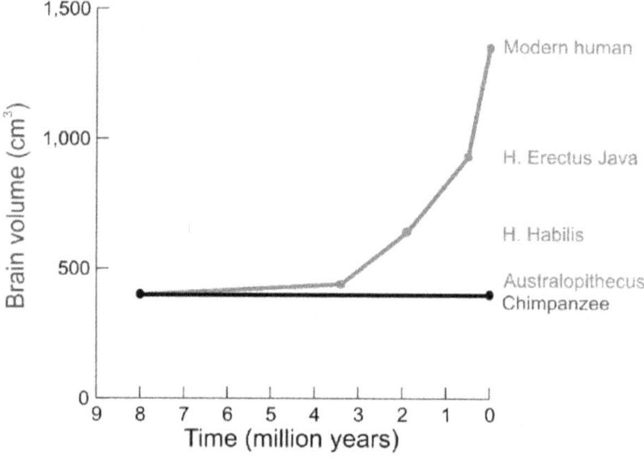

Figure 2. Evolution of brain size

I.2.3   Human Evolution Begins With the Emergence of Homo Erectus

In the metaphor I used above when puzzling over the evolution of the eye, the apprentice works by successively adding functional modules under the continual control of master selection, by trial and error, working without insight, but being corrected at each step. Selection compensates for the randomness of mutations. As the growth of brain volume suggests (see Figure 2), this process took off with the emergence of Homo erectus, a name that lumps up fossils found across Africa, Europe and Asia, some as old as 1.8 million years,[18] and continued through many branching points down to the modern human. Only three of the side branches are known for sure: Denisovan, Floresiensis, and Neanderthal, all of which became extinct in the last one hundred thousand years.

---

[18] 'Homo erectus' (from Latin erectus = upright) designates the first recognizable members of the genus Homo. Note that upright walking is not the defining feature of H erectus, as the term might suggest. Fossils show that ape-like creatures that walked upright appeared long before H erectus. All the skeletal features that characterize upright bipedal walking, from head to toe, are found in fossils of Australopithecus afarensis who lived between about 3.8 and 2.9 million years ago in Eastern Africa, and the analysis of petrified footprints from that era has confirmed that those Southern apes walked bipedally like humans. Thus, species that walked upright are at least 1.8 million years older than Homo erectus, but they had brains no larger than those of chimps. See J DeSilva, "First Steps. How Upright Walking Made us Human." Harper Collins (2021).

The chapter of human evolution, one could say, begins with the emergence of Homo erectus (whatever this term implies; probably multiple species). Gene analysis of extant species indicates that the last common ancestors of chimps and humans lived about six million years ago, and fossilized bones of Homo erectus are about two million years old. Thus, at some time during those four million years that we know little about, our ancestors abandoned the forests, where chimps continued to live, and took to the plains.

Descending from the trees changed everything. The diet: fruits are plenty in forests, but scarce in the savannah, so they had to be substituted with berries and roots, and increasingly with game. One problem was that the new diet had less water, and consequently, the 'descendants', whose physiology depended on large quantities of liquid from fruits, would need a continuous supply of clean water, which means they had to stay near springs or running waters. This and the new ways of gathering food meant that they had to be able to move fast and over long distances, which put evolutionary pressure on the development of legs quite different from those of the apes, and big lungs to supply their muscles with sufficient oxygen when running. These dramatic modifications of the body took place within a period of a few million years, which is quite short compared to the 40 million years (or more) it took for primates to develop.

I think Homo erectus was so successful for a number of reasons that they had no serious natural enemy.[19] From some point on, they no longer struggled fighting nature, as most species do; their main struggle was now competing with their own relatives. The change from a plant-eating arboreal animal to a hunter that used weapons and made meat a main part of its diet was a dramatic turn in evolutionary history.

---

[19] Which kind of animals constituted a danger to our ancestors can be inferred from our emotional reactions to the sight of animal shapes. Fear or disgust is produced by the shapes/movements of snakes, spiders, and rats, as well as masses of ants and maggots. Among the larger animals, the shape of hyenas is particularly repulsive. But lions, tigers and bears are not perceived as repulsive, except for the threat of gaping teeth in general, the most common being the fangs of dogs. This suggests that lions, tigers, and bears did not present much danger to early humans, in contrast to snakes, spiders, rats, and hyenas, which might have frequently caused death of babies and children. Filmmakers have also tried to create dinosaurs that are scary, but with little success; the view of a dinosaur is not hair-raising. Interestingly, a kind of monster that plays most effectively in many horror movies has the appearance of an ogre looking like the Neanderthal as rendered by artists based on paleontology. Might the hundred-thousand-year long struggle have created a collective memory like the ones that make us fear snakes and spiders?

First, the use of weapons makes hunting much easier than using body parts (fangs, claws etc.) to kill prey as all other predator animals do. Homo erectus also used tools to butcher their game and fire to cook it.[20] The turtle who defied all enemies for millions of years had no chance against two hands that turned it over and put it on the ember.

Second, for hunter-gatherers to raise offspring is most efficient when both parents cooperate. In other hunting mammals like cats or bears the offspring is raised only by the females. The males provide little more than their sperms. Homo erectus developed the two-parent family which was vastly more efficient. The two-parent family is unusual among primates. It was invented by the dinosaurs and still is the basis of reproduction in most bird species. This is of course why we sympathize with birds and adore them. Watching a bird couple breed and raise their chicks we feel as if they were our relatives, quite at odds with the biological tree of descent. The family, of course, is also the basis of more extensive social organization.

Some authors have hypothesized that early humans were not "at the top of the food chain" (where modern humans are), but rather in the middle, consuming meat, but also being consumed by others, and that they were scavengers, leaving the hunting to more powerful predators and waiting for their turn after the predator was satisfied. I don't subscribe to this hypothesis. For one, the human physiology is not that of a scavenger; unlike for dogs, rotten meat is poisonous for humans. Second, using tools, however primitive, and group collaboration, made killing animals easier for early humans than for other predators. They could easily ambush large plant eaters like Bisons and kill them. Why would they have to wait for other predators to do it? It is more likely that early humans mastered the hunt better than other predators of their time. In fact, lions become an important theme in cave art by Homo sapiens during the late Paleolithic. The depictions of cave lions, a species of large lions that became extinct about 14,000 years ago, one might think, were of ceremonial nature. But recent discoveries show that much earlier already Neanderthals hunted cave lions, pierced their rib cage with wooden spears, and used their pelt.[21]

---

[20] S Hlubik, F Berna, C Feibel, D Braun, JWK Harris, "Researching the nature of fire at 1.5 Mya on the site of FxJj20 AB, Koobi Fora, Kenya, using high-resolution spatial analysis and FTIR spectrometry." Current Anthropology 58 S243-S257 (2017).

[21] G Russo, A Milks, D Leder et al. First direct evidence of lion hunting and the early use of a lion pelt by Neanderthals. Sci Rep 13, 16405 (2023).

Hunting with weapons and the use of tools require intelligence, and so does the use of fire. And social organization is also intricately linked to intelligence. Thus, both tool use and social organization exerted strong evolutionary pressure for the development of intelligence which presumably resulted in the rapid increase of brain volume; rapid compared to the evolution of primates, but still slow enough to provide sufficient time for testing a large number of mutations related to brain development. While intelligence emerged also in several other species, for example in parrots and dolphins, it did not exert much evolutionary pressure, because, lacking the versatile hands of primates, there was little the intelligence could be applied to. Having keen senses and being able to move fast remained more important than being able to communicate, think, and plan ahead.

The evolution of brain mechanisms involved improvements of perception, communication, and action planning, which means improvement of the computational algorithms of the brain. In modern computer jargon this is called software development. And just as computer software is developed much faster than computer hardware, we can assume that brain mechanisms evolved much faster than anatomical structures did. Indeed, the skeletons of the homo species are rather similar, but their mental capacities probably differed significantly.

I.2.4   Group Selection

Since the motor of evolution is selection, the rapid evolution of the brain must have been achieved by intense selection, which probably meant fierce competition between the homo species. Because fossils are petrified bones that do not contain DNA anymore, we will never know the details of the lives of Homo erectus. How many species existed, and when each went extinct is not clear. It is now believed that migration out of Africa began approximately 2 million years ago with the early expansions of hominids of the type of Homo erectus. This initial migration was followed by other archaic humans including Homo heidelbergensis, which lived around 500,000 years ago and was the likely ancestor of both Denisovans and Neanderthals. There were probably many more homo species, and extinctions occurred all the time; but this is speculation because fossils do not provide enough information for reliable classification of species. For a long time there must have been several rivaling homo species in Africa, and Homo sapiens, who split off as a species around 300,000 years ago, was one of them. Finally, Homo sapiens also emerged outside Africa beginning about 70-50,000 years ago (and perhaps earlier in sporadic migrations). They dispersed across Eurasia where they gradually replaced the previous immigrants, such as Homo neanderthalensis.[22] Thus, Sapiens is the latest branch from the large tree of Homo erectus.

When Sapiens 'replaced' the Neanderthals, as paleontologists put it, it means they drove them to extinction. The two must have been competing for hunting grounds, shelters, and other resources. We do not know if it happened by direct confrontation or by gradual marginalization. Why did they have to compete? Some authors portray hunting/gathering as a paradisiacal state of human existence. There may indeed have been phases when life of the hunters was paradisiacal. All homo species evolved first in Africa where they may have competed with each other, and where the species they hunted were used to being preyed on by human hunters for hundreds of thousands of years and had therefore evolved corresponding flight instincts. But when humans left Africa, they would encounter species that did not have those instincts, species that had never been confronted with a two-legged running animal carrying a spear. They encountered large plant eaters that had lived millions of years with no such deadly predator. This means that the new hunters could just walk up to them and spear them down. Excavations have shown that this happened when Sapiens first invaded Australia around 40,000 years ago, and then again 15,000 years ago when they set foot on the American continent, and each time dozens of large plant-eating species vanished, and with them many other species.[23]

But the hunters' lives were not always so easy. As for any large predator, a given area of hunting ground can only support a limited number of individuals, and each species is constantly trying that limit, meaning that each such species alternates periodically between affluence and starvation. During periods of affluence, populations grow; during periods of famine, selection takes place. Imagine that a people of hunter-gatherers had adapted to hunting species of large animals, like the various mammoths that thrived in Eurasia during the last 5 million years, but a change of climate made their population dwindle. Then the hunter-gatherer people would migrate to wherever they could still find them, adapting to life in colder climates, improving their hunting techniques, etc. But, inevitably, different groups (tribes, peoples, or species) of hunter-gatherers

---

[22] Genetic evidence shows that present-day humans outside Africa carry about 2% Neanderthal genes, which means that Sapiens must have interbred with Neanderthals. Africans carry 0%, which is obviously a consequence of the fact that people in Africa had no opportunity to meet Neanderthals.

[23] For a detailed account see Jared Diamond, "The Third Chimpanzee. The Evolution and Future of the Human Animal," Harper Perennial (1993, reissued in 2006), and Elizabeth Kolbert, "The Sixth Extinction," Picador (2015).

would come into conflict and eliminate one another. Because the homo species are socially organized the competition is between groups. It is not the typical kind of 'survival of the fittest' that selects among individuals, for example, those with the best hunting skills. It is between genomes of groups. I argue that there was competition between related species as well as between groups within species. The groups that survived prevailed because their genes gave the group superior qualities for competition. Over time this enhanced those qualities. It may not have improved the skills for hunting or gathering or building shelters, but it improved skills in competing with other groups (reflexive evolution).

This may appear like mere speculation since there are no documents about the lives of hunter-gatherers in the paleolithic. Neither, I think, can we learn much about those previous eons by studying the last surviving hunter-gatherers which have taken refuge in the few remaining pockets of undisturbed wilderness of the globe today. But recently, the extension of gene science into paleontology ('paleo-genomics') is giving us amazing new insights. Studies of the collected remains of hunter-gatherers in European museums are shedding light on genetic diversification and group replacement among Homo sapiens in the upper paleolithic.

Recent studies analyzed the genomes from the remains of 356 individuals spanning between 35,000 and 5,000 years ago; essentially all ancient bones and teeth that had been collected, and dated, from Europe and Western Asia.[24] Previously, paleontologists who studied European hunter-gatherer societies based on found tools and other cultural indicators had classified them uniformly as 'Gravettian' and 'Epi-Gravettian' cultures (referring to periods before and after the last ice age, respectively). But, to their surprise, the genetic studies identified at least eight different genetic clusters, some more genetically distinct from each other than modern-day Europeans and Asians. People to the east were light-skinned and dark-eyed, and people to the west probably tended to be dark-skinned and blue-eyed. And, no doubt, they also spoke different languages.

What struck me most are the indications that some of the populations identified by genetic cluster analysis disappeared, leaving no trace in the genomes of succeeding populations. The last ice age, which covered large parts of Europe with ice between 25,000 and 19,000 years ago, made humans retreat to southern ice-free pockets of land, until the climate warmed again and glaciers retreated, when they were eventually able to expand northward to recuperate

---

[24] C. Posth et al. "Palaeogenomics of Upper Palaeolithic to Neolithic European hunter-gatherers," Nature 615, pages 117–126 (2023)

lebensraum. In the Italian peninsula, one of the ice-free pockets that had been populated continuously, the inhabitants after the ice age belonged to a different genetic cluster than the previous inhabitants. And the genetic signature of those original inhabitants was not found in any of the subsequent hunter-gatherer populations of Europe/Western Asia. Apparently, when a passage to the Italian peninsula from the North-East opened up after the ice age, new immigrants replaced the local descendants. People that had survived the ice age were exterminated when the climate warmed up again.

This finding, that a local genetic cluster was 'replaced' by a cluster affiliated with geographically distant people is direct evidence for group selection in the age of hunter-gatherers. In this example, selection took place within the species of Homo sapiens. A few thousand years before, Homo sapiens had 'replaced' Homo neanderthalensis. It is the kind of process that, by reflexive evolution, creates the 'society forming engenes' that we will discuss below.

I.2.5   The Evolution of the Human Brain Is a Mystery

Compared to our closest relatives, the apes, our brain has superpower. How is it possible that evolution endowed us with a super brain in such a short time span, a couple of million years, while our monkey ancestors were already around for 40 million years? And why are we the only species on the planet to possess such an organ? Regarding intellectual capacity, there is a halo around Homo sapiens like the halo around a colony of Streptomyces griseus in a Petri dish full of growing germs. What was it that sparked from God's finger to the finger of Adam?

During my years in the Department of Neurology of the University of Zurich I had the chance to join dinners for the invited speakers of the "Wednesday Colloquium of Neuroscience" which were often hosted by my mentor, the neurologist Professor Günter Baumgartner. On one occasion the party discussed the puzzle of a brain area specialized for reading. Most of us have extensive experience looking at visually presented words, so it is no surprise that our brains have special circuits for reading. But evidence from neurological patients who lost the ability to read seemed to indicate that there was a small region in the temporal lobe that serves this specific function. Now, the existence of areas with specific functions is well known for language: there is one for language understanding and one for language production, named 'Wernicke' and 'Broca' after the neurologists who discovered them. But language has been used by Homo sapiens for a long time, like a hundred thousand years, or perhaps since the origin of the species. A reading area would present a puzzle. How can a brain region have evolved for something that humans have practiced only for a few thousand years? Such a short time is generally not considered long enough for the evolution of a complex structure. In the dinner discussion, the possibility was raised that a specialized brain region for reading might have evolved a long time ago for a different function, namely for reading animal tracks as practiced by hunters, and that in today's life the circuitry of that region is most suitable for word recognition. Thus, when children learn to read, this particular region would be engaged and its circuits trained for word recognition, which of course depends on the specific language and thus can only be achieved through experience.

It happened that shortly after that dinner evening I contracted a flu and so did my wife and our two children. It was a memorable experience; all four of us had high fever, I measured my temperature as 42 C (as an experimental physicist I know how to read scales, even in delirium) and we, the parents, scrambled to see that the children got enough to drink. I vividly remember a sleepless night when I felt that my brain was working at feverish speed. I found that quite pleasant and went through many thoughts. One that I remember related to the evolution of brain mechanisms. It suddenly became clear to me that there is a link: it's the brain power that caused our loneliness as humans. At some point intelligence made Homo erectus so powerful that they had no serious enemy other than themselves, and the ensuing fierce competition drove the evolution of intelligence – and eventually made us the lonely species.

In my feverish state I also saw clearly how this could have happened: mutations leading to new brain mechanisms can accumulate in the population over a long time, perhaps several million years; and mutations can remain dormant, that is, without yielding a reproductive advantage, for a long time until becoming useful at some point, perhaps in combination with additional new mutations, or when living conditions change. It is a common pattern of evolution that it creates innovations that only much later come to serve some important function. In dinosaurs, evolution invented feathers before any dinosaurs could fly: mutations created genes for beta-keratins which later became part of the unique amino acid composition of proteins that determines the hardness, resilience and elasticity of bird feathers.[25] Brain mechanisms may have evolved similarly, step by step. As every programmer knows, a program serving some function usually has several parts, and if only one part is faulty or missing, the entire function fails. The same is certainly true for brain functions. Mutations

---

[25] Y Pan et al. The molecular evolution of feathers with direct evidence from fossils. Proceedings of the National Academy of Sciences 116 (8) 3018-3023 (2019). https://www.pnas.org/content/116/8/3018

occur one by one, and a number of specific mutations may be required for a new function to emerge. This conjunction effect is certainly ubiquitous in brain evolution: a language production area is of little use without a language understanding area, and vice versa. Thus, only when a number of mutations are carried along in the population genome is there a chance that two such mutations combine in an individual zygote. At that moment, a brain mechanism may emerge that suddenly gives a huge reproductive advantage and will thus spread quickly through the population genome. Or a complex mechanism develops because it provides reproductive advantage for one function but is later used for a different function.

Recent brain imaging studies have actually confirmed that there is a small area that shows special reading activity, a tiny patch within the fusiform face area (a larger region that lights up in the scanner when a person sees a face). And not only has it been demonstrated to respond strongly during word reading. A follow-up study using a method that allows tracing the neural fibers in the brain also showed that this patch has a special connectivity with the rest of the brain, and this connectivity is present in children before they can read. But the specific activation of the patch occurs only after they learn to read. In fact, from the connectivity pattern in a 5-year old child that could not read, the researchers were able to identify the location of the patch that would later show word-reading specific activity when the child was 8; an amazing result.[26] This is perfectly consistent with the above hypothesis that the 'reading area' is actually an ancient structure, a visual processing tool that the brain evolved for other reasons than word reading, quite plausibly for track reading through thousands of generations when hunting was vitally important.

To summarize this section ("Where we come from…"), what I am arguing is that, compared to other brains, and in fact anything we know, the human brain is a monster of intellectual power, and key to understanding how this monster brain could have evolved in a period as short as two million years are two circumstances: the first is that mutations encoding new functions may remain dormant for a long time and accumulate until the new functions start producing positive selection pressure; and the second is that Homo erectus was so powerful that the direction of Darwinian selection shifted from adaptation to the environment to competition within the species.

---

[26] ZM Saygin, DE Osher, ES Norton, DA Youssoufian, SD Beach, J Feather, N Gaab, JD Gabrieli, N Kanwisher. Connectivity precedes function in the development of the visual word form area. Nat Neurosci. 19(9):1250-5 (2016).

I.2.6   Nature Versus Nurture

Everybody knows that human babies are born with a number of reflexes, such as the grasping reflex: a baby closes the hand with a firm grip when something is touching its palm. But the story of innate behavioral patterns is more complex. When my daughter was three months old, I happened to come across an article in a magazine that described an 'experiment' a student of Piaget had performed on newborn babies. The experiment consisted in the experimenter sticking out her tongue and watching the baby. She observed that, after a few seconds, the baby would try to stick out its tongue too. The young researcher eagerly told Piaget about her experiment, asking what he thinks about it. His answer was "I think it's quite rude." – Although my daughter was not new-born anymore, I did try out this rude behavior on her, and, to my joy, after a few seconds I saw her tongue appear between the lips. What can we learn from this experiment? The baby is obviously imitating the movement she sees. But how is that possible? The sensory stimulus is processed in the baby's visual brain, but how does the motor center of the brain know what muscles to activate to produce a movement that would result in similar processing by the visual brain of the experimenter? Apparently, newborn babies already possess an elaborate mechanism that links the center of visual understanding of a movement to the center for production of the corresponding movement of its own. The brain can reproduce what it sees. Because sticking out the tongue is an arbitrary movement, apparently without any use for infant or mother, the experiment demonstrates the universality of the linking mechanism.[27] It is the basis of learning to speak and of human communication in general. This simple experiment also makes clear why teaching animals a language is difficult and tedious; the ability to learn a language requires much more than the capacity to learn the meanings of tokens.

How much of human behavior is inherited and how much is the result of experience? This question has been debated ad nauseam. The answer is of course, both. In fact, I think, the way nature has packed the blueprint for an immensely complicated organ like the brain into a comparatively sparse genetic code is one of the great mysteries of nature. As we will see, many behavioral traits, perhaps all, have a genetic origin. Language is perhaps the best example. Of course we don't inherit our language; a child learns the language that it is immersed in during its first years of life. But, as Noam Chomsky and others have

---

[27] Neurons of this mechanism have aptly been called 'mirror neurons', G Rizzolatti, L Fadiga L Fogassi, V Gallese, "Premotor cortex and the recognition of motor actions." Cogn. Brain Res. 3:131-41 (1996).

shown, the principles underlying the structure of language are biologically determined in the human mind and hence genetically transmitted. All humans (with very rare exceptions) are born with basic brain mechanisms that enable them to pick up a language by listening and observing. (The rare exceptions of people who are unable to learn a language occur in families carrying a genetic defect.) We find such interdigitating of inherited factors with experience in virtually every kind of human behavior we look at. Thus, the question "how much?" is simply not the right question. It's like asking: how much of a railroad is tracks and how much is train? Are the tracks 50% of the railroad? For someone at home planning a journey it may seem that the tracks are the most important, but for a person waiting on the platform the train seems more important. Thus, the answer to the question depends on where you stand and what you look at.

It is surprising how often this obvious fact, that both contribute, is phrased the wrong way in public discussions. In a TV show an author is introduced who emphasized the importance of environment and experience in child development, arguing that personality is not determined a hundred percent by genes. However, the moderator of the show summarizes the author's work as showing that personality is determined a hundred percent by environment and experience.

Once in a while I see researchers present their studies on identical and fraternal twins on TV, every time revealing, with ever greater certainty than previous studies, the "controversial result" that the genetic influence on human behavioral traits accounts for over 50% of the variation between individuals.[28] Apparently, these researchers expect reluctance of their audience to accept such a result. On the other hand, many broadcasts tend to downplay the role of inheritance in child development and the formation of human society, perhaps for fear that biologists will claim too much territory for the genes, which in turn will lead the public to neglect learning and education; or because of the belief that the problems of society must be resolved by improving education and training. Thus, despite the work of Konrad Lorenz and Edward O. Wilson, the claim of a genetic basis of social behavior continues to meet fierce resistance.

But I think it is very important also in the realm of education to appreciate that genetic basis. Even if its influence would be small compared to the environmental influence it cannot be neglected, because the two types of

---

[28] Twin studies draw their results by determining correlations, e.g., identical twins growing up separately show higher correlations in their behaviors than fraternal twins growing up separately.

influence have vastly different impacts on the progress of society: Education always starts from scratch, whereas the genetic factor, whether small or large, is always born anew in a hundred million babies per year. Thus, reforming a society by education is a task of Sisyphus (the figure of Greek mythology who was condemned to roll a boulder up a hill, and every time he had the boulder close to the summit, it rolled down again). Every time feminists have fought a victory for gender equality, the success seems to slip away in the next generation.[29] And every time political revolutionaries have fought a victory against social inequality, the achievement seems to dissipate in the passage of a generation.

Those twin studies are narrowly focused on the variation within the human population, but do not look at the difference between the human and other species. Darwin and generations of naturists were fascinated by the question of how much we differ from, or resemble, the other species around us. Indeed, the evolutionary perspective provides much stronger arguments for the inheritance of behavioral traits than those twin studies.

I.3 Engenes Of The Brain / The Great Parliament Of The Instincts

I.3.1 Emotions and Drives

There are innate behavioral mechanisms that we are usually not aware of. In certain situations we are surprised by an unexpected emotion. As psychologists and ethologists have pointed out, emotions often indicate the presence of an ancient instinct[30] Many years ago I wanted to visit Lake Kinneret, the Sea of Galilee. I took a bus from Haifa, but that dropped me off in Nazareth, a small town in an arid region midway between the Mediterranean and the Lake, where I had to spend a few hours. My guidebook mentioned a place called Mary's Well. It was a hot morning in June, the sun burned, and the dusty road was lined by houses and walls of white stone. A sign marked a small entrance beside the road. I entered a cave, and, coming from the glistening light outside I could not see anything, but I heard the sound of running water. Now, finding water in a place called Mary's Well is hardly surprising; what surprised me was the intense

---

[29] Michelle Goldberg: "The Future Isn't Female Anymore."
https://www.nytimes.com/2022/06/17/opinion/roe-dobbs-abortion-feminism.html
[30] William McDougall, "An Introduction to Social Psychology." Methuen, London (1908); Konrad Lorenz, „Über den Begriff der Instinkthandlung." In: Folia Biotheoretica. volume 2, Nr. 17, 1937, S. 17–50; Nikolaas Tinbergen, "The Study of Instinct" Clarendon (1951).

pleasure that the sound of the water down in the cave gave me. When I remember this experience now, it strikes me that finding drinkable water is vitally important for primates, especially for those that have descended from trees, where fruits provided plenty of water, to live in the plane. Thus, the sound of running water is an appetitive stimulus. It signals the presence of fresh water, and hearing this sound gives us pleasure and peace. That is why we like to have fountains in parks and gardens. The pleasure that flowers can give us has a similar origin. It goes back to the life in trees when our ancestors depended on fruit trees. They were attracted to regions of forest with lots of flowers because flowering trees would provide fruits. Even more basic is the effect of light. Because we are a diurnal species, as were our ancestors, light wakes us up and gives us joy and energy, whereas darkness induces rest and inhibits activity to the point of being scary or even causing depression, as the winter in northern countries does. Also the colors related to morning and night affect the mood, as Goethe noticed; yellow activates and excites, while blue calms down and instills peace.

We have a strong feeling of home and homeland. The urge to build a house is deeply rooted in human nature; no child that does not take pleasure in making her or his own little house, be it chairs with a blanket or a hut made from twigs in the forest. It does not have to be a big building, children love camping. A house stands for family and being sheltered, the antidote to feeling lonely. When preparing food, some people purse their lips. This may be more common among women, but I noticed that when I prepare fruit salad, my lips move. When we stumble we instinctively grab a handrail or other things in reach, which is reflexive. But for objects we use a different kind of grabbing which is more under conscious control; an object is something we interact with. Sports are popular in today's societies, and they often involve throwing or hitting something, actions we inherited from stone age hunters. In today's urban societies many people love to go hunting or fishing. Also collecting (should I rather say gathering?) mushrooms or berries can be a passion. Most sports also have the form of a fight, either between two individuals or, even more popular, between two teams. Of course, this is because humans sometimes need to act out like this, as psychologists know, but the need comes from the long evolution of humans competing with each other. The crave for fighting and hunting is more common among men, the passion for shopping, more among women. All these passions remind us of our hunter-gatherer ancestors of millions of years of the past.

The discussion of whether human behavior is learned or based on innate mechanisms has a long history. In particular the term 'instinctive' has been used to assess how much Homo sapiens differs from the other animal species; various authors have stated that instincts in Man are fewer and weaker, claiming that human behavior is controlled more by conscious reasoning rather than innate mechanisms. Both the definition of the term instinct and its philosophical discussion in the 19th and much of the last century were often framed by the intention to define "the difference" between Man and other creatures, and the desire to prove Man's intellectual and spiritual superiority and disprove the Darwinian theory of evolution. In general, the discussion portrayed a simplistic picture of innate mechanisms, underestimating their sophistication, and specifically their importance in human behavior. On the other hand, it has long been recognized that conscious control is limited and much of what drives human behavior is unconscious and has roots that are shared across people. The psychiatrist Carl Gustav Jung called this the "collective unconscious," a component of the human psyche that is inherited.

Today, concepts like instinctive versus conscious behavior appear in a new light because of progress in two areas of science in the second half of the 20th century: One is the advent of neurophysiology methods that made it possible to study brain functions at the neural signal level, which has given us a fairly good idea of how the brain represents and processes information. Although we are still far from understanding brain processes comprehensively, the 'computational algorithms' underlying certain brain functions have been clarified in some cases and can be modeled, for example, perceptual and cognitive functions in vision, audition and touch. The other milestone of progress is the advent of the computer. Now, in the 21st century, it is clear to everybody that machines can think; there is artificial intelligence. Although by design computer and brain are as different as they could possibly be, computer science and brain research have fertilized each other; understanding brain functions was helped by comparison with related computer functions, and the development of computer algorithms was influenced by the insight from neurophysiological research.

One surprising result is that we now understand the extent to which the processing in our brains is unconscious; not only the subcortical, which has traditionally been associated with 'the unconscious', but also the processing in cerebral cortex (the big mushroom-like structure at the top of the brain) which has been considered the seat of consciousness.

In vision, conscious perception typically involves selective attention, which has been likened to a spotlight that illuminates a small patch of the image containing the object of interest, thus screening out everything outside the patch. But neurophysiology has shown that the visual cortex sets up object representations not only for the one attended, but also for the many ignored objects.[31] The cortex first individuates objects and creates representations from which attention can then select. Thus, representation comes first, selection next.[32] Representing objects from the chaos of millions of pixels streaming from the eyes into the brain at every moment is a formidable task, still a challenge for computer vision algorithms today. Our brain represents objects in a snap. What we consciously perceive is a selection from visual input that has already been massively preprocessed by unconscious, 'instinctive' mechanisms; an internal model of the outside world, in terms of the engineer. And the similarity of visual processing between human and monkey brains shows that it's been designed by evolution – we inherited the algorithm. Evolutionary algorithms also underlie our behavior. We may think that we have our behavior under conscious control, but in fact we act according to motivations largely created by unconscious mechanisms.[33]

I.3.2 Humans Are Born With a Number of Anlagen That Develop Into Behavioral Faculties

Many behavioral patterns are not learned, although their development may be influenced by learning. The so-called instincts in the animal domain are much more than just chains of reflexes.

An instructive example is the eggroll movement by which wild geese roll an egg that has accidentally fallen out back into the nest. This behavioral pattern was studied by Konrad Lorenz and Niko Tinbergen.[34] They found that it has 3 phases: first, the goose, sitting on its eggs, spots the strayed egg and is aroused by this sight; it then gets up and turns its body to face the egg; and finally it performs a movement with its beak that rolls the egg back into the nest, upon which the goose calms and settles down on the eggs as before. The authors

---

[31] Object representation involves lumping together the features of an object, such as border lines, curves, and corners that make up its contour, as well as colors, textures, and its location and motion; everything we can know about an object by seeing.

[32] Fangtu T. Qiu, Tadashi Sugihara and & Rüdiger von der Heydt, "Figure-ground mechanisms provide structure for selective attention." *Nature Neuroscience* 10 (11): 1492-1499 (2007). This result and most of what is known about visual processing comes from studies of visual systems of macaques which are similar to those of apes and humans.

[33] Robert M. Sapolsky, "Behave: the biology of humans at our best and worst." New York, Penguin (2017).

[34] K. Lorenz & N. Tinbergen, "Taxis und Instinkthandlung in der Eirollbewegung der Graugans [Directed and instinctive behavior in the egg rolling movements of the gray goose]." *Zeitschrift für Tierpsychologie, 2,* 1–29, (1938).

showed that this behavior is not based on 'understanding' the situation. They placed a decoy egg next to the nest which looked like the other eggs but was attached to the ground with a rubber band. In this situation the goose performed the three phases of the behavior, just as with the real egg, except that it did not succeed in the third phase where its beak slipped because the decoy egg was attached. But the goose nevertheless appeared satisfied after performing the movements and settled down on the eggs as if the operation had been successful. After a while, it 'discovered' the decoy egg as if it had not seen it before and was aroused again, and then performed the entire sequence of movements again, etc.

This experiment shows some features that are typical also for other innate behavioral patterns. Particularly interesting is the apparent emotional process: the arousal or unrest at the beginning after the cognitive trigger event, and the apparent satisfaction after the completion of the response. Another insight to gain from this experiment is that innate behavioral patterns are generally more complex than just "a chain of reflexes", as instinctive responses have been described. After the cognitive initiation of the pattern, the system collects sensory information (the location of the target) and uses it to adjust the body posture, until the final motor response is executed.

Even the most basic instinctive responses have a similar complexity; for example, the so-called 'escape reflex', which is ubiquitous among animal species, also consists of a cognitive trigger event followed by sensory processing: evaluation of current body position, possible flight direction and its relation to body position, as required for calculating the necessary movements to be performed, and the final motor response. This response pattern also includes the emotional phases: arousal at the beginning and relaxation at the end (in case the escape succeeded).

I.3.3   The Two Desires That Drive Behavior

As in the example of the egg-rolling response of the goose, instinctive patterns of behavior generally start with an appetitive phase in which the organism becomes unquiet, as if searching for something. Typically, when it finds the object of the search, a specific response sequence is launched which is directed towards an evolutionarily defined goal. Once the goal is achieved the organism calms down, assuming a restful state which terminates the behavior pattern.

We know from our subjective experience that successful completion of a sequence of instinctive behavior that gives us pleasure, also motivates us to perform it again and again. This is certainly so also in other species, and for good evolutionary reasons. If a monkey had no pleasure jumping around in the trees, it would just sleep on a branch all the time, and when getting hungry it would look for fruits, but at that point it would not have enough energy reserve to search and find the quantity of fruit that it needs. Instead, the drive to roam about, a behavior that may look like curiosity and playing, serves the animal to explore its surroundings and plan foraging trips. In fact, also in humans many behavioral patterns are sequences of several stages, each of which involves some pleasure when executed. While great pleasures are rare, life offers lots of small pleasures all the time. How many a husband has put the peace of a day at risk just by looking at a beautiful woman in the presence of his spouse – small pleasure.

Some instinctive behavioral sequences may not give pleasure, but rather relief from stress or anxiety. The most basic of these is certainly the drive to live. Danger of death produces fear and anxiety, calling for a response to avert the danger – flight, defense etc. – which, if successful, relieves the stress. The structure is similar, but rather than longing for something, the motivation comes from the desire to leave a stressful or frightening situation.

The two desires, seeking pleasure and avoiding displeasure, are the forces that pull and push us around all day. Both are based on ancient physiological mechanisms of high complexity. Since prehistoric times humans have found ways to activate the reward mechanisms deliberately by taking substances they found in plants, like opium, or that they prepared, like alcohol, and modern humans have also synthetic drugs at their disposal. All these drugs mimic substances the brain normally uses to steer behavior. In the 1970ies it was discovered that opiates are molecules that stimulate a class of 'receptors' that the brain normally activates with its own specific molecules to produce pleasure. Certain nerve cells excrete these substances in situations when the host has completed a biologically important behavioral sequence, such as mating, finding a spring of water, killing an animal in the hunt, or simply when getting up in the morning and seeking rest in the evening. The resulting pleasure is the incentive to perform those behaviors; its memory will induce the behavior later again. The underlying brain mechanisms are highly complex. There are many classes of molecules, each molecule acts on specific receptors in different parts of the brain, and each action has its characteristic dynamics. Thus, although much of this is known today, it is still very difficult to predict the behavioral effects. And, of course, stimulating those receptors directly by taking substances that are similar to the brain's own, or mimic their effects, yanks out the gears of the complex machinery of motivation and inevitably destroys its functioning.

The behavioral patterns of the brain, or 'engenes', as I call them, are complex programs with several components, including perceptual and motor mechanisms. Like in a technical engine, there is a trigger mechanism that initiates execution of the program and a motor that produces an action; and ahead of the action there is sensory processing to plan the action; and following the action there is a positive feeling of pleasure, or a relief from negative feelings like tension, distress or anxiety. Many times each day (or night, in the case of a nocturnal species), an organism chooses which of the available engenes to activate. The choice may be a routine that can be innate or formed like a habit, but often it is a decision based on a motivational state or even an abstract rational plan. In humans the choice of engenes is extraordinarily complex. In general, one could say that every choice we make, even the habitual, is driven either by seeking pleasure or by avoiding displeasure.

Engenes of the brain are not like reflexes. The difference is the emotional component. Grasping a hot object produces pain and triggers a release response. When an object approaches the eye, this triggers a lid closure response, but no pain. Why does one experience involve pain, but not the other? The answer, I think, is that the sensation of pain leaves a memory trace which later serves to avoid situations similar to the one that caused the pain. The release or withdrawal response is not a simple reflex; a reflex loop requires sensory signals traveling up to a response center and motor signals traveling down to the appropriate muscles, and this would take too long (most of the nerve fibers signaling pain are very slow, and even the fastest pain fibers conduct only half as fast at the fastest motor fibers). The lid closure reflex, involving a short loop, is fast enough to protect the eye, but the response triggered by burning the skin generally comes too late to prevent the damage; therefore, evolution has come up with a more intelligent mechanism involving pain and memory.

It is important to see that the behavioral engenes are not under voluntary control, and the choice which engene to activate is not so much a rational decision but an emotional choice. An infant does not think about standing up and walking on two legs when the time comes. Nor does it copy adult behavior; I'm sure Romulus and Remus, who were raised by a four-legged mother, a wolf, started to walk on two legs in due time. One only needs to watch an infant at that age, the urge to get up and the great satisfaction when it succeeds, to convince oneself that this is the expression of a fundamental instinctive behavior, just like the ability to fly and the urge to do it in birds.

We have passions and aversions, pleasure and disgust, and most people would agree that these are generally not based on rational thinking. In many cases it is also clear that they are not based on education or experience. Children need not be taught to avoid eating something that stinks, and they spontaneously reject food that is sour or has a bitter taste, but crave for sweet. For primates it was always important to find spring water, which is pure, and avoid surface water which can be contaminated. Thus, we prefer to drink water cool, presumably because spring water is cool, in contrast to surface water, and modern humans (at least in the U.S.) are obsessed with ice water.

Taste and smell provide many examples where pleasure and disgust are obviously preprogrammed since ancient times. The pleasure of sweet and the displeasure of sour we have obviously inherited from our arboreal ancestors for whom sugars were a main source of calories. It made them search for ripe fruit with high sugar content and avoid unripe fruit which has little sugar. The Sour receptors signal acidity. Interestingly, adding sugar neutralizes the sour taste; that's why we sweeten a sour drink. But every chemist knows that sugar is a neutral substance that cannot change the acidity; the drink is as acidic with sugar as it is without. That sugar cancels sour is the result of neural computation.

For us, as for our ancestors, sugars and fats are sources of calories and until modern times they were hard to come by in sufficient quantities. They are still potent sources of sensory pleasure. As every mother knows, adding sweet + fat + cold together is most attractive for children: it's ice cream. It is often said that taste is idiosyncratic, "*de gustibus non est disputandum*", but why do we all love the taste of vanilla?

Why do people enjoy fireworks? To the dismay of their parents, little boys love to play with fire. The attraction of fire seems irresistible. Animals are generally afraid of fire; of course, because wildfires are extremely dangerous. But to humans, fire has been a friend, a companion for more than a million years.[35] At some point, evolution flipped the sign of the emotion from fear to fun. Films and computer games target this emotion with the sound and sight of explosions. Note that the sound of the entertainment products resembles more the blaze of a fire than the bang of a real explosion.

I.3.4   Based On Genes Does Not Mean Stereotyped

Anthropologists of the early 20th century assumed that innate behavioral mechanisms must be the same in each individual, and, therefore, the observed

---

[35] S Hlubik, F Berna, C Feibel, D Braun, JWK Harris, "Researching the nature of fire at 1.5 Mya on the site of FxJj20 AB, Koobi Fora, Kenya, using high-resolution spatial analysis and FTIR spectrometry." Current Anthropology 58 S243-S257 (2017).

differences between people must be attributed to influences of environment, culture, and tradition. They were right about the diversity of human culture, but the assumption that the innate behavioral mechanisms are the same in all people is wrong. The science of heredity has shown that the genome varies across the human population, and this variation includes the genetic basis of behavior.[36] This is of course what the twin studies show: Fraternal twins (who share their genomes partly) show more variance than identical twins (who share their genomes entirely). Thus, the claim that a certain behavioral pattern has a genetic basis does not imply that everybody has that behavioral pattern, or has it to the same degree. No two brains have the same genetic code, except for the rare occasions of identical twins (0.3%), and even those that share an identical code develop differently because of variable gene expression and variable influences of environment and education.

Pointing out that many people do not have a certain behavior does not prove that it must be entirely the result of tradition or a special environmental influence. Take for example height fear (or vertigo). I personally have strong attacks of vertigo when I climb metal grid see-through stairs outside of a high building such as the tower of St. Stephan in Vienna, but many people do not have this problem at all. For example, roofers are known for lacking height fear. Now, to the point: nobody would argue that height fear is the result of tradition or an environmental influence. It is an elementary reaction that is hard to control, although it can be weakened (adapted) and overcome by practice. Height fear is either a relic from the arboreal life of our remote ancestors that warned them not to climb too high, or a pattern that evolved as a protection when early homo took to prairies, which strengthened the legs but weakened the arms, leading to Homo erectus, and climbing trees was no longer safe. I found that the sensation of vertigo was enhanced to a degree of nausea when I was with my little children who were running up and down the stairs, even though these were completely encaged and safe, so there was no rational reason to be worried. This again argues for a protective function of that emotional reaction.

The example of height fear shows that behavioral mechanisms that clearly have an ancient genetic basis can nevertheless vary in strength across individuals in today's population. Studies of heredity have also shown that behavioral traits are generally based on multiple genes, typically hundreds, each of which may contain a mutation. Therefore, although the genes are discrete, engenes have essentially continuous distributions of strength.

---

[36] R Plomin, "Blueprint: how DNA makes us who we are." MIT Press, Cambridge (2018).

I.3.5   How I Learned To Appreciate the Power of Pink

Individual differences are often used as an argument that certain preferences reflect just the influence of the environment, gender stereotyping and the wrong education. For example, a mother sighs that her daughter always wants to wear pink, and another mother shrugs it off as a fad, because "my daughters don't have that fad, it's just peer pressure and the prejudice that girls have to wear pink." I'm not sure. But when my grandson Jash turned nine I decided my present for the day would be a Meccano, because Meccano had given me many happy hours when I was nine. So, there it was, a box with lots of pieces and an instruction booklet with pictures. To begin, I suggested that we build a car according to the instructions, and we would do it together. He did fine with the screws, but of course it took time. Meccano is not like Lego, and into the second hour, I noticed that he lost steam. But all the time his little sister Simie, who was four at the time, had been watching us with interest, and when her brother lost interest, she was eager to step in. I was amazed how skillful she could put nuts on the screws almost immediately and knew how to use wrench and screwdriver, none of which she had ever done before. We made progress and soon finished the car (well, it did take a while). We tried it out and it worked, and we were all proud, brother, sister, and grandfather. And at the end, Simie said: "For my next birthday I also want a Meccano – but in pink!" That's how I learned to appreciate the power of pink. I then remembered that my daughter, Simie's mother, had loved pink almost from the time she was a baby – pink and purple. Interestingly, Simie's sister who is two years younger does not have the obsession with pink, although she tries to imitate her sister and the two always play together. This disagreement between the sisters as much as the agreement between mother and daughter convinced me that the pink preference has a genetic basis (see Gregor Mendel).

I'm aware there is an organization named "Pink stinks" that tries to combat gender stereotyping, but I think they put the wrong label on a noble undertaking. It seems obvious to me that the attractiveness of pink relates to the fact that pink is one of the distinctive features of babies, activating a cognitive mechanism that is deeply rooted in human heritage, probably reaching back to our oldest primate ancestors (I wonder if there are behavioral tests in monkeys of this). A famous brain scientist and psychologist, a woman I greatly admire, contradicted me on this. She thought that the alleged preference of girls for pink is a fashion as arbitrary as any other fashion, referencing a 19th century newspaper article that proposed pink for baby *boys*. But I have never heard of a boy with a pink obsession. In contrast, prescribing baby blue for boys is probably nothing but a fashion; the favorite color of boys is not a nice color; it's battle-ship gray. Lego, after many years of resisting gender stereotyping, finally succumbed to competition and consumer demand and now makes different sets of bricks, either colored or battle-ship gray. In any case, the attempt to ban pink reminds me of Don Quixote fighting the windmill.

I.3.6   Of Men And Mice

Here is another emotion whose origin is a puzzle: young children love to stroke little furry animals. For a three-year-old, touching a kitten or a dog puppy is heaven. Why do children have that craving? It's actually a passion that some people carry on to adulthood (see John Steinbeck: "Of Men and Mice"). The craving for baby animals certainly relates to the 'Brood-care engene' that we will consider below under 'Society forming engenes'. But human babies don't have fur; the craving for furry animals is a puzzle. It is obvious to me that for children the fur is important, naked baby animals like newborn rabbits are not attractive. Also, many people love dogs, but the same people rather react with discomfort when they come across a Xoloitzcuintli, the Mexican hairless dog: the skin feels warm, but not pleasant like fur. They are good foot warmers in bed, but they are not cute. – Here is my speculation: The passion for furry baby animals comes from one of those ancient mutations that were long dormant, a result of molecular gambling that first conferred neither advantage nor disadvantage for survival, but at some point became important, just as the emergence of a 'reading area' in the brain mentioned above. And in this case the molecular gambling resulted in a mechanism that gave humans pleasure when they picked up pups, perhaps after killing the mother animal, and cradled them. It might have been the beginning of the long friendships between dog and human, and between cat and human. Dogs became useful as watch dogs, and cats as protectors of grain storages, and both became men's first companions when humans switched from a life as hunters and gatherers to farming, an incredible change of lifestyle that has been called the Neolithic Revolution. The passion for cuddling animal pups was a prerequisite for animal husbandry and the basis for the domestication of goats, sheep, pigs, cattle, chickens and more. Thus, the cuteness of kittens and the power of pink are just two obvious manifestations of ancient engenes.

What is significant is that the transition to agriculture actually happened within a few thousand years, and independently in several locations across the globe, an accomplishment of unprecedented speed in all evolution on earth. The agricultural revolution spread over Europe only 6-4,000 years ago, but European children are attracted to animals even before they can speak. We see how happy children are if they can cuddle an animal – and feel pity for those whose parents don't like pets. My point is, changing the mind of a hunter to that of a shepherd is not an easy thing, it's a big mental transformation that does not occur at a snap just when people decide to do agriculture from now on.[37] In the Bible, the good shepherd who lays down his life for the sheep is the symbol for altruistic behavior. And such a transformation does not occur within a few thousand years. Homo sapiens must have been able to activate faculties of the brain that had been established long before. Just a change of tradition and lifestyle would not transform hunters into farmers; it needs passion and a lot of intuitive understanding of growing plants and animals to be a farmer. Indeed, still in today's urban civilization many people have a passion for gardening; one can see how having their hands in the soil gives them pleasure; others have a passion for breeding animals. Talking to people on a family farm, like an Amish family or farmers in the Swiss mountains, makes one realize that farm life is something deeply rooted in human nature. It is one of the tragedies of modern industry-style agriculture that it deprives those people of their vocation.

I.3.7   The Pursuit of Happiness

Although we cannot say for sure, the principles of motivation—seeking pleasure and avoiding displeasure—seem to drive the behavior of animals as well as ours. But, of course, the ability to reason, communicate and interact in a society makes human behavior more complex. Still, it is based on ancient engenes of the brain. These engenes give us the enchantment of the babbling spring, the beauty of a flower, the sweetness of a child and the pleasures and pains of love. They give us joy and happiness.

Thus, to be happy we feel that we need to satisfy our desires. But our desires are the desires of our engenes. Since sugars were once an important source of calories, but were hard to come by, sweet is pleasure, and today's market provides it in abundance. Not only do we find (cane) sugar added to all kinds of food, but fruits have also become richer in sugars than ever. What once pleased kings, today's consumers find too sour. The oranges in the orchard of King Pedro's Alcázar of Seville would not sell in any supermarket today.

Since we are descendants of hunter-gatherers it is no surprise that the corresponding engenes influence us in our daily activities. If you have ever collected mushrooms or berries in the woods you will remember the satisfaction

---

[37] That's how the historian Yuval Harari sees it: a mere decision.

of hitting a trove. After spending days gathering, the pleasure intensifies. This activity was once the main source of food: search, hit and enjoy.

The freedom and right to follow the call of these engenes is explicitly recognized in the Declaration of Independence: "We hold these truths to be self-evident, that all men are created equal, that they are endowed by their Creator with certain unalienable Rights, that among these are Life, Liberty and *the pursuit of Happiness*."[38] This is certainly a great formulation of the basis of political order. To have the right to pursue happiness stated explicitly with the foundation of a country is perhaps unique.

But the feeling that we need to satisfy our desires to be happy is at the root of much unhappiness. Our desires are the desires of engenes that were designed by evolution, and happiness has never been a concern of evolution. This basic truth was clearly formulated by Buddha who preached that nothing is permanent and that a life based on possessing things or persons doesn't make us happy, and that the cause of suffering is greed.[39]

Since we attempt here to examine the engenes of the brain in a scientific way without the usual prejudice, we may wonder if the pursuit of happiness is really an unalienable right in general. For example, the drive to seek power in society is an engene that is strong in some people, especially men, and it gives them pleasure. This may be a fundamental condition for serving important political

---

[38] https://en.wikipedia.org/wiki/Life,_Liberty_and_the_pursuit_of_Happiness

[39] Buddha advised us to ignore those desires to become happier, until ultimately, if we succeed, we will reach a state of complete happiness: nirvana. That suppression of desires makes happy is a remarkable insight. It is physiologically plausible. The various engenes all use common neural circuits to produce desires or anxiety, and others to produce satisfaction and pleasure. But these neural circuits adapt. An example is taste: diluted raspberry syrup may taste sweet and delicious, but after drinking a more concentrated solution, the same syrup tastes like water. Adaptation is a general property of neural circuits, including pleasure mechanisms, for example the opioid receptors which are naturally stimulated by neurotransmitters produced in the brain (endorphins): after repeated stimulation, their activation tends to get less and less, such that ever stronger stimulation is needed to produce the same degree of pleasure. The converse is also true, after a period without stimulation, the receptors become more sensitive. Thus, continuously satisfying the demands of all those engenes will adapt the pleasure receptors, and to satisfy their owner will require more and more of the actions these engenes ask for; in the case of the engene that manages nutrition, craving for sweet; in the case of the engene that strives for possession, greed. And conversely, ignoring their demands and suppressing the actions will sensitize the pleasure receptors and may eventually lead to complete happiness, as Buddha predicts.

functions, but it can also entail the abuse of power. There is no question that wielding power gives political leaders pleasure, and can lead to addiction. An image comes to mind of Stalin watching a huge military parade on the Red Square, smiling and obviously happy. Also Hitler depended on the pleasure of giving speeches to huge crowds, using the newly invented loudspeaker, to show his power. He got used to this excitement and apparently depended on it, taking more and more to psychoactive drugs when opportunities to address big crowds became rare. The engene of wielding power may also underlie the drive to make money, because money is power. It seems to me that the drive to accumulate wealth is largely based on this addictive pleasure of power. Accumulating wealth is perhaps people's most common attempt to pursue happiness.

I.3.8   Engenes That Move Us Around

We will now look specifically at human behavior under the aspect of where its motivations come from, trying to identify the engenes and their evolutionary origin.

Observing the development of children can give hints at innate behaviors that are no longer visible in adults. Genetic patterns that were once useful can remain in the genome even after the environmental conditions have changed, often for a long time. This is also true for the engenes of the brain. When a certain function has become obsolete, instead of removing its genetic pattern, evolution may add a new pattern that produces a mechanism that inhibits the old function, as in the example of vertigo mentioned above (the unpleasant feeling that inhibits the habit of climbing), or it may modify the existing pattern to serve a new function. Often these additions and modifications develop later during infancy than the original functions. That is why one can observe inherited behaviors in infants that later disappear when the child grows up. A simple example is the grasp reflex in babies, an ancient coordination used to hold on to the hair of the mother who had to have her hands free when moving in trees, as can be seen in monkeys. Interestingly, in premature babies the reflex is so strong that one can let them cling to a rope and suspend their body entirely. The reflex later weakens and disappears after a few months. Adults who have not learned to swim will drown in the water, but babies produce the ancient swimming coordination (like that seen in dogs), and they hold their breath when the face is under water and breathe when they come up. Apparently, we are losing these innate mechanisms later during development.

While all other primates are quadrupeds, our ancestors became bipeds at some point during the last 5 million years, which was a dramatic change. It involved pronounced modifications of the anatomy, especially in foot, knees, hips, and spine, but also new brain mechanisms. Walking on two legs is qualitatively different: while four legs provide static stability, remaining upright on two legs requires dynamic control: the support surface continuously needs to be brought vertically under the body's center of gravity. Except under the unusual condition of standing still on our feet without any disturbance, we continually need to make steps to keep the balance. Our brain uses sensors in feet and legs as well as signals from the vestibular organ and the visual system that together tell us exactly the direction of the force of gravity and where it is moving to predict the adjustments. Moreover, when we are walking, running, or jumping, or when disturbed by an external force like when picking up a load, the brain adds inertial and external forces to the gravity vector to maintain equilibrium. When you throw a ball, the first muscle that is activated is your gastrocnemius, a muscle in the back of the lower leg. The engene works so well that it almost never fails (except when we are drunk, or getting old). Besides enabling us to walk upright, it is the basis of bike riding and some of the amazing acrobatics seen in modern sports, as we will see later.

Several of our emotional reactions remind us that our remote ancestors descended from trees. How much our children love climbing and swinging can be appreciated from the billions of dollars communities spent on playgrounds with swings and structures for climbing. In those ancient times, climbing a tree meant escaping to safety, and the swinging movements signaled to the little ancestor "here are you safe, you can relax." Clearly, the reward part of the ancient engene is still intact. Being carried by the mother may be the primary source of evolution of this engene; an infant put down and left alone will soon start to cry. To stay close to the mother is vitally important for the infant. Also, hearing people talking induces sleep, whereas silence wakes the baby up. Many adults sleep with the radio or TV on.

The drive to explore has enabled humans to spread all over the globe, even crossing the vast space of the Pacific Ocean in small boats. Without the marvelous engene of curiosity and exploration this would not have been possible and Homo sapiens would never have become what they are. Again, this drive is not rational. Pondering the chance of success of an expedition into the ocean would have led them to stay where they were. Today, the quest to go to the Moon, Mars or other, is the nonsensical product of activating this irrational ancient engene. Just like other engenes, the 'Curiosity engene' works with negative and positive feelings, creating an urge to explore and the satisfaction of success. Interestingly, in this case language has a special term for the negative feeling:

boredom. Watching young people, I convinced myself that being bored is painful to them. For better or worse, this problem has been eliminated by the advent of smartphones.

Compared to the apes, humans are a restless species. Life as hunters and gatherers required movement. It is thought that the reason for humans being almost hairless is that this way they can have sweat glands all over the body which allows them to dissipate heat more efficiently when running. This enabled early hunters to run fast for longer durations. Hairy animals must dissipate all the heat through respiration when running and thus have less endurance. Early humans also had to move frequently over long distances while gathering food and searching for hunting grounds according to seasonal variations and in response to changes of climate. Early humans may have been even more mobile than hunter-gatherer societies found today that have been marginalized and had to adapt their lifestyle to the conditions of the rainforest. Being confined to life inside houses in the modern urban societies, many people feel the urge to escape, leading to seasonal mass migrations during vacations, and people finding pleasure in camping outside.

I.3.9   Home

Wer jetzt kein Haus hat baut sich keines mehr,
wer jetzt allein ist wird es lange bleiben,
wird wachen, lesen, lange Briefe schreiben
und wird in den Alleen hin und her
unruhig wandern, wenn die Blätter treiben.

From Rainer Maria Rilke: Herbstag

Who has no house now will build none anymore,
who is now alone will be so for long,
will stay up, reading, writing long letters,
will wander in the alleys to and fro
restless, when the leaves are drifting.

From Rainer Maria Rilke: Autumn Day

The house is an important part of human life. Children love building and inhabiting toy houses. The fun generated by the 'Housing engene' makes people go camping. A house means family, homelessness means loneliness. This has certainly been so for ages, with caves providing shelter for families since the time of Homo erectus. They were a precious asset, providing room for social life and for maintaining a fire that kept animals away. The limited number of available caves may have set a limit to population growth. Early hominids certainly competed for the best caves in the best situations. A home is the most basic good in modern societies too. The home is protected against trespassing by law, and homelessness is the bottom of poverty. The pleasure of a home is an important affordance of cars (I wonder when cars will be equipped with coffee makers).

I.3.10   Learning a Language

Humans know how to communicate virtually from birth; within hours, or a few days, a baby recognizes a smile and smiles back. Language requires the ability to form abstract concepts. Simie, a little girl still at the age of 1-word sentences, points up to the transparent corrugated plastic roof on my pergola and says: "dirty." It was the first time she saw that roof (or any transparent roof I presume). Her response shows that her brain had already formed the highly abstract concept of "dirty" and was happy to apply it at this occasion (I was less happy; I had to clean the roof).

The inherited brain structures are responsible for the similarity of language production and the basic grammatical rules in all languages. The existence of two specialized brain regions for language production and language understanding in specific locations of the cerebral cortex, as known from studies of patients with focal brain lesions, shows that there is a basic structure for language processing that is genetically programmed. The concepts of nouns and verbs come with the genes. Some of the genetic code required for learning a language has been identified.

As with other engenes, the 'Verbal-communication engene' generates an urge to talk, and talking yields pleasure. The cell phone age provides an impressive demonstration. There is also an interesting gender difference. I see female students being attached to the phone more often than male students. 'Urge to talk' may not adequately describe the negative feeling associated with this engene. For humans, being deprived of communication is unpleasant to the extent of causing suffering and depression. In fact, it has been used as a method of torture.

I.3.11   What the Brain Can, And Cannot Do

The fact that newborn babies have the ability to communicate clearly shows that the basic mechanisms that enable us to learn a language are innate. Without these mechanisms, humans cannot learn to speak. Recently a family was discovered in England in which some members cannot learn to speak a language, and this inability was found to be inherited. In fact, the language disorder is related to a mutation in a gene called FOXP2. The inheritance is dominant, that is, damage to one copy of the gene is sufficient to derail speech and language development. This shows that FOXP2 is necessary for language development, but several other genes are also required.

While there is clear evidence for genetic factors, language is also the prime example for the influence of tradition. A child will pick up whatever language it hears early in life. And, just as for language, humans can learn many other skills. We can run, swim, climb and ride bicycles. Skateboarders can jump performing the most incredible loops in the air. Driving cars, we move much faster than walking or running, even through traffic in crowded cities, and pilots learn to fly airplanes at speeds a hundred times faster than walking. Isn't that proof that our brain can learn anything? One might think that modern civilization demonstrates that our brain is infinitely versatile because it can learn.

But let's look at some of the examples more carefully. Because our ancestors lived in trees for millions of years, evolution has endowed us with a powerful vestibular system. This is the organ that registers at any moment the orientation and accelerations of the head. In combination with the visual sense, the brain computes how the head moves and what forces are needed to move in the desired directions. These are complex computations that mathematicians call tensor algebra. Using millions of stress receptors in the tendons the brain keeps track of the rest of the body, the positions and movements of the limbs, and how to create the forces for the intended movement. One can imagine how much the life in trees has honed the underlying algorithms. Not all animals have such a fantastic computer for movement. While bears can stand up and walk on two legs for a short time, their movements are slow and clumsy. With a lot of training they can learn to ride a bike for a brief period. In fact, the vestibular signals and the computations for bike riding are largely the same as required for bipedal walking and running: how should the center of gravity move and where should we place our feet to exactly oppose the vector sum of gravity and force of acceleration. If the feet are under the center of gravity, posture is stable (labile equilibrium). Placing the feet at some distance away from the point where they oppose gravity lets the force of gravity accelerate the body in the desired direction, and once it moves, a step is made that places a foot under the center of gravity again, and so forth, repeating the sequence. This is walking or running. When riding a bike, the computations are very much the same, the only difference being that the movement of feet is replaced by the movement of a wheel. To learn bike riding we have to learn to anticipate the movements of the front wheel and to move the handlebar so as to make the wheel perform the same movements as the feet in walking. And of course we have to suppress the ordinary movements of the feet. Our exquisite movement system enables dancers to move elegantly and divers to perform the most complex jumps. Also when skiing, snowboarding and windsurfing we use the same engene; the dynamics are the same, and the engene uses the same algorithm: it anticipates the vector sum of gravity and acceleration forces and moves the feet where the vector points.

We are amazingly skilled at moving fast; cars and planes move much faster than our biological ways of moving. How is that possible? How can our perception cope with speeds that evolution could not anticipate? Sensing our speed of movement relies primarily on the visual system, mostly on processing the transformations of the images in the eyes caused by our own motion. Because in the images, near objects stream by at higher speed than far objects, the images are transforming in a way that informs the brain about the speed and direction of self-motion. This is called motion parallax. Now, it is a simple physical fact that the motion parallax caused by fast self-motion in a large environment is the same as the motion parallax caused by slow self-motion in a small environment. For example, when we are driving on a highway the parallax is the same as when we are walking on a narrow trail. In one situation, speed is high and objects are distant, in the other, speed is slow and objects are close. That means that the brain can use the same algorithm to compute our movements. Thus, we are well prepared by evolution for car driving. What we have to learn is just to cope with a limited view in the car seat and, of course, to suppress the walking movements.

The above examples show that many of the skills we developed to cope with the modern world are actually based on engenes of the brain prepared by evolution through millions of years. So, is the brain really the freely programmable multi-purpose computer that it appears to be? Closer scrutiny shows that this is an illusion. There are limits of what we can learn that are rooted in the ancient design of our brain. The magnificent vestibular system that enables the most complex movements is designed only for movements on time scales that were important for the life in trees. It has its limits for slow movements. In engineering terms, the lower 'cut off frequency' is about 1 Hz, which means that changes of velocity that take place over periods much longer than a second, the vestibular signals are inaccurate, and for very slow changes, they fail completely. In the laboratory, this is commonly demonstrated by seating a person on a rotating chair that is enclosed in a cylinder that rotates with the chair so that the person cannot see the outside world. When the chair is set in motion, the person first experiences the acceleration and perceives herself as rotating, but after a while the vestibular signals fade and the perception of motion ceases so that the person has the illusion of being stationary. This pleasant state ends abruptly when the person tilts her head, because then the head rotates about a different axis and the vestibular sensors for rotation about the vertical axis of the head (whose signals had vanished) are suddenly stimulated, resulting in a vivid response which typically makes the subject vomit.

One consequence of this limitation is that pilots, however experienced, cannot keep the plane on course in a cloud without instruments. If the vestibular system sensed accelerations (changes in speed, and also rotations) accurately like technical navigation systems do, it would not need vision and should thus enable the pilot to fly in clouds. The problem is that the brain cannot integrate the acceleration signals it gets over longer periods of time. The pilot needs such integration to convert the acceleration signals into velocity and orientation of the plane. As a result, without vision, the pilot cannot distinguish a horizontal flight direction from a flight that is losing height. The brain does this fine for short periods, as during the jumps of a diver, but to get a sense of direction for more gradual turns it needs visual input. Technical systems can accurately integrate acceleration signals over days and weeks, as demonstrated in 1958 by the submarine Nautilus that crossed the north pole under the ice in a voyage that took 19 days with no vision. Our vestibular system has been honed by evolution during 40 million years of arboreal life of our monkey ancestors; it's accurate for the duration of a triple toe loop, but cannot keep the direction of flight straight for more than a few seconds.

In fact, more generally speaking, the world that we experience, our intuitive world, is entirely created by our brain. In the language of the engineer, the brain computes an internal model and updates it continuously based on the incoming sensory signals. We rely on this model all the time, it predicts exactly where to land our next step and even the over next step. And when driving it tells us where the wheels of the car go although we cannot see them. It enables us to grasp objects, hit a golf ball with amazing precision, unfailingly pick the ripest apple from a basket, and all the other tasks of daily life. It is extremely useful, but it is idiosyncratic, specifically human. As mentioned, when walking in a moonlit night we see the moon following us. Of course, rationally we know that it must be an illusion. But this does not change our perception.

The illusion of the movement of the moon is but one of many consequences of the peculiar representation of space in the brain: The maximum distance it can represent is finite and fairly short, no more than about 30 meters (100 feet). At small distances, that space is nearly veridical (consistent with physical space); we do not err when reaching for an object, and people that walk by do not change in size. But when we stand on a mountain looking down at the bottom of a valley, people look small like ants; and a parachutist seen jumping from a plane appears to shrink rapidly after a few seconds. All this follows from the finite size of the internal space model which is like a dome that we carry along with us. The brain 'projects' the visual image onto that dome like a projector onto a screen. Therefore, because the moon is 'projected' onto the dome, and the dome follows us, so does the moon. And the apparent size of distant objects is given by the size of their 'projection' onto the dome. When an object moves away, its image in the eye (as in any camera) shrinks, and so does its 'projection' on the dome. Beyond a certain distance, we see it shrinking accordingly. At close distances, within a range, the brain computes the size of the object accurately, and within that range objects do not appear to shrink or expand.

We learn in school that the colors of the world are the different wavelengths of light. We got that: Newton has shown that light is composed of a spectrum of colors. But where is brown in the spectrum, or gray, or purple? No, the colors we perceive are not related in a simple way to the physical wavelengths. Colors, like space, are computed in the brain. In fact, sunlight has an infinite number of wavelengths, and each object surface absorbs some wavelengths more than others; it has a characteristic absorption spectrum. Objects in the world come in a sheer infinite variety of absorption spectra, and our visual cortex categorizes them in a peculiar way that is much simpler than the physical manifold. This is why our colors can be simulated by electronic displays. It requires only three signals per pixel. The displays simply mimic the light absorptions that real objects produce in the three cone types of the retina. Fortunately, we have only three, which simplifies the technology. Most animals have more. The humble goldfish has four color receptors, and he/she uses them: The biologist Christa Neumeyer designed behavioral experiments showing that a goldfish can distinguish colors that to humans look identical.[40] We can accept that, but we cannot imagine the colorful world of goldfish. Also birds and insects have more advanced color vision than humans. As mentioned above, our color vision is modest because in the Cretaceous period dinosaurs ruled the day and forced our

---

[40] Christa Neumeyer, "Tetrachromatic color vision in goldfish: evidence from color mixture experiments." J Comp Physiol A 171, 639–649 (1992).

little mammalian ancestors to live underground and come out only in the dark, but color vision needs plenty of light.

I.4 SOCIETY FORMING ENGENES

Clearly, the one trait that makes our species the most powerful is human society. The evolution of the society forming engenes gave Homo sapiens superior power and eventually led to the extinctions of the other competing species, leaving us the only species in the genus Homo, indeed, the only species capable of culture in the universe, as far as we know.

Human society is also the most difficult to understand. Its nucleus, the two-parent family, is a phenomenon. If an extraterrestrial being would visit our planet, it would certainly be astonished to see those creatures sticking together in pairs, often walking hand-in-hand. If the extraterrestrial were familiar with sexual reproduction (which is likely for theoretical reasons of evolution), it might think that this is how humans copulate, like the dragon flies that do it in flight.

I.4.1 The Two-Parent Family

The reason for this behavior is obviously another. We cannot know for sure when the two-parent family was invented, but I think it might have been when Homo erectus emerged. Given the new lifestyle of hunter-gatherers, it must have been advantageous that the male contributed to alimenting the offspring, which, as mentioned, is unusual among mammals. We are not descendants from lions where the females procure the food for the family while the male defends the territory, but from ape-like creatures which stick together in clans. The two-parent family is highly efficient, especially in raising offspring that mature slowly. Hunter-gatherers must cover the distances involved in hunting and searching for edible roots and seeds or drinkable water, which means that a mother had to carry her baby on foraging trips until it could walk on its own. But when the group changed territory, the family had to carry children that could not run fast enough to keep up with the group, that is, children under the age of about four. Thus, only with the father participating, a family could have a baby and a toddler at the same time. How important it was to be able to run and cover large distances on the ground is obvious from the anatomy of the skeleton of Homo erectus which is optimized for bipedal walking and running, in striking contrast to those of the great apes. Therefore, while the male with his stronger upper body was obviously better equipped for hunting, both male and female needed good legs for running. This is why women, while overall smaller than men, tend to have similarly long legs (and it's probably also the reason why women with long legs are attractive to men; more about attraction will be said later). The amazing speed that five-year-olds can run attests to the successful adaptation to a mobile lifestyle.

But how did evolution create the two-parent family? Today's people often lament about the high divorce rates, but what is truly amazing is actually how long the marriage bond lasts, usually for decades, often long after the children have grown up, or even for life. Despite the stubborn individualism of human nature, and despite the differences in personality and mindset between men and women, they stick together like north and south poles of magnets. How did evolution create this durable bond? How did the new engene of pair bonding evolve? As usual, by gradual modification of existing genetic material. There are two ancient engenes that evolution adapted.

The first was obviously derived from the seasonal attraction between sexes during the fertile period of the female, perhaps the strongest drive in all sexually reproducing species. The Sex engene is strong, because if it fails, the genes will be lost. But in most species it occupies the partners only for a relatively short time, compared to the time they spend on finding food and raising offspring. The act of copulation is generally short, and once it's over, both go back to business as usual.

In humans, this engene has been expanded, from being seasonal to almost continuous (two copulations per week recommended by Luther), and it became universal, penetrating both body and mind. One could say, evolution hijacked the sex drive to create the strong bond that underlies the institution of marriage which exists in all cultures around the globe.

The other engene that evolution adapted is the brood care instinct. It shows up in behaviors like mouth-to-mouth kissing which is obviously a relic of the mother-child feeding relation, and feeding behavior is also part of the role playing in marriages. With men appealing to the childcare instincts of women, the latter often take over a motherly role in the relationship. Conversely, women may seek protection, and some women assume childlike behavior during courtship, thereby appealing to the childcare instincts of men (*die 'Kindfrau'*).

The Brood-care engene has been hugely expanded in humans. Many species have elaborate brood care, especially birds, but it is active only until the offspring are fully fledged, or weaned, after which the engene is stopped and reset. I'm not a zoologist, but examples of bonds lasting across generations seem to be rare; chimps exhibit lasting mother-child bonding, and elephants too. But strong bonding of parents to their offspring over several generations seems to be unique to humans.

A loving relationship between spouses is not the mammalian way of life, and certainly not that of the apes. In a TV documentary about orangutans a young scientist commented on pictures showing a dominant male with the characteristic cheek flaps and his 'resident females'. She said that usually there are also several adolescent males around who keep a distance, but sometimes a female sneaks away and has an affair with one of the young males "because often the way the dominant male behaves is really not nice." This is certainly the view of Homo sapiens: Not nice.

Within a couple of million years (H erectus), or perhaps within as little as 0.3 million years (H sapiens), evolution broke with the 40-million-year-old rule of promiscuous and dominant-male polygamous sex relationships. It invented love. That is to say, it added *agape* to *eros*. The Greek made this distinction which comes handy to our discussion. The orangutans have *eros,* but no *agape.* A female might have moments of pleasure once in a while, when it's her turn mating with the resident male; but how does that compare with the joy of a romantic love and the continuing pleasures of marriage (or displeasures, for that matter)! The orangutan mother does care for her child, and mother and child certainly have a strong bond – for a limited time; but how does that compare with the lifelong love between parents, children, and grandchildren!

How did evolution come up with *agape*? When the apostle Paul writes (1st Corinthian 13): "Love is patient, love is kind. … It keeps no record of wrongs… It always protects, always trusts, always hopes, always perseveres," his description clearly fits human mother love. Only mothers always protect, always trust, always hope for their sons and keep no record of their wrongs. How many a mother has loved her son even when he was a criminal. Thus, by adapting and combining two big instincts, sex and mother care, evolution created the two-parent family.

Interesting is that the change took place mainly in the male behavior. The silverback gorilla happily watches his family and defends it if necessary, he takes care of inseminating his harem, but otherwise contributes little to rearing his offspring. In the society of our closest relatives, the chimpanzees, females accept several males to inseminate them (polyandry), whose sperms then compete in the uterus; as a result, reflexive evolution has blessed the males with extra-large testicles.[41] In Homo erectus, the role of the male changed drastically; he is now responsible for the alimentation as much as the female, besides his role in providing shelter and defending the family. The comparison with the societies of our ape relatives shows that human society took a different path since those species diverged.

The creation of the caring father is unprecedented not only among the apes, it is also highly unusual across the entire kingdom. In 95% of mammalian species the males do not cooperate in raising offspring, in striking contrast to birds where both parents tend to the young in over 90% of the species. In birds we see many examples of amazing parental cooperation, like in Emperor Penguins, where the male incubates the egg for two months through the freezing dark of the Antarctic winter while his mate goes off to sea to feed, until she returns and tends to the chick. And just like in birds, having the fathers care for the family also made the human line of primates highly successful. Among the rare species of mammals, besides humans, that adopted the two-parent family model are the Titi monkeys (Plate 2). But in most mammals the males bitterly fight each other, competing for a chance to have it with the females. Evolutionarily they would be much better off if the effort spent on male competition over mating was redirected to increasing the chance of survival of the offspring.

Why did all those mammal species not adopt the two-parent family model which is so much more efficient than the standard model of male competition? When evolution created mammals, it enabled females to feed the newborn, and the role of males shrunk correspondingly to merely contributing semen, and they began to compete with each other for inseminating the females. Strong pair bonding would have reduced the chance of males to spread their genes by inseminating multiple females. To enable the two-parent family model, evolution had to develop specific mechanisms that counteract the opportunity of polygamy.

A recent modeling study,[42] examining standard population genetic models for various conceivable scenarios, found that the transition to the two-parent family type of society cannot occur because males are locked in a social

---

[41] Without polyandry, there is no evolutionary pressure to increase testicle size because sperms are abundant; it is only when sperms of different males compete in the uterus that testicle size matters: the male whose sperms outnumber those of the competitor has the greater chance to become the father.

[42] Sergey Gavrilets, "Human origins and the transition from promiscuity to pair-bonding." PNAS 109(25) 9923-8 (2012)

Plate 2. The two-parent family model of reproduction, which is so successful among birds, is rarely found in mammals. Among the rare exceptions, besides humans, are the titi monkeys. These small monkeys have overlong tails that are 'non-prehensile', that is, not used for grasping. But the tails serve a function in pair bonding. **A.** Bolivian titi monkey couple. **B.** Their baby, cuddled by the father.

dilemma, where shifting one's effort from 'appropriation' to 'production' would give an advantage to their competitors. In other words, inseminating more than one female is so efficient in spreading one's genes that it blocks a transition to the more efficient type of society. The reason why this is so in mammals, but not in birds, amphibians, or reptiles, is the gender asymmetry in mammals that burdens the female with a monopoly in nurturing the newborn. Because of this asymmetry, there is no evolutionary pressure towards male participation.

But the transition can happen if the model accounts for male heterogeneity, *assortative pair formation*, and *female choice* and *faithfulness*. These are the three terms that distinguish that mathematical model from simpler standard models of population genetics. The names of the terms hint at actual behavioral traits found in today's human population relating to the social engenes. The two-parent family society could spread in the model population thanks to evolution on both sides, modifications of male and female behaviors that mutually reinforced each other. It is fascinating how much a mathematical model can reveal about the behaviors of humans that we know only by their fossils – mathematics, which is pure reasoning.

The term *male heterogeneity* is the precondition for the change in male behavior from the standard role of the inseminator in mammals to a responsible father as in birds. There must be genetic variance to allow the transition.

The term *assortative pair formation* points to the miraculous invention of personal bonding between two individuals, the romantic love. In Homo sapiens this is an important phase in life in which the individuals search for a partner. It starts with a characteristic unrest and a mental state of longing, or even depression, that finally, once the search has settled, leads to strong bonding. We may call this mechanism the 'Bonding engene'. I think there is no parallel to this in apes. The intense love is a transient phase that many people regard as the happiest period of their lives. Again, the evolutionary innovation affected primarily the role of the male in that the strong bonding to one female reduced the opportunity of polygamy (more about this later when we will discuss the wider society). Whenever a genetic program unfolds in the individual during development, it incorporates information from experience. Extreme cases of such intertwinement of genes and experience are called imprinting. The 'falling in love' is such a case. All hopes and desires are fixed on one single person, a state that can last for years. As said already, this phase is generally transient; after about three years, the Bonding engene hands control over to another engene that includes children, grandchildren, and other kinship: the Family engene.

Looking at the behavioral modifications brought by the transition to the two-parent-family society, it becomes clear that the new Bonding engene modified not only behaviors of the individuals, but also the embedding society. While creating the bond between partners, it also produced manners to signal the bond to other members of the society. That is the origin of the institution of marriage that seems to exist in all cultures. Short of the beautiful tails that enable titi monkeys to signal their bond, we need wedding bands. Marriage often involves also other visible social indicators, like wedding celebration, honeymoon, having the young wife move in with the husband's family, or the reverse, and change of clothing or hair style of the married woman. While these may seem like mere traditions, considering the evolutionary conundrum of mammalian societies we see that all these 'traditions' are based on an engene whose evolution achieved the transformation from the standard mammalian model to the two-parent-family model of society.

So much about the Bonding engene which corresponds to the term *assortative pair formation* in the population genetic model. We will have to say more about the term *female choice and faithfulness* later when looking at another invention of evolution, the beauty of women.

I.4.2   The Family Engene

There is little doubt that the two-parent family revolutionized the life of Homo. It provided the ground for a stable family in which infants and children that need many years to mature could be raised, allowing complex brains to unfold. More than that, evolution extended parent care to include children, grandchildren, and great-grandchildren. I call this the 'Family engene'.[43] The power of this engene can be seen at the time of the tax return, when people take pains to save for their offspring rather than give to the community. It is the Family engene at work, not simple selfishness, as old people try to shelter their wealth from tax far beyond the needs of their own lives.

Again, as in the case of falling in love, the genetic program unfolds with imprinting. Parents do not recognize the genetic makeup of their children (Plate 3), but rather *learn* their faces, voices, and the way they move. I don't think the intensity of parents' love differs between natural and adopted children. Two children of different colors growing up together can bond as well as siblings of the same color, and when a White person falls in love with a Black person, their

---

[43] I avoid the term 'kinship' here which is the general concept in anthropology. I want to emphasize that what drives this engene are the emotions imprinted by upbringing and family experience; it relies on face-to-face (or ear-to-ear, to include the blind) interaction. Familiarity does not necessarily depend on biological relationship; it can also be friendship. The meaning of 'familiar' includes experience, like when we say, I am familiar with something.

emotional valuation of skin color changes, the White person develops affection for brown skins, and vice versa. The ability to form specific bonding between individuals is rare in the animal kingdom. Even when relationships between two partners appear to be personal, as in birds, it is often a non-specific bonding that can easily be transferred to a new partner when the first partner disappears. No doubt, the ability to develop personal bonding is also the basis of friendship and the foundation of human society.

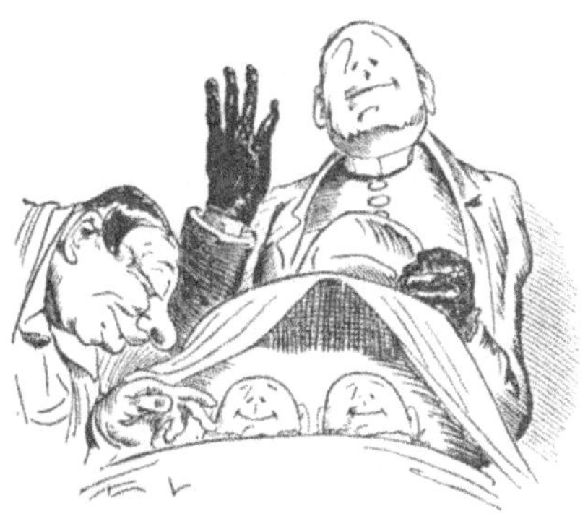

Plate 3. Parents do not recognize the genetic makeup of their children. Mr. Schmöck (left) greets his newborn twins, the result of a pilgrimage his wife Helen undertook nine months ago, accompanied by Cousin Francis (in back). Francis congratulates, "This is truly twofold blessing."

From: Wilhelm Busch, Die Fromme Helene (The Pious Helen), 1872.

Lifelong care of children and grandchildren seems unique among all animals. It has given human society superior strength, enabling the species to expand across the globe, occupying diverse climate zones and habitats. And it still does today; consider how much modern economies depend on grandmothers taking care of the family's children, enabling both parents to work.

While it evolved as an expansion of the Brood-care engene, the Family engene also produces mutual bonding, implanting into children love for the parents, which is a puzzle. The evolutionary advantage of extending the duration of brood care is easy to see; human children need support and protection until adolescence, and grandparents can shoulder some of that burden, thus freeing father and mother time for procuring food and housing. But why do humans care about their parents? We take it as the norm that children love their parents, assuming it to be the result of the experience of family life. Indeed, should children not be grateful for what they received from their parents? But why is a cat not 'grateful' to its mother? Most animals are not grateful to their mothers after they have grown up. The offspring are attached to the mother only as long as she provides nourishment and shelter. After weaning they leave to start their own life. In fact, mothers help the weaning by rejecting the young when the time comes rather than expecting reciprocity. Caring about their mother, not to mention the father, would provide no advantage for their genes; it would be a waste of time. But humans generally feel love for their parents and care for them. The evolutionary basis of this reciprocity is not easy to understand. But it is not merely a tradition. We will come back to this enigma later in the discussion of religion.

The other important aspect of the expansion of the Brood-care engene is that the bonding now includes not only the direct line of progeny, but also other kinship such as siblings and cousins and uncles and aunts. This is how a clan forms.

I.4.3 Inter-Individual Variation of Social Attitudes

It is the nature of behavioral engenes that they involve desire and satisfaction. Our social engenes make us feel lonely and enjoy company; just being with friends is pleasure. So does the expanded Brood-care engene. For many people, just being with children is a pleasure. It is this engene what makes children cute and beautiful and the subject of our hopes. Women are excited when they see a newborn and they claim to see specific features (whereas for men newborns all look alike). The emotional changes associated with becoming parent are more surprising for a man than for a woman. I had very little interest in children until I had one. I experienced the change as a new fundamental biological feeling. Suddenly, just being with children and doing childish things was pleasure. But people are different, not all men have such feelings, as I can see watching some of my close friends. Even men that are highly social and engaged in education or community activity may not feel strong pleasure in rearing their children. As pointed out before, inter-individual variation is typical for inherited mechanisms; the genes differ, and the expression of genes during development creates additional variation. Mother love is perhaps the most reliable, but there are also mothers who do not love their children, it's just not in their nature. Lack of motherlove is uncommon, but certainly not rare.

Newly formed engines can be flawed

Much of the changes in social behavior discussed above, especially those concerning males, are relatively recent in primates. I tentatively associate them with the era of Homo erectus, but some may even be more recent. As with computers, software can be changed more readily than hardware. The human body did not change all that much between Homo habilis and Homo sapiens, but the brain changed a lot. Simply its volume more than doubled (see Figure 2) but the amount of 'software' may have increased a hundredfold. As we all know, new software comes with flaws. So, it may not be surprising that the new behavioral engenes also have flaws. The engene underlying the two-parent family consists of many components. The two main components were adapted from the ancient engenes of sex and mother care.

The combination of these two may seem like an unholy alliance. To create a strong bond between parents, evolution has boosted the sex drive so much that men need to satisfy it continuously, more than once a week, which often meets difficulty. Also, it is not a simple bodily function, but something that also involves the mind and the psyche. The desire has many objects: breasts, long legs, a beautiful face, soft skin, a loving voice, or a smile. The engene is composed of many parts and each of them has its variations. Evolution has also boosted the Brood-care engene and extended it to the male, creating fathers who love their children. Males to have feelings for their offspring is highly unusual among mammals. This engene also has its variations.

So, it should not surprise that in some phenotypes these complex engenes are mixed up, producing, for example, pedophilia. All behavioral engenes involve sensory mechanisms which necessarily have limited specificity. One source of confusion might be that women share features with children, such as smooth skin, they are smaller than men, and their voices have a higher pitch. Thus, a mix-up of perceptual mechanisms might be at the root of this disposition and the crimes it fathered. But that's just speculation.

The variable representation of the inherited engenes is the reason for the individual differences of human inclination and behavior, as can be seen, for example, in the case of sexual orientation. As said, in creating the two-parent family, to provide the necessary glue between partners, evolution has enhanced and protracted sexual attraction – evolution hijacked the Sex engene for that purpose. But this engene is not monolithic, it's complex with various components in each, the perception-, action-, and satisfaction parts of the machine. So, it is no surprise that boosting the sexual appetite has not only strengthened the bonding between husband and wife, but has also produced variability, leading to the appearance of different phenotypes. One example is homosexual orientation which is found in a substantial percentage of today's people, a fact that is hard to reconcile with the law of natural selection. It contradicts the most fundamental principle of evolution, that only genes that proliferate can survive.

I.4.4   Formation of Society

Group competition

Because the new Family engene that created the two-parent family also extended childcare into adulthood and even beyond, it would soon give rise to larger clans, leading to an early human society. It is obvious that having society made the human species immensely powerful. Organized groups were able to hunt big animals, and hunting big animals only made sense if there was a large group to be fed. Being a member of a clan had many advantages besides alimentation; a group can protect and provide shelter for the weaker members like women with children, build houses, share a cave and protect it, which all would be difficult for a single family. A large group can also roam a larger space to find new resources which was essential in times of shortage of food. Armed with clubs and spears Homo erectus probably did not have to fear animal predators. Even lions are easily scared by a mere stick. Hyenas and bears might have been serious enemies, and again, the group could defend itself more easily than a single couple. Mechanisms of group bonding evolved. As a consequence, when the population grew, different clans began to compete for hunting grounds and other essential resources, like caves and access to clean water.

If Homo erectus was so powerful compared to other species, one might think that these early humans must have had a happy life. Did they have to compete at all? This is one of the mysteries of human evolution: the population of Homo erectus and its branches down to Homo sapiens remained rather constant at a size well below a million[44] until quite recently. It did not grow exponentially as expected it would under conditions of affluence. The population did not explode after humans left Africa and spread over the globe, and remained low even after the transition from hunter-gatherer to agricultural society about 13 thousand years ago. Exponential growth took off only 7 thousand years ago, virtually in the last minute of human existence. The limited population size over millions of years shows that humans, like other species of large animals, were under constant pressure to survive. Whenever conditions became favorable and the population grew, it soon reached a limit and starvation slowed its growth. Humans did not escape the iron fist of natural selection. The competition must have been within the species and between closely related species.

We do not know for certain how the social and political structure of the early hominid people looked like, but we can assume that groups with a high degree of organization prevailed over less organized groups, and as this happened over eons, the genetic code for social engenes evolved. Competition would always occur when the local population grew or the climate changed. Groups had to cede regions to others and emigrate, and if they found virgin territories with favorable conditions, they thrived. If they found territories that were already occupied by others, they would try to supersede them, which was often successful because the newly arriving people were hardened by the previous struggle and better organized for the fight than the people they encountered.[45]

In this competition, intelligence became more important than ever because intelligence enables communication and anticipation of looming dangers. Thus,

---

[44] Based on the diversity of the present human genome and the mutation rate, it has been estimated that the size of the human population remained relatively constant on the order of 10,000 breeding individuals throughout the last two million years. H. C. Harpending, M. A. Batzer, M. Gurven, L. B. Jorde, A. R. Rogers, S. T. Sherry, "Genetic traces of ancient demography" Proc. Natl. Acad. Sci. USA Vol. 95, pp. 1961–1967, February 1998. The corresponding 'census population' is roughly ten times larger, that is, on the order of 100,000 individuals.
For Homo sapiens 200,000 years ago an effective population size of the order of 10,000 to 30,000 breeding individuals has been estimated, with a corresponding 'census population' of roughly 100,000 to 300,000 individuals. P. Sjödin, A. E. Sjöstrand, M. Jakobsson, M. G. B. Blum, "Resequencing Data Provide No Evidence for a Human Bottleneck in Africa during the Penultimate Glacial Period" Mol. Biol. Evol. 29(7):1851–1860. 2012.

[45] For example, in the Migration Period, Germanic peoples, under pressure from invading Huns and expanding Slavic peoples to the east, had to cede territory in north-eastern Europe, but when migrating South and West they conquered much of the Roman empire: today's Italy, France, England, Spain, and even North Africa.

the next couple of million years (from the time on that Homo erectus people essentially competed only with themselves) put strong evolutionary pressure on brain development. Although two million years is short compared to the total era of primates, it is long enough for useful mutations to accumulate, and the continual emergence of variants and branching off of new hominid species, with the ensuing competition, created the brain of modern humans. The long intense competition left its footprint, creating society forming engenes that are still with us today.

Fairness and responsibility

When the Brood-care engene expanded its scope from immediate offspring to broader family and clan, this was particularly important for the competition between groups within the species and between closely related species; and the competition, in turn, accelerated the evolution of the social engenes. Hence evolution strengthened feelings of fairness and responsibility for others within the clan and even for the larger group. Still, their scope is limited. One can easily see that there is a gradient of emotions when considering the strength of our feelings for a close relative who gets ill or dies, compared to an acquaintance or someone we merely hear about in the news. Evolution endowed us with a strong sense of fairness and justice, but when it comes to practice, we notice that relational distance matters.

Recognition by the group

Next to the love for family and friends, perhaps the most basic source of social motivation is the desire to be recognized by the community. Children already show this at a young age, and it shapes human behavior throughout life. The mother needs recognition for giving birth to children and raising them, the employee needs recognition for her/his work. Recognition motivates the health service worker, the artist, and the scientist. That there is an underlying engene can be seen by looking at the emotional sequence: a phase of unrest and yearning, then a phase of activity, eventually followed by satisfaction if the goal of recognition is achieved. No writer who does not write for the sake of being recognized. A composer may suffer for years without recognition, but continues to create music that she/he thinks people will enjoy one time. All artists, be it writers, musicians, composers, painters, actors, or dancers, need recognition like the air to breathe, and suffer when recognition is lacking. For many people, recognition by the society is the greatest pleasure. Even the most solitary scientist who takes pleasure in the lonely discovery, enjoys the feeling of being the only one to know it who someday will be recognized for it. In a bizarre twist, even Hitler in his 'Political Testament' written two months before his end, knowing that he was responsible for the deaths of millions and for Germany being destroyed, asked for recognition.

I.4.5   Power Relations

Leadership

A basic inclination of human society is to produce leaders and accept the authority of leadership. People in Bavaria call the authorities the '*Grosskopfeten*', which is Bavarian dialect, meaning something like the big-headed guys, the men of power. My first love made me realize how important the shape of a man's head is for women. She adored a classmate named B just for his head. She said otherwise she thought there was nothing of him that impressed her, but the look of his head. She lamented about that, and then looked at me and sighed: "Why can't you have a head like B! I want to cut his head off and put it on your body" (after first severing off my head, I suppose).

The inclination towards authoritarian rule must be ancient. Already in the early days of hunter-gatherers, groups chose a leader. Again and again during the unfathomably long prehistoric era, groups that felt the urge to choose a shrewd leader and obey him prevailed over groups that lacked such leaders. More specifically, an engene evolved that drives some members to assume the role of a leader, and at the same time instills loyalty into the other members. The roots of this engene may go back to the time before hominids split off from apes, as the gorilla society also has a strong leader, the silver back. In human society also it is predominantly males that have the drive to become leaders. Whether obtained from ape-like ancestors or not, the desire to have authority and the inclination towards obedience has become part of our inheritance.

One indication that authoritarian rule in the human family has an ancient origin is the act of weeping. Weeping is a peculiar social behavior that is obviously related to the crying of infants which serves to communicate distress and pain to the mother. Evolution probably extended this behavior to juveniles and adults as a protection against the aggression by the dominant male and authoritarian rule in general. Weeping signals pain, pleading for mercy and submission of the weak under the strong.

The willingness, and even desire, to submit under the rule of an authority is deeply rooted in human nature. Even people living in egalitarian modern democracies indulge in reports and pictures about the royal family of England. A recent exhibition in Switzerland[46] documents the historical visits of members of various royal families to Switzerland and the fascination and excitement among the Swiss people about these royal visitors; the Swiss who pride themselves as citizens of "the oldest existing democracy." The longing for a predestined leader who rules and does not respond to any other authority is deeply rooted in human nature, and is of course in conflict with modern democracy. The inherited pattern is irrational; rationally, people want their leaders to be responsible and committed to the wellbeing of all, but emotionally, they want someone they can look up to, and can identify with in their dreams. Rather than a representative who would raise them out of poverty, people may elect a billionaire who gives a tinker's damn about the poor.

The popular epic products of modern entertainment exploit this inheritance. But there is another ingredient of those entertainment products that is no less important, the religious setting. The ultimate leader must also have the divine blessing. The most appealing configuration is centered on a young boy who is endowed with the divine power to grow into that role and thus save his people (or the universe, for that matter). The Psychologist C.G. Jung uses the term 'archetype' for those inherited engenes, and modern entertainment businesses diligently exploit them.

Ranked society

Early human societies certainly had a hierarchical structure with some families claiming privileges over others, and both claiming privileges over newcomers, migrants who joined the group and who occupied the lowest ranks in society. This is what we can still see in societies that have grown organically over thousands of years (before they were overrun by the modern civilization) like, for example, the social organization of the '*ayllu*' of indigenous people in the Andes that still exists today. Also Rome had an organization like this for hundreds of years, where elder members of a small number of families constituted the senate. The senate in turn selected two consuls who ruled the state, controlling each other, and the persons for the other offices. Before, in older times Rome had been ruled by kings, the more primitive social organization. The history of Rome is an example of the struggle to create a form

---

[46] Exhibition "Die Royals kommen (The royals are coming)", Forum Schweizer Geschichte, Schwyz, 3/13 – 10/3/2021.

of society that respects human dignity against the force of the evolutionary engene that simply calls for an autocratic leader.

Indeed, human society appears as a balance between mechanisms of cooperativity striving to create an egalitarian society, and power-struggle mechanisms striving to create an autocratic rule. Because the evolutionary advantage of cooperative mechanisms is that a group whose members feel responsible for each other will prevail, the cooperative mechanisms must be widely distributed across the population to be effective.

In contrast, power-struggle mechanisms strengthen aggressive behavior of certain individuals, leading to a struggle for dominance within the group. These mechanisms are driven more by reflexive evolution because they enable the dominant individual to proliferate his (not her!) genes within a group without necessarily strengthening its fitness in the struggle to survive. Whether the resulting autocratic organization improves fitness of the group is not clear; the one-leader organization might have been advantageous in combat with competing groups if the rest of the group was loyal to the leader and followed his commands. In any case, the one-leader organization, which is probably ancient because it resembles the group organization found in gorillas and orangutans, continued to be strengthened by reflexive evolution across the ages, making it a strong alternative even as the cooperative mechanisms evolved.

I.4.6   Gender and Society

Rilke's *Gegenstrophen* is the song of the rift between the minds of girls and boys and how it forebodes their fate in life.

> *Wo wir als Kinder uns schon*
> *häßlich für immer verzerrn,*
> *wart ihr wie Brot vor der Wandlung.*
> *Abbruch der Kindheit*
> *war euch nicht Schaden. Auf einmal*
> *standet ihr da, wie im Gott*
> *plötzlich zum Wunder ergänzt.*

From R.M. Rilke, Gegenstrophen

> Where we as children already
> ugly forever disfigure ourselves,
> you were like bread before consecration.
> Childhood's breaking-off
> did you no harm. All at once
> stood you there, like in God
> suddenly completed to a miracle.

From R.M. Rilke, Antistrophes

As we saw above, when evolution introduced the two-parent family it changed the role of both women and men. For women the primary responsibilities remained the same, choose a partner, establish a home, give birth and raise children. The change was that they would now apply different criteria for selection of a partner. Before, that was simple and casual, now it became a choice for life. Rather than simply following the male attraction, they now had to consider which candidate would provide the best protection in the clan and whether he would collaborate in raising children. Sexual attraction between the partners became continuous and much stronger than before. The emerging clan structure introduced other social bonds that grew ever stronger, lifelong attachment to the parents and other relatives, and lifelong attachment to their children, grandchildren and more. Thus, development became more complex for girls: as children the girls are primarily attached to a female, the mother, as are the boys, but with sexual maturation their bodies switch the preference over to a male. For boys, the development is simpler; with sexual maturation they just need to switch from one female to another.

Wir, wie gebrochen vom Berg,
oft schon als Knaben scharf
an den Rändern, vielleicht
manchmal glücklich behaun;
wir, wie Stücke Gesteins
über Blumen gestürzt.

From R.M. Rilke, Gegenstrophen

We, as if broken from cliffs,
often as boys already sharp
at the edges, perhaps
sometimes luckily hewn;
we, like chunks of rock
dumped over flowers.

From R.M. Rilke, Antistrophes

The engene that drives competition and combat makes itself visible in boys already at a young age. Even the sweetest four-year old suddenly indulges in striking the air with a stick and chopping off heads of flowers and poking with pointed tools whatever suits poking, behaviors that are rarely seen in girls. Hitting and poking are his favorite sports. Later he will join a sports team and fight with comrades against the opponents. Being a member of a team and fighting alongside friends will be his dream into adulthood. Seeking adventures and the urge to realize this dream produce emotional pressure that needs to be released. Young men need to be challenged, they want to explore the unknown, to the extreme of climbing rocks and diving into caves. Young men under 25 like to take risks, as the insurance companies know. Modern society offers sports, but it also takes advantage of that pressure when recruiting young men for military purposes. "Transform Your Life and Become Part of Something Bigger. Explore the Navy SEALs. Online Application. Extreme Challenges. The Best of the Best" is the call. Young men are needed to fuel the war machine. What the government pays for the service does not nearly compensate for the actual risks of entering the service. If salaries and social benefits were determined by supply and demand on a market that was not biased by the attraction of comradery and adventure, Navy Seals (or any military service for that matter) would be much more expensive. Thus, society shamelessly profits by appealing to that innate behavioral engene.

Every teacher knows that boys are more aggressive than girls. Attempts to promote gender equality in modern sports cannot make us blind to this difference. Car driving is more stressful in European countries where male drivers are in the majority, than in the U.S. where about 50% of the drivers are women.

Not unlike chimpanzees, humans tend to form groups that compete with each other. Group competition presumably characterized other Homo species too. And evolution has given men a special role in these fights, they are the warriors. The omnipresence of war on earth is a horrible source of gender bias. A recent television report shows a Taliban gynecologist, a woman in her 40ies who has seen nothing but war in her lifetime. She examines a pregnant woman who wants to know the sex of her baby. Scanning the patient's uterus with ultrasound, she exclaims: "Wow, this is another boy! Here are the two testicles, and here is the penis." To the journalist she adds: "Families with many boys are strong because men can fight, families with only girls are weak." Times of war create misogyny.

When reflecting about evolution of gender differences one must always begin with the basic asymmetry of sexual reproduction. Although this seems like a wide field, it all boils down to the simple fact that females can pass on their genes only to a limited number of offspring while for males the number is almost unlimited. For example, August 'The Strong', king of Saxony, is said to have fathered 300 children, Genghis Khan probably has more. Thus, when males and females are about equally frequent, like in human society, males compete for access to females. This is an iron law of evolution: genes of males that father many children will spread more than genes of males that father few. Therefore, the genome of the species will enrich with genetic traits that enhance behavior to this end, an example of reflexive evolution.[47]

The evolution of the two-parent family contradicts this general law. So strong must have been its reproductive advantage that it largely outweighed that of the standard male behavior. But clearly, there is a conflict, and human society has reached a balance between the two. The advantage of impregnating more than one female is still a factor, but evolution has designed barriers against this behavior to protect the two-parent family, like moral concerns, the behavioral pattern of jealousy, and the rules imposed by the society. So much about the consequences of the basic asymmetry for the *male* behavior.

---

[47] Some authors have phrased the asymmetry between genders by saying the female, contributing her precious egg, makes a *higher investment* than the male who contributes only one of the virtually infinite number of his sperms. I don't like the investment metaphor because it suggests that the behavior of the genders is based on reasoning like calculating the risk of an investment, whereas the behavior of both sexes is influenced by engenes that are irrational.

But what about the female behavior? Given the basic asymmetry, how has female behavior been shaped by the evolution of the two-parent family? The conflict is similar, but the effect of the ancient pattern on shaping female behavior is indirect. Choosing a husband that collaborates in raising the kids has a direct advantage. But choosing a womanizer has the indirect advantage that, in passing on *his* genes, there is a chance of reproducing his behavior in the sons, and thereby increasing the propagation of *her* genes as well. This is why women often fall for that type of man. The extreme form of male behavior with the effect of enhancing gene propagation is rape, and, although women detest it, many women marry men they know have a tendency towards violence or rape, and patiently endure abuse to an extent that is hard to understand. Psychologists have coined the term 'martyr complex' for this pattern of passive suffering and regard it as pathological. In fact, it is probably just an extreme expression of an ancient engene that enhances propagation of their own genes. Also the tendency of societies to turn a blind eye to violence in marriages reflects a mentality of tolerance of both genders rooted in that ancient engene.

Shame

In the above discussion we skipped an important dimension of the evolution that led to the emergence of the two-parent family. The creation of a new kind of bonding between partners is one dimension, the other is suppression of older patterns of behavior. Evolution had to get rid of the ancient mechanisms of promiscuous sex life and polygamy. For this, evolution invented shame. In our society, showing male sexual organs is gross, or porno, and is illegal in public. The ancient Greek accepted them in sculptures and paintings, but even they depicted the penis tiny compared to the muscular bodies, neatly resting on the testicles. To my knowledge, they never depicted erected penises. Why is this so? I don't know of any kind of animals that show even a hint of shame in their behavior related to sex. They might choose a secluded place because of fear of predators, but I don't see any indication of shame when animals copulate. Why do humans have shame? Sexual shame seems to be universal across cultures. And, like many other expressions of emotions, it is obviously genetically programmed. Until one or two years of age, children are perfectly comfortable being naked on the beach. But by the age of four they definitely care about clothing, becoming extremely careful to be properly dressed. Many people think that this is a matter of education,[48] but it's not. Studies by Eibl-Eibesfeldt have

---

[48] That sexual shame is learned is a wide-spread opinion. On the internet I found this: "All of these examples of sexual shame are learned. They came from somewhere. You picked

shown that this is so in many cultures all around the globe. Even in the rain-forest where people wear little clothing, in some cultures men cover their penis with a tube of cane held in place with a string around the hips and they feel naked without that piece of clothing. Shame simply develops; parents don't have to call out "shame, shame!" to teach their toddler.

Shame is also felt as humiliating. Just as children feel embarrassed, adults feel chastised being naked in public. In the antique, victorious potentates humiliated the defeated enemies by having them parade handcuffed and naked (see Sargon's victory stele, Plate 1; depictions of naked defeated enemies are also found on ceramics of the Mochica[49] and in other cultures). Forced nakedness is often used for torture.

Exposing genitals in public is taboo (and generally a legal offense). Where does this taboo come from? Evolution rarely creates new mechanisms from scratch. I remember when I was a student that two of my friends, two girls, told me they witnessed an indecent exposure on the street. I was amused, I simply found it bizarre and never thought about it, until one day in the Zoo of Indianapolis, which has pretty nice outside spaces for the animals, I was watching a group of rhesus monkeys in their rocky environment. A big alpha male was surrounded by his harem, and there was also a young single monkey at some distance who seemed lost and desperately trying to get closer, but every time he approached, the big alpha viciously scared him away. The young monkey was a male, as I soon noticed, and ostentatiously presented his erected organ, which glowed in the afternoon sun like a neon advertisement. Every time the big male charged at him, but could not leave his ladies too far behind, the young guy retreated, climbing up on the rocks to a safe distance, and then teased the colossus again. Although the crowd of visitors found it entertaining, families with children were visibly embarrassed.

Clearly, among rhesus the dominant male will furiously punish exposure that he considers inappropriate. It makes sense because keeping the genes of other males away increases survival of his own genes. From the level of fury one could guess that any perpetrators would be punished harshly and possibly injured

---

them up along the way. And they can be embarrassing, confusing, or even downright scary to look at in yourself. The good news is that since they were learned, thankfully, they can be unlearned. However, that is no easy task; it doesn't happen overnight and takes courage to do." – Of course, that's how many therapists make their living.
From   https://www.psychologytoday.com/us/blog/underneath-the-sheets/201908/no-one-is-immune-sexual-shame, accessed 2/3/2021.
[49] Ceramics collection in the Larco Museum, Lima, Peru.

lethally. As a result, the young outsider 'knew' his limits quite well. His behavior also made sense in terms of spreading his genes. Exposing his organ signaled potency to the females and presumably attracted them, so at the next occasion when the dominant male was distracted, he had a good chance to impregnate one of them. For creating the two-parent family, this behavior, which was so advantageous in rhesus society, became outlawed by one of the strongest taboos in human society. Even the gesture of a stretched middle finger is perceived as a gross offense, and little children know that sticking the tongue out is an insult.

People who think that taboos need to be broken down are misled by the doctrine that the human mind is totally malleable and that irrational needs to give way to rational thinking. Despite the considerable liberalization of visual publishing in the Western world, most people are appalled by pictures of sexual intercourse. They may even feel slightly uneasy just watching movie scenes of a kiss between conventional lovers, and are surely disgusted by footage showing a mouth-to-mouth kiss between two men. The problem is that there are innate mechanisms of shame that are similar in most of us. To the authors and artists who are trying to change this: good luck Sisyphus!

The tits taboo

But why did showing female breasts become shameful, these life-spending organs, one of the most wonderful inventions of evolution? The prohibition to expose this part of the body that defines the animal kingdom that we belong to – the mammals – is one of the most bizarre features of our society. Next to the sexual organs the female breasts are the most shamed body parts. A Baltimore nightclub owner eagerly advertises his business as "No tits" to assure customers that it is entirely legal according to Maryland law. Once in a while, there are revolts against this taboo. In the late 1800s, the invention of the bra was celebrated by women as a great progress and a victory for their gender. But in 1976 a Swiss woman queried the government whether women are obliged to wear bras on public beaches, and a court in Bern responded: No, there was no such law. In the following, thousands of women bathed topless in the public baths all over Switzerland. This again was celebrated as a victory. The invention of the bra did make the breasts more conspicuous, but also relegated them to the monotony of industrially shaped spherical cups, designed to optimally activate the convexity detector of male brains. The topless revolution in Swiss public baths eventually revealed the interesting variety of shapes.

Why then is showing these life spending and kingdom-defining organs inappropriate, or even sinful and illegal? And why do men have that irresistible desire to see them? I remember that once in the summer when I boarded the streetcar in Zurich going to work, I noticed a young woman standing next to me who wore a simple blouse that was held in place by just an elastic seam above her breasts. I was so thrilled that when she unfortunately got out at the next stop, I seriously considered getting off too and following her. Well, I followed her, but only with my eyes as far as possible. How can a man with a brain have such silly ideas? I did have a brain, and even a PhD, and a wife to whom I was happily married. Later, after explaining how the social brain engenes create a hierarchical society, we will see that the shape of female breasts and their irresistible attraction have a history in evolution. We will also have to talk about other taboos in a later chapter.

Why is the beautiful sex not male but female?

As we have seen above, sexual evolution creates beautiful animals like the birds of paradise with their amazing plumage. Among animal species with few exceptions the 'beautiful' sex is male. It must be so in general, because generally the males compete for the females, and the better the chance for a male of being accepted for mating by a female, the greater the number of possible offspring that inherit his genes. In contrast, for a female attracting multiple males does not pay off this way, it does not multiply the number of offspring that carry her genes. The creation of the attractive features is an example of reflexive evolution (see section I.1.3 "Reflexive evolution"), because wearing them does not make the animal more fit for survival; in fact, it usually does the opposite: it decreases the chance of survival. Both sexes contribute to reflexive evolution because both, the visible feature and the neural mechanism to perceive it, are genetically coded. The visible feature is expressed in the males and the perceptual mechanism in the females. Thus, a male that displays a highly attractive feature has a higher chance to attract a female, and conversely, a female who mates with a highly attractive male will tend to produce male offspring that are highly attractive, thus increasing the chance for *her* genes to be passed on.

Human society is a peculiar anomaly; in all cultures and at all times the beauty of women is praised, but for men, beauty is not regarded to be important. "*El hombre y el oso, lo mas feo lo mas hermoso*" (The man and the bear, the uglier, the prettier). Even language sidesteps giving the attribute 'beautiful' to a man, substituting 'good looking' or 'handsome' instead. Admittedly, beauty is a matter of taste, and *de gustibus non est disputandum*, but there is no doubt that women are more concerned about their beauty than men are. It is truly amazing how much importance women give to their appearance. Not only young unmarried women, but even children and old ladies. Hardly any old lady who does not appreciate a diamond necklace. Today I was watching a long political debate on TV. The anchor, a woman with a really beautiful face, wore super large eye lashes which must have been quite inconvenient during the broadcast that lasted for hours. Another woman, a journalist who seemed very intelligent as she made excellent comments, used a sophisticated lid paint I had never seen (or noticed) before: a blue color painted on the tiny rim of mucosa of the lower lid which enhanced the blue color of her eyes (based on a phenomenon called 'color bleeding', or 'assimilation', in perception science; the chromaticity of small regions tends to 'bleed' into near-by larger regions; watch the plastic nets of oranges in the grocery store: the red of the net bleeds into its surrounding, making yellow fruits appear orange). Of course, people on television always wear makeup, also men, although that's usually quite discreet, and even Angela Merkel wears eye makeup and a little lipstick, and so did Ms. Thatcher. However, for an intellectual woman like the journalist to go to that length is remarkable. Isn't the impact of her words the main purpose of her appearance? How much does she think that impact is enhanced by the eye shadow? Probably not at all, or perhaps negatively as the visual signal tends to distract from the spoken message.

Why is it that the coin of beauty is flipped in Homo sapiens compared to most other species? The answer is surprising: It is the reproductive bias of the society. First, in the two-parent scheme, the male partner has an important role in maintaining the family, so it is important for a young woman to choose the most promising collaborator. Second, raising offspring is more successful if you have a high rank in the society. High ranking members enjoy better alimentation in general and are better off in times of famine or war. Therefore, if a woman chooses a man of high rank (a behavioral pattern called 'hyper marriage' by sociologists), the chance that her children survive and grow up healthy is high. As we all know this is much easier if she is attractive. Evolution has played this game since the earliest days of human society, indeed, from the day when the two-parent family was created. Since a couple of million years is relatively recent on the evolutionary time scale, there was not enough time for women to develop attractive plumage, so they are putting on jewelry which attracts gaze: Primate eyes have high acuity at the center of gaze which they move around in jerks called saccades to sample high-resolution information from many locations, and they have a corresponding brain mechanism that directs gaze to those locations that appear to be of interest (visual attention). This mechanism works fast and largely involuntarily, directing attention automatically to the most salient points in a scene. Putting on something glittery creates salient points, thus exploiting that mechanism of the male viewer.

There are of course a number of natural female features that attract the interest of males, and males have features that attract females, and either sex has the corresponding perceptual mechanisms. These are genetic programs that are expressed in a gender specific way, comparable to those in other species. What is special in Homo sapiens is that the female actor gives much less importance to the standard signals of males compared to how our ape relatives do. The importance has shifted to signals indicating rank in society. Meanwhile, the male actors continue to respond to the standard sensory signals in the traditional way. The traditional way is superficial and primitive, focused on external features. In contrast, the female mechanism of selection is sophisticated, focusing on indicators of social rank.

Reflexive evolution has honed and exaggerated both the signaling and the perception, just like in other species, but with reversed roles. Like orangutan males developed cheek flaps that make the females happy, women developed large protruding breasts that make men happy. Men developed the corresponding perceptual mechanisms that stimulate desire. Originally, this was a mechanism to select a partner that would provide good nutrition to her babies, thus enhancing survival of the children. But, because women with large breasts were attractive, they also had more choices for selecting a partner of social rank which enhanced survival of their children independently of the quantity of milk they could provide; and a male who chose an attractive woman enhanced the chance of proliferating his genes because his daughters would also tend to be attractive and have good choices; and so on. Through evolution, this mechanism became so strong that the desire in men can overrule all rational intentions. It is easy to see that the attractiveness of full breasts is not simply the result of the basic mechanism selecting for good nutrition, because women often have breasts big enough to hold milk for three babies. Also, having large breasts is obviously not necessary for sufficient feeding, as women in some parts of the world have small breasts and their children grow up fine, for example in Japan.

I called evolutionary development reflexive if it enhances proliferation of genes without improving fitness for survival. Genes for full breasts do provide a nutritional advantage and one might think that they spread just because of that. But there are female features that enhance attractiveness without any value for survival, like clear skin and a small waist; at least, one would be hard pressed to find their value for improving fitness. The waist is invariably a female feature because, relative to body size, women tend to have wider hips than men. And because the presence of a waist is easily detectable by perceptual mechanisms, it has been a key for gender recognition since ancient times. Thus, women with pronounced waists stimulated the male gender recognition mechanism more strongly than women with less pronounced waists and were thus chosen more often for mating. That is the direct effect, and just like in the case of breast size, there is an indirect effect that enhanced the male perceptual mechanism: since women with smaller waists were more attractive, men who were strongly stimulated by that perceptual mechanism would choose more attractive women on average than men who were less stimulated, and joining their genes with those of the attractive female feature provided an advantage in reproduction. My classmates in high school would chant "Gina Lollobrigida!" (a famous Italian actress at the time) and call out her bosom-, waist- and hip measures.

Factors of female beauty also include the absence of negative features, i.e., features whose presence reduces attractiveness. No doubt, absence of a waist, or a tire of fat around the waist are such features, because they indicate pregnancy or motherhood. Other negative factors for female beauty are features that are characteristically male, like a big nose, a strong lower jaw, and body hair.

In short, reflexive evolution has made women ever more attractive and men ever more attractable. However, because reflexive evolution may eventually lower the chance of survival, producing too many offspring with insufficient fitness, it seems that evolution developed specific mechanisms to limit the strength of the reflexive factor. By erecting moral barriers, the society took over control, as will be discussed below. This explains the peculiar taboos mentioned above, like the no-tits rule. Exposing the female breasts became sinful: "Son of man, there were two women, daughters of the same mother, who acted like prostitutes in Egypt, behaving promiscuously in their youth. Their breasts were fondled there, and their virgin nipples caressed."[50]

Female beauty is a capital for the ones who have it. A woman with a pretty face and round breasts can go and pick a man of high rank, for instance the president of the United States. A French king built a castle for a beautiful young peasant girl. The beauty of a young girl can easily confuse even a smart man and derail his life, like the famous filmmaker who, when interviewing a teenager, found that she had nice breasts, so he made love to her, but she was legally minor, he got sued and convicted and had to flee the country. Female beauty is a windfall, and nature is arbitrary and unfair. If I imagine what a young girl might feel the day when she suddenly realizes that she is pretty and can buy anything

---

[50] Ezekiel 23:3, Holman Christian Standard Bible

she wants, and what another girl who is not so lucky feels, it makes me sad. Speaking of capital, it really means money if *he* is a billionaire. It also means money if you look at the billion-dollar porno business.

The funny thing is that beauty in the eyes of men has so many requirements that it becomes difficult for a woman to pass for beautiful. Either her face is ordinary, or the nose is too big, or too pointed; or she does have a beautiful face and long hair but has relatively short legs. In the end it becomes clear that women who would satisfy all the requirements may be one in thousand. What is funny is that, after all, none of this matters. If she cooks well and smiles, everything is fine.

The above picture is of course a caricature of human society. There are many women who have the capital, but do not exploit it that way, and they have my greatest respect. But the shallowness of the perceptual trigger mechanism of the male sex is certainly true. And women do exploit that weakness. But women have that power only for a limited time; limited in life as well as in the relationship. Once they have made their choice and the family is founded, that power quickly dwindles, but is then replaced by other sources of power, the convenience of home and food, and the bond of both parents to the children.

I am always amazed about the sophistication of the Female-choice engene. Women keenly intuit the social rank of a potential mate. They value the pitch of his voice and the way he speaks; they observe his interaction with other males taking into account *their* ranks. And they even take into consideration the future potential of a young man who is still not fully developed. All these factors contribute to her emotional state that leads to her final choice. Women are also keenly aware of their own attractiveness. They are aware of all the attractive features that women possess, their own features as well as other women's features, and evaluate their effects on the male observer. Which is interesting, because they do not feel the attraction of a competitor woman with the passion that men feel, but can gauge her strength.

It is amazing how this engene shines through the façade of modern western civilization. Hardly any woman who does not care about her hair style. Wearing long hair untied in public, frowned upon not so long ago in Europe, and still today in many cultures, has become common. Fashion of clothing and shoe wear accentuates female features of attraction. Among students and young people in general, females expose more skin than males. And when women lose one of their breasts (e.g., because of cancer surgery) it causes them depression, even at old age. The market offers all kinds of tools and tricks to enhance women's attractive features, such as invisible shaping bras and underwear, face make up, perfumes and jewelry. Many women have the attitude of raising the pitch of their voice, to the extent of speaking like Mickey Mouse, which enhances the difference to the male gender and also mimics children's voices, thus stimulating the perceptual mechanisms of the male brood care instinct. These are all ways to make up for the lack of strong anatomical features like colorful plumage or the antlers of deer that eons of evolution created in (males of) other species. The relatively short period of the evolution of Homo erectus did not allow for such 'hardware' to evolve (except perhaps the strong and long hair that women inherited from our tree-bound ancestors where it served for the babies to hold on), so evolution designed 'software' instead: the brain engenes. Typical for an innate behavioral pattern, the Vanity engene remains active even when it no longer serves the function it evolved for: providing choices for selection of the man with whom to produce offspring.

The corresponding engene of men is much simpler. But it has some sophistication in evaluating the health and youth of a woman. Youth has become important since evolution developed the specific bonding of marriage, meaning that the woman of his choice may be his only chance to procreate his genes. Because the number of children a woman can have is limited, her age is critical. The younger his choice, the more children can carry his genes. This follows from the iron law of sexual reproduction. This evolutionary logic accounts for many features of beauty, like well proportioned, firm breasts, slim figure, child-like elegance of movement, innocent smiling, giggling and expression of shame, as well as the absence of gray hair and wrinkles. Gray hair and wrinkles are strong inhibitors of attraction (except in wives, who remain beautiful because when they get wrinkles their husbands are presbyopic and cannot see them). When people are lamenting about the 'cult of youthfulness' that supposedly is a fad of modern times created by fashion and entertainment industries, they should be reminded that the male preferences that the industries relentlessly exploit simply reflect the ancient law of sexual reproduction.

It is important to realize that both, the female behavior of attracting and choosing a mate, as well as the male behavior of being trapped, are engenes that function by themselves and are only partially under the control of conscious reasoning. They are based on relatively simple inherited mechanisms that produce emotions which in turn influence our decision. And sometimes they lead us to make the wrong choice, "love makes blind" one says. Or a choice that is dangerous, for example when a woman marries a man who tends to get violent. The Bonding engene makes us feel love, but we should remember that its evolution was guided by nothing else but the effectiveness in enhancing reproduction of the specific set of genes. It *was*; it all happened in the past; we inherited the result.

When writing these pages my thoughts drifted off... The curious reversal of 'the beautiful sex' produced by a hierarchical society... What about other species that also have a hierarchical society, like wolves for example. Wolf packs have a pronounced hacking order. If my theory is right, there should be a similar inversion of the role of the sexes in displaying attractive features. Female wolves should display attractive features in order to mate with the alpha male. Where are these features? Should they not have beautiful fur coats? We don't see any eye-catching features. If anything, female wolves look less conspicuous than male wolves. – But that is what Homo sapiens sees. How ignorant are we about canine culture! The canine beauty is not visual, it's olfactory! Dogs are descendants from wolves, and anyone who has taken out a male dog knows how much he needs to sniff out: gosh, just one block of a little street requires half an hour of sniffing! He is sniffing all the interesting messages, and once in a while – he is texting back. We cannot imagine the beauty of the scents. For the dog, some streets may be as exciting as a bikini fashion show for a man. Female canines evolved a chemistry for producing fascinating scents, just like male birds evolved to produce wonderful colors of plumage; and male dogs have evolved a keen perception for scents that gives them pleasure, just like the female birds evolved a taste for beautiful plumage. These evolutions did not improve fitness for hunting or any other useful skills, but just optimized the chance of procreation of the genes of the individual, relative to its species consorts. It's reflexive evolution.

To summarize, the reason why not men, but women are the beautiful sex is an anomaly produced by the power of human society. Being attractive to men afforded women the ability to choose a man of high social rank which created advantage in raising offspring. The inversion is an anomaly in the animal kingdom (where attracting the opposite sex is usually the task of the male) although it may not be unique.[51] It's a phenomenon of societies with hierarchical structure.

---

[51] See also M Andersson, "Evolution of reversed sex roles, sexual size dimorphism, and mating system in coucals (Centropodidae, Aves)." *Biological Journal of the Linnean Society* (1995); and C Voigt and W Goymann, "Sex-role reversal is reflected in the brain of African black coucals (Centropus grillii)." *Developmental Neurobiology* 67(12):1560-1573 (2007). doi:10.1002/dneu.20528.

Guadalupe

A family in the city of Cochabamba had a maid, Guadalupe, a young woman who had been raised in the family since she was an infant. Indios from a community in a remote valley of the mountains had brought her because they knew the head of the family who had been their patron, a landowner in that valley before the revolution. Guadalupe was the younger of two sisters, the older of whom had also been raised in the same family and had then left to find her own life. When I asked the head of the family, a man of age at the time, why the Indios brought those children, he said the community did not want them, "*mala sangre* (bad blood)." I looked puzzled, and he added, their mother was "*demasiado detras de los hombres* (too much after the men)". Like everywhere in the world, women who excessively exploit their beauty and the responsiveness of men to it, if they are not courtesans of the king, are outlawed and regarded as low class and dirty. The indigenous communities exert strict control over the morals; they do not tolerate extra marital sex, that is, the respective women are stigmatized and their children expelled, because they believe it's in the blood. What is actually in the blood, I think, is the moral control; it's a function of the engene that protects the two-parent family.

Of course, this kind of moral control is not a specialty of indigenous people but exists in all cultures around the globe. What appears like a moral commandment is in fact a simple law of evolution: children of parents who respected marriage had a better chance of survival than children of parents who did not. In addition, children from extramarital relationships were a burden for the group, reducing their chance of survival as a group in times of famine and war. Thus, humans came to inherit respect for the marriage, a behavioral pattern that is the basis of the two-parent family. Respect for the marriage is but one example of mechanisms by which human society took control over reproduction. Others are the delayed sexual maturity with a marked threshold for having the first sexual intercourse, and a continued protection of adolescents against sexual aggression even after the age of sexual maturity. These may all be mechanisms to stabilize the population. As mentioned above, the population of the homo species remained rather constant over millions of years, continually challenging the limits set by the hunter-gatherer lifestyle. Certainly the exaggeration of sexual attraction that evolution invented to cement the two-parent family aggravated the situation by increasing the chance of pregnancy. As a compensation, social control mechanisms evolved to avoid overpopulation and the ensuing famines. Having few well-nourished offspring was a better guarantee for survival of a species than having many debilitated offspring.

The anecdote of Guadalupe indicates the presence of a social 'Moral engene' that acts to protect the two-parent family. But why does the Moral engene punish the women, but not the unfaithful men? The Jealousy engene gives the genes of a married woman a reproductive advantage because it enhances the proportion of the children of the man of her choice that carry her genes. This is the counterpart of male lions killing the pups of their mate from a previous relationship. The Jealousy engene has the same effect in men, it enhances the proportion of the children of *the woman of his choice* that carry *his* genes. Thus, the Jealousy engene works symmetrically for both genders. But the Moral engene is biased: females who have sex with a married man are stigmatized in society as whores, but their male customers have little to fear. Even in today's society women of that profession have a much higher risk of being murdered than women of other professions. Their customers might be punished by their wives at home, but that's all.

To understand the Moral engene, remember that being attractive affords a woman choices of men and the chance of hyper marriage, joining her genes with those of a man who is successful in society. The whore tends to join her genes indiscriminately. She does not select men who will likely be responsible and engage in an exclusive relationship. In doing so, she weakens the genetic basis of the two-parent family that is so important for a group to be successful. Only a married woman has fulfilled the evolutionary duty of a wise choice between men. The Moral engene may also be at the root of the psychological trauma of rape (orangutan women are typically being raped and apparently without trauma). So, the Moral engene does more than reduce the number of children from extra marital relationships. It strengthens the genetic basis of the institution of marriage. The wise choice of women in selecting a partner is essential for maintaining this pillar of society.

The reason why the same does not hold for men is simply that men's choices are not wise. Men's desires are simple and their choices more superficial on average than those of women. The bizarre cohabitation of evolutionary programmed motivation and rational mind leads to strange conflicts in human love affairs. I cannot think of a better exposition of such conflicts than Luis Buñuel's movie "That Obscure Object of Desire."

The game of female beauty and male responsiveness to it can lead to a peculiar inversion of dominance (in comparison to male dominance, as observed in apes) in which the man submits under the rule of the woman, at least at home. In the family, the woman has more power than it appears. The revolution of the role of the male has created mechanisms that suppress the ancient pattern of male behavior and reward the new role with strong positive emotions. Part of the bonding mechanism is that he finds pleasure in obeying her. And she of course also finds pleasure in ruling. Indeed, the pleasure of submission can be so strong that men find it erotic being physically 'abused' by a woman. The abuse is more symbolic than real; a woman slips into the role of the 'Domina' to satisfy the masochistic desire of the man and may find it erotic too. To some degree, the pleasure of the weak ruling over the strong is probably an ingredient of all marriages; and it's also the reason why in our modern culture women like to practice horseback riding generally more than men: the pleasure of dominating a strong animal.

Many cultures explicitly impose moral sexual laws; and they weigh more on women than on men, which follows directly from what was said above: Women are the attractive gender, and therefore women must control themselves – or must be controlled – to protect the two-parent family. In some cultures the burden of restrictions placed on women is extreme. Since they have many features that attract and arouse the lust of men, some cultures require that women not display any of them, imposing long dress with long sleeves and tight collar to cover all skin. And because the face is the strongest of all attractors, women must veil their face wearing a burka. Still, the female voice is attractive too, and because the acoustic burka has not yet been invented, and because the female gait might also stimulate the male desire despite dress and burka, women are not allowed to walk on the streets unaccompanied. Only in the company of a brother or the husband can they go shopping.

The switch of gender regarding the perception of beauty is but one aspect of the peculiar organization of human society. But revolutionary as it was, slipping into the role of the attractor did not alleviate women from the iron law of sexual reproduction: that women can only pass their genes on to a limited number of offspring. With all their cunning tricks and despite some commanding power in partnership, family and house, women could not escape the curse of that law. To procreate their genes, they must give in to the unfair conditions of the society. When the time comes, they must succumb; that's why the bride weeps on the day of her wedding. And the society knows and exploits this weakness. As a result, women are constantly undervalued on the job market and wherever they compete with men. Because this disadvantage stems from an irreducible biological condition, there is little hope that education or progress of civilization will remedy it. It can only be compensated by the institutions of the society, that is, by specific legislation.

I.4.7   Culture

We tend to think that culture is a matter of tradition. But more than is generally assumed, culture is also based on evolutionary engenes. When I 'discovered' the Americas it opened my eyes for the miracle of human culture. When the Spanish discovered the New World in the 1500s, they found, and destroyed, two great civilizations, Ēxcān Tlahtōlōyān, the Aztec empire in Mesoamerica, and Tahuantinsuyo, the Inca empire in the Andes. People in the Americas had lived completely separate from the rest of the world for 15 thousand years, but their cultures, as far as we know them from Spanish and Indigenous chronists and from monuments and artifacts that survived, were strikingly similar to the ancient cultures of the Old World. Both Worlds developed agriculture and animal husbandry, both had kings and emperors, kingdoms that fought wars against each other, and empires that merged different peoples into an overarching political structure. Both had religions and their priests that were powerful, sometimes as powerful as the king, and both built monumental temples for their gods. The Egyptians built pyramids, and so did the Mayas and Aztecs in Central America, and the Chimu in South America. Like the Egyptians, the Aztec and Maya societies distinguished nobility and commoners, revered a pantheon of deities, and had a calendric system. Following separate traditions for many thousand years, the dynasties of both, the Pharaohs and the Incas were revered as descendants from the sun god, representing power and justice. Both the Pharaohs and the Incas ruled over vast empires that were hierarchically organized.

These similarities between cultures produced by people that were separated for 15 thousand years, a time span that no prehistoric tradition could ever bridge, these similarities, to me, are convincing evidence that culture is not merely tradition, but is anchored in the genes. True, one can argue that developments in agriculture and technology were driven by similar needs and somewhat similar natural conditions in both parts of the World, but the environment of the Andean civilizations is very different from that of Mesopotamia: Here, the Altiplano, a high plane 12 thousand feet above sea level, framed by snow capped mountains and steep valleys; there, an alluvial plane between two rivers close to sea level. Consequently, the plants that were domesticated and the type of agriculture were quite different: potatoes here, cereals there. But the religions, the organization of states, and the rules of power were surprisingly similar.

Present day sociologists seem to conceive the evolution of human society as a gradual process that began in the Neolithic age when the introduction of agriculture led to settlements and population growth in certain regions such as

Mesopotamia and the Nile valley. The growing populations and the new ways of producing food called for higher levels of social organization with division of labor and centralized power structure. Authors use the term 'evolution' for a process of transition to higher organization arguing that the various prehistoric groups competed with each other, and the better organized societies prevailed over other societies that were still more primitive.[52] Viewed superficially, this process resembles Darwinian evolution: mutation and gradual differentiation of societies, competition between societies of different organizations, and selection of the most efficient organization. But this is only as it appears. 'Social evolution' is only a metaphor, an analogy. The difference is that this kind of 'evolution' takes place in traditions, not in the genes; it lacks the durable memory of genetic coding. Tradition certainly has memory: memory of oral tradition, of technological advances, traditions of organization of communities and of the rule of power. Only very recently, since the invention of script, memory is also in written documents.

The significant difference is that memory of tradition is frail compared to the genetic code. Oral tradition lasts only a few generations. When the Spaniards established their rule in the Andes in the 16th century, native peoples only remembered the succession of Inca rulers since the 12th century, plus some legends of their origin. Nobody knew anything about the majestic ruins of Tiwanaku, a civilization that peaked around 800 CE. Although the Inca, and probably already the Tiwanaku civilization, had writing in the form of quipus, knotted strings, only a small number of scribes could read them, and they vanished after the conquest and most of the quipus were destroyed before anybody made efforts to understand them. The Maya had a thriving civilization around 800 CE, but remembered virtually nothing of it when Central America was conquered by the Spanish in the 1500s. The Mayas did have extensive literature, but it was nearly all purposely destroyed under the catholic rule.

So, if the emergence of human societies of high organization is entirely the 'evolution' of tradition, as modern sociological theories have it, how can we explain that similar societies evolved in people of the New World and people of the Old World that lived completely separate for 15 thousand years? Here again, we need to look at the evolution of genes.

---

[52] Steven K. Sanderson "Social Transformations," Rowman & Littlefield, Lanham (1999). But see also Johannes Fabian "Time and the Other," Columbia University Press, New York, (1983).

Weeping and laughing as protections against authoritarian rule

So let's begin by looking at behaviors that are obviously not acquired through tradition, but inherited. I have pointed out above that weeping is a peculiar social behavior that evolution created probably as a protection against the aggression by the dominant male and authoritarian rule in general. Weeping signals pain, pleading for mercy and submission of the weak under the strong, but is also a display of deep emotion in general. Nobody would doubt that weeping has a genetic basis. Weeping tends to be suppressed in males, but the inhibitory mechanism apparently weakens with age so that some old men start weeping when they hear their national anthem.

A complementary function is that of laughing. It's another important part of social behavior that also has its basis in the genes. As always, observing the development of children is instructive. The primordial joke perhaps is the fart. Babies and young infants are totally oblivious to the sound of a fart as if they were deaf, which is interesting. But for older children, it is amusing and they break out in laughter. I remember as a little boy together with a friend I entered the machine room of an old sawmill, which was of course forbidden. When we suddenly heard the owner enter the room, we were scared half to death and crouched behind a machine. But then the old man let off a fart, and we burst out in laughter. We simply could not suppress the urge.

The primordial joke may help us to understand the evolutionary origin of humor. The key, I think, is understanding the hierarchical society. The authoritarian rule can be unfair and detrimental, and submission under the absolute power of the leader can jeopardize the needs and rights of the weaker members of society. An antidote to absolute power is humor. A joke can challenge the authority.[53] Laughing eases the tension of a confrontation. It is a defense against the power of the authority. Not surprisingly, women use it more often than men. In a tense situation, when a dominant male, such as the head of a clan, is annoyed and going to punish a lower ranking member, a woman might

---

[53] The challenged authority can be abstract, for example, the respect for a severe medical condition. A little joke that invariably wrings out at least a smile from even the most serious person is this German *Schuettelreim: "Frage: was ist der Unterschied zwischen 'nem Kaiserschmarrn und 'nem Epileptiker? Antwort: Der Kaiserschmarrn liegt in Zucker und Zimt, der Epileptiker liegt im Zimmer und zuckt."* This cannot be translated, but here is a quote from the psychologist/psychiatrist Karl Pribram who, referring to the frontal lobe extirpation procedure that became fashionable in the 1950ies, supposedly to free creative powers of the brain, said that he'd "rather have a bottle in front of me than a frontal lobotomy!"

make a funny remark and start to laugh, and everybody watching the precarious situation will start to laugh. This immediately lets the steam off the authoritarian engene (which is a component of the Strife engene discussed below). Thus, humor is effective against the authoritarian rule. Young girls laugh and giggle a lot, and among adults, laughing alludes to childhood. When women are present in a party, men are typically trying to make them laugh, and they gratefully respond. This way, a male occupying a lower rank in society can score points and win the admiration of the females even in the presence of a higher-ranking male. The court jester had the freedom of making fun even of high-ranking persons at the court. Today, comedians give the political opposition effective weapons against the ruling regime.

Looking back at evolution, a plausible explanation for the emergence of humor is that members of the clan that would have been losing in a confrontation (and be deprived of reproduction or even killed) could evade the sanctions by humor and thus procreate their genes. The 'Humor engene' probably evolved by modification of mechanisms of child-mother interaction. The spirit of humor that challenges the authority lives on today in many personifications: the *Kasperle/Kasperli* in puppet shows of German language regions, in *El Chabo del Ocho* in Latin America, as well as in the protagonists of comedians like Buster Keaton, Charlie Chaplin and others.

Universality of culture

The discussion of the previous sections suggests that some aspects of human culture have their basis in the engenes of the brain and are thus inheritable. There is no doubt that weeping is an innate instinctive behavior. For laughing this may seem less obvious, but we have seen above that laughing and sense of humor most likely evolved in tandem with the strengthening of autocratic rule in human society.

Virtually every ingredient of culture that produces similar emotions in the various cultures around the globe probably has its underlying engene. All cultures around the globe have weddings:[54] some kind of ceremony by which society authorizes and gives its blessing to a sexual relationship, converting a taboo into a virtue. It is the social function of the engene that forms the two-parent family which is the basis of human society and the most important factor in the success of Homo sapiens.

---

[54] Irenäus Eibl-Eibesfeldt "Human Ethology." Aldine de Gruyter, New York (1989).

Also dance and music are cultural phenomena shared by people around the globe. People are longing for music and feel the urge to dance, and both give pleasure and satisfaction. The ubiquity of these specific human faculties and their similarity across cultures points to basic inheritable engenes. The Bach family used to be the example for hereditary mental functions in humans in biology textbooks; it may not be any more because of the post-WWII trend to downplay inheritance. The pedigree of the Bach family shows a number of outstanding musicians – Johann Sebastian Bach is considered by many the greatest composer of all times – and it also shows other members that did *not* have that gift, similar to Gregor Mendel's pedigrees of peas. If musical talent were entirely a matter of education and environment, then all the sons of J.S. Bach should have become musicians, but in fact, of his nine surviving children, only four became significant musicians. His first wife was also his second-degree cousin, and two of their three surviving children were musicians; with his second wife, herself a gifted soprano and daughter of a musician, he had six surviving children of whom two were significant musicians. This variation within the family is strong evidence for a genetic code.

Not only the faculty of producing music but its appreciation varies greatly between people. Most of my family loved music, but there was a granduncle who did not appreciate it at all; on the rare occasions he visited us, the first thing he did was to switch off any music we happened to be listening to. A friend of mine in Israel, a psychologist and a bright and educated woman, says music to her is like noise and confessed to me that she could not even recognize their national anthem. But non-musical people seem to be in a minority.

The enormous consumption of music today testifies to the importance of the 'Music engene'. Both the Dance- and Music engenes probably served their function in social gatherings which enhance the bonds within a clan. Evolutionary drive may have also come from their role in facilitating sexual relationships and helping to overcome rigid social taboos.

On the genealogy of music

I find the Music engene particularly interesting and mysterious. Music has specific structures, like melody, rhythm and harmony that are universal. While there are differences between cultures, like prevalence of the pentatonic (five-tone) scale in East Asian and native American music, versus the harmonic (seven-tone) scales in Western music, and the prevalence of rhythm in African music, these are merely differences in emphasis, and most music has all the different ingredients.

The harmonic scales come in two variants: minor and major keys, the minor provides feelings of desire, longing and sadness, while the major key is assertive, providing joy and satisfaction. Interestingly, many forms of music have a structure of dialogue, two phrases in sequence, like question and answer. One example is a motive in the first movement of Mozart's 40th symphony that nowadays many people have on their cell phones. The first phrase moves up in scale and has the character of a question, and the second phrase moves down and is affirmative (how fitting for a cell phone!). Similar patterns are common in Beethoven's music, in fact, I would say, in all kinds of music. In the sonata form of classical music the first movement has two themes that are first presented each by itself, and then both interwoven. This specific structure suggests that music originally served as communication between lovers, the minor scale expressing uncertainty of a question, the major scale, affirmation of the answer. Still today, music serves asking for, and granting love. In Latin America it is common for a young man to give a serenade with friends in front of the house of his love.

There are a few observations that make me think that music is actually a form of communication that is older in evolution than language and has been superseded by language. First, music seems to have direct access to emotions. Everybody knows that; it is the reason why music plays such a big role in entertainment. There is no movie without music (in the time of silent movies, a pianist accompanied the presentation), and composers for movies have developed music to be most effective in creating feelings of anxiety, fear, joy or triumph. Interestingly, the composer who was borrowed from most is Brahms, a classical composer of the late romantic period. But hardly any movie uses 12-tone music. There must be a reason why music has that easy access to the emotion centers of the brain. Another observation is that young people, especially boys, feel uncomfortable when asked to sing solo for a group, like in a school class. There is an inhibitory mechanism that hinders singing, as opposed to talking. The inhibitory block goes away in group singing. It is plausible that when language developed as a new communication channel, music had to be inhibited. But it continued to play an important role in the communication between mother and child. Finally, a third point, neurologists have described patients who lost language because of a stroke but could still sing. Such patients cannot speak the text of a poem but can sing it. This shows that music and language are supported by separate brain structures.

The evolution of the Music engene may have begun from lullabies that mothers used to calm their baby. The productive and the perceptual mechanisms mutually honed each other by reflexive evolution. The special use of the voice imparted happiness and calm, introducing sleep. Because of this emotional attachment the specific auditory mechanism then lent itself easily to a role in courtship, which influenced the choice of partner, giving the corresponding genes a reproductive advantage that led to further strengthening of both the productive and perceptual mechanisms. This is another example of the strategy of treating the loved one like a child, appealing to the mother-child emotional bonding. That is why the Music engine has a direct path to the emotional centers.

Performing music is the art of activating the structure of the brain that has this specific affinity, and composers like Mozart, Beethoven or Brahms were gifted in writing music that is especially effective in stimulating those brain structures. Some themes are immediately pleasurable and stick in the mind. One might even say, composing music is like an act of discovery more than of creation, and it seems to me that Beethoven discovered more themes than any other composer. Different styles of music stimulate the music centers in different ways. The pleasure produced by Bach's music is different from that of Brahms' or Wagner's music, which is again different from that of pop music. But what they all have in common is that they activate the Music engene.

Composers, and the arts community in general, always want innovation. The pleasure function adapts: when hearing a piece for the second time, the experience is not the same. It may feel like magic the first time, still a great pleasure the second time, and after many times it becomes just a pleasant habitual piece of consumption. Adaptation or habituation are typical in the responses of neurons in cerebral cortex. A neuron that responds strongly to a certain visual stimulus generally responds less to a second presentation of the same stimulus. Adaptation probably underlies curiosity which is an important part of primate behavior. Its counterpart is boredom, which can be like a pain. I think adaptation also underlies the appetite for something new in the arts, and it was probably driving composers like Mozart to write thousands of compositions. The brains of both the composer and the audience adapt, and that is why composers at all times explored new ways, so that the character of the work of each composer changes over her/his lifetime, and the general style of music changes across the ages.

In the progress of innovation then came a point, around 1900, when the music community felt that the traditional forms had been exhausted. Perhaps the number of emotionally active themes that the brain can distinguish is limited; listeners may notice a similarity with the themes previous composers discovered, and composers may feel constrained by it. So, it seemed like there was no point in adding more of the kind. Assuming that the limitation was the convention, the community tried to break free from the previously accepted schemes. People began to think that art is nothing but convention and everything could be defined as art (Marcel Duchamp). Composers invented 'atonal music', trying to break with all traditional forms, composing according to new rules that they invented.

This way of conceiving art is based on the belief I have criticized before, that the brain is a tabula rasa at birth, and all our mind is a product of environment and education; thus, the perception of art is also learned or acquired by training. Composers of modern music explored this idea, convinced that listeners will get used to the new rules and structures and find pleasure in the new music just as previous audiences found pleasure in the traditional music, which however had been exhausted. But the result was that the modern music largely lost its audience. This is because the audience does have basic inherited mechanisms that are stimulated by the traditional music, but not by the modern 'atonal' music. Of course, the brain can learn, and in the course of composing atonal music the composer gets used to the new harmonies and time structures. And also the audience can learn them, but it requires intensive training, and few listeners ever achieve the training level of the composer. The result is that the audiences shrink and may eventually consist of people who like the surprise and the experience of the new, no matter if they can perceive it as music or not. Defining itself by the negation of traditional structures and rules, modern music reduces the experience of the listener to the perceptual mechanisms her/his brain has built up by learning or training, excluding all the inherited mechanisms. Unfortunately, the brain, which comes with lots of room for processing the traditional music, has little space to house modern music. I think the difference in brain space is big, like the difference between a palace and a garden shed! We should not ignore the existence of inherited engenes and their role in the consumption of art.

Art as a product of reflexive evolution

Art has played a role in human society long before historic times, as documented, for example, by the magnificent paintings discovered in the Chauvet Caverns which are about 30 thousand years old, and by little sculptures found in graves that are over 50 thousand years old. But the existence of arts seems like a divine feature of mankind, and may appear as something incompatible with the Darwinian theory of evolution. The reader might be puzzled by me associating something as cultural as music with the Darwinian theory of evolution. – In terms of fitness for survival, what could be the benefit of music? If some genetic mutation produced musical talent, what would be the survival benefit for the offspring?

In the context of sexual evolution, R.A. Fisher remarked "although the offspring show no general superiority in the ordinary course of life, they retain their ascendancy in sexual selection," and have, therefore, a better chance of passing on their genes. In birds, males with feathers of a certain color attract females that are sensitive to that color, thus selecting for a perceptual mechanism, and those sensitive females choose males who display that color more than others, thus selecting for the color. Over many generations this feedback loop (or rather spiral) reinforces both the external feature and the corresponding perceptual mechanism. This is how the Sex engene evolved.

The same is true for cultural engenes. A variety of evolutionary spirals have created the basis for the diverse phenomena of arts. If, for some reason (which could be a random mutation), certain tones evoke a pleasant feeling, an individual who can produce those tones will be liked in society, and the society will honor that capability with generosity, giving that individual a chance to procreate her/his musical gene. Unlike sexual selection, where a perceptual brain of an individual selects a partner and with the partner the gene, here, the perceptual brains of the community select an artist and thereby give the artistic gene a chance to procreate. This is because perception and production of music share common genes. So, when a community likes music and pays, it helps musical genes to survive. Because this kind of evolution involves the ears of the community, it can only occur if there is a society.

In general, to set off a reinforcement spiral, there must be genetic codes for a production mechanism and the corresponding perception mechanism, and inheritance of these two pieces of code must be positively correlated, that is, inheriting one of them must not be completely statistically independent from inheriting the other. In the case of musical talent, this is intuitively plausible because the ability to produce music requires an ear for music, and consequently the passion for listening to music correlates with the ability to create it. Similar correlations exist for other kinds of art.

The correlation between the genetic codes for objective feature and subjective preference has been studied scientifically in animals, for example the European crow, where it was found that some of the genes that determine the pigments of the feathers code also for the photo pigments in the eye.[55] Thus, inheriting a specific feather pattern correlates with inheriting a corresponding visual preference. As a result, two distinct populations of crows coexist in

---

[55] J.W. Poelstra et al. "The genomic landscape underlying phenotypic integrity in the face of gene flow in crows." Science 344(6190), 2014.

Europe, the Carrion crow, which is all black, and the Hooded crow, which has only a black head while most of the body is gray. The carrion crow is found in western Europe, the hooded crow in Eastern and Northern Europe, the border running North-South through Germany. The two populations remain stable despite frequent interbreeding in the border zone. This genetic scheme is paradigmatic for the schemes that gave rise to reflexive evolution of music and other cultural phenomena.

The merits of women in preserving cultural genes

I have argued above that the formation of human society virtually from the beginning involved competition between groups, tribes and peoples. Some peoples had to cede regions to others and were pushed to migrate, but migration required new organizations: the formation of a warrior guild, structured command chain, and new ways of securing food supply during migratory expeditions. It probably led also to improvements of weapons. Clubs gave way to stone axes, and spears to bow and arrow. Innovations in war technology spread through the world like wildfires. The emergence of metallurgy led to the invention of the sword in the bronze age, and once humans mastered the iron metallurgy, of swords and bows of steel. The use of horses for transportation and the development of spoke wheel chariots led to sweeping conquests; around 3,650 BCE the Hittites sacked Babylon, and the Hyksos invaded Egypt, establishing the 14th dynasty. Although we know little about the prehistoric ages, episodes of mobile, war savvy people conquering peaceful sedentary civilizations were probably a common pattern in human evolution.

If the civilized were constantly being replaced by the aggressive, how could civilization ever happen? How could the brain ever accumulate sufficient genes to support arts and science? When the invaders conquered a country, they would usually execute the elites to eliminate resistance, like Genghis Khan did when he devastated Persia, and Charlemagne after defeating the Saxons. This means that some of the best genes for civilization got lost. Over thousands of years this should continuously reduce the chance for civilizations to emerge. But civilizations did emerge, and especially in prosperous regions that were heavily embattled, like Mesopotamia and the valley of Mexico City. Perhaps the answer to this riddle is that the extermination of the elites was limited to the males, while women were spared. Indeed, in war times, women were usually raped en masse, but did also engage in consensual relationships with the conquerors, which led to amalgamation of the genomes of the two populations. This certainly happened when the Goths invaded Italy and Spain in the 5th century, which became the cradles of high civilizations in Europe in the Middle Ages. Just like women are generally attracted to high-ranking men within society, women of the defeated were attracted to the victors, and those who had children with them saved their precious genes for civilization. Of course, when women engage with the conquerors it is not looked upon well by their people, and often in history, when the tide of power turned, these women were prosecuted and publicly punished by flogging and shaving their heads to expose their behavior as shameful. But looking at their achievements for civilization, one cannot help but admire the evolutionary wisdom of women's choosing.

I.4.8   Religion

Religion is an important part of human culture. Wherever we look across the globe people are religious. There is a great diversity of religions, and people generally adopt the religion of the people they grew up with. But all religions have similar moral laws, and people, whether religious or not, have moral values.

We know from observations on patients with brain lesions that the frontal lobe[56] of the brain holds important functions that determine our personality as we act in society and seem to represent our moral values. This became first known through the incredible story of survival of Phineas Gage, an American railroad construction foreman who had an accident in which dynamite drove a large iron rod completely through his head, destroying much of his brain's left frontal lobe. After the accident Gage's personality changed so much that friends saw him as "no longer Gage." The pre-accident Gage was described as hard-working, responsible, and "a great favorite" with the men in his charge, his employers having regarded him as "the most efficient and capable foreman in their employ." While Gage's memory and general intelligence seemed unimpaired after the accident, he was now described as "fitful, irreverent, indulging at times in the grossest profanity (which was not previously his custom), manifesting but little deference for his fellows, impatient of restraint or advice when it conflicts with his desires…"[57] Apparently, with his frontal lobe, Phineas Gage lost much of his personality and values. The involvement of the

---

[56] The frontal lobe is the largest of the four lobes of the cerebral cortex, the large, corrugated structure that sits on top of the brain like the hat of a mushroom.

[57] John Martyn Harlow (1868). "Recovery from the Passage of an Iron Bar through the Head". Publications of the Massachusetts Medical Society. 2 (3): 327–47. Reprinted: David Clapp & Son (1869)

frontal lobe in ethical social behavior has been confirmed since by neurologists who found similar personality changes in patients with frontal lobe damage.

A hint at brain processes related to religious experience is the observation of neurologists that some patients with epilepsy report having intense religious experiences during a seizure. A famous epileptic, the Russian novelist Fyodor Dostoyevsky, has described his seizures as blissful: a "happiness unthinkable in the normal state and unimaginable for anyone who hasn't experienced it… I am in perfect harmony with myself and the entire universe." The patients reporting intense religious experiences generally had seizures in the temporal lobe[58] and some brain researchers have concluded that there is a "center of religious belief" in the temporal lobe.

An epileptic seizure starts when large numbers of neurons in a small region, the 'epileptic focus', all become active at the same time and begin to fire rhythmically. Normally neurons in the brain fire impulses, or bursts of impulses, individually when they are activated by other neurons, for example sensory receptor neurons, and send these impulses through their axons (the nerve fibers) to again other neurons. That is how information is processed in the brain. But neurons also fire impulses when they are injured, as I know from neurophysiological experiments. When a neuron is accidentally punctured by a micro-electrode it fires impulses in rapid sequence, like 300 per second or more, until it dies. During a seizure, the neurons of the epileptic focus also fire abnormally, but synchronously in short bursts of impulses with pauses in between. The activity spreads to other parts of the brain and ends only when the neurons are exhausted. There are different kinds of seizures, from 'grand mal' which makes the patient fall down unconscious with terrible convulsions, to 'petit mal' seizures during which the patient may be conscious, but has delusions, perceptions that seem real but are not based on the senses like normal perceptions. A neurologist studied the case of a patient who reported that, when she saw a rose, the next moment, to her bewilderment, roses appeared everywhere around her in the room. Bystanders might have shrugged this off as just a fantasy, but there is a plausible neurophysiological explanation. It could be that, when she saw the rose, neurons in the visual cortex were stimulated, as they normally are, but it happened at a moment when a seizure was imminent in a pathological region, a region that is connected to the visual cortex and normally processes signals from those visual neurons. But now, because of its labile state, those visual signals triggered the seizure. The neurons in the epileptic focus then

---

[58] The temporal lobes are the lateral lobes of the cerebral cortex. The temporal lobe is the most common origin of epileptic seizures.

transmitted their frantic activity back to the visual areas that signal the shape and color of roses. To other brain centers this appears exactly like activity that would be produced by roses in the visual field, roses scattered across the room. Thus, the seizure neurons can set off delusional activity in some area that their axons are connected to. Similarly, when patients report religious experiences, the localization of the epileptic focus may not be the 'center of religious belief'. Rather, the experience could come from neurons somewhere else, a place where religious information is stored, and these are activated by the epileptic neurons (or might be activated by the power of God, – we do not know).

Only a small percentage of patients report religious experiences related to epileptic seizure. But some people without epilepsy also have intense religious experiences, and it is not clear if such experience is more common in epileptics than in the general population. Perhaps those patients come from particularly religious families. No study has carefully examined these factors. Several authors have claimed that the site of the epileptic activity that leads to religious experiences is the temporal lobe, but again without unequivocal evidence.

Recently, psychoactive ingredients of 'Magic Mushrooms' have been found to mimic religious experiences. A close friend of mine participated as a subject in a study with such a substance (psilocybin) performed in a prestigious medical school. She said that she saw God, and that it was totally amazing, "a once in a lifetime experience." – I am rather worried because of the experiences of epileptic patients that are caused by the hyperactivity of neurons during seizures, which exhausts the neurons and eventually kills them. The religious experiences induced by the 'Magic Mushrooms' might also be caused by such rapid firing of neurons when they are dying, like in epileptic seizures.

To a neuroscientist who is convinced of the doctrine that any experience, be it from perception or introspection or memory or dreams, has its underlying neural activity, those observations on religious experiences, though interesting, are not really surprising. They do not provide a cue to whether such experiences come from family tradition and religious education of the individual, or whether there is also an inherited collective component. Since the various religions differ in their specifics, their beliefs, and their rituals and moral rules, and since children adopt the religion according to the traditions of the people with whom they grow up, it is clear that, to the most part, religion is defined by tradition. So, does it matter if there is also a small part that comes from the genes? What's the point of digging for the evolutionary roots of religions? Perhaps it's all just tradition.

Some intellectually progressive people think that religious beliefs stem from the desire to 'explain' natural phenomena that are otherwise hard to understand. Or that they originate at a moment in life when the infant, who has no memory yet of the past, starts wondering, where do I come from? These attempts to explain the emergence of religious beliefs entirely miss the point. They ignore that being religious is a natural part of the human inner world, a force of formidable strength, like a hurricane in the external world. For the 'progressive', religious taboos are obsolete cultural remnants, nuisance obstacles that need to be taken down, and 'progressive' people have tried to break taboos for a good part of the 20th century. But taboos are made of unbreakable material. A group of intellectuals around the French magazine Charlie Hebdo made breaking down religious taboos their mission, believing that such taboos are irrational and detrimental for society, with the result that the magazine was attacked by terrorists who killed 12 people, among them the publishing director and several prominent cartoonists. The terrorists defended their religious taboos.

In Marx' theory of society, the unfair capitalist system of exploitation of humans by humans will eventually transform into a classless communist society, and Marxists generally view religion as an obstacle on the way to the ideal society. In Marx's words, "religion is opium for the people." He argued that religion is part of the ideology promoted by the ruling class to stabilize their grip on power and reinforce the order of inequality, injustice, and exploitation, because religion promises compensation for the unfair conditions in this life by future justice in the afterlife – indeed, a cheap way to pay off their immense moral debt.

Different people have different religions, but all have certain aspects in common. In all parts of the world people have a fundamental longing for the spiritual, for something that transcends human existence; they venerate gods, or the one God, or they desire to become one with everything, a state of the mind that unites us with others. In all parts of the world people respect their parents, venerate the elderly, and revere the dead. Unless one thinks that there is only one true religion and the others are just misguided beliefs of heathens, one would conclude that religiousness is much like language, a human faculty whose specifics are filled in from experience after birth. Just like language, religion must have a genetic basis. And much like in the case of language, inherited brain mechanisms enable the acquisition of a detailed pattern from the environment. The process builds in part on general social behavioral foundations, like the ability to perceive love and to feel and give love, the value of honesty, the desire to feel joy in a group, and the need to be accepted as a member of the group; but the specific features of religion are the longing for spiritual experience, the awe of the supranatural, and the belief in life after death, including the belief that the dead can influence our life.

As we saw above when introducing the concept of engenes, behaviors driven by engenes have three phases, an emotional phase of unrest and searching, followed then by production of a specific action, and after conclusion of the action a final emotional phase of calm and satisfaction. Religious behavior also shows these characteristic three phases: the longing for God or spiritual elation; the specific actions which may be prayers, religious service, or meditation; and finally the experience of comfort and satisfaction. The three phases, which characterize religious behaviors all around the world, I hypothesize, are the expression of the Religious engene. Like other engenes of the brain, the Religious engene varies in strength between people. Some hear the voice of God; others do not have such experiences at all.

What are the evolutionary aspects of religion? How could evolution design something as complex as the Religious engene? Where did it start and what might be the selection pressure that led to its evolution?

Afterlife

A central part of all religions is the recognition of some spiritual authority that represents moral values, guides our destiny, and gives meaning to life. This authority is generally seen in the wisdom of the elderly and the enduring spiritual power of the deceased. To some extent, the parents already represent this authority, a source of guidance and spiritual force. Humans generally feel love for their parents and care for them. This is not a rational behavior. Love and respect for the parents is a strong emotion, and neglecting to care for them produces the feeling of guilt. I think it is no accident that the commandment "Honour thy father and thy mother" follows right after the commandments that refer to God, before the other moral laws. All religions include veneration of the dead, including one's ancestors, and request love and respect for the deceased. And the belief that the dead have a continued existence, and may possess the ability to influence the fortune of the living, is a central part of many religions. Indeed, we do not need this commandment to honor our parents, it's the opposite, the commandment reflects our inborn moral feelings. All this indicates that love for the parents is programmed in the human genome, it has an evolutionary origin.

Now we can see the solution to the puzzle posed above, why evolution made the Family engene reciprocal. It not only expanded brood care in time (giving lifelong support to the children) and across generations (including grandchildren and great grandchildren), but made it also bidirectional: imparting to children the faculty of love for parents and grandparents. A cat mother gives self-sacrificing love, suckling her kittens, brushing their fur, doing their toilet, and hunting to provide them meat. But when the kittens grow up they don't care about their mother. Cat love is not reciprocal. In humans, evolution made brood care reciprocal. Parents give shelter and constitute authority. They guide the children's behavior, introducing them to the society and teaching moral standards. The child in turn feels protected and perceives its moral judgments reinforced, in particular the system of social norms. The feeling of being sheltered and embedded in a system of moral laws comes from this engene (the Family engene) that has become a pillar of human society. It enables humans to behave responsibly and unselfish, thus giving strength to the community.

The expansion of the Brood-care engene producing life-long bonding and reciprocal affection between generations is a unique achievement of human evolution. This expansion, I think, is the origin of the evolution of the Religious engene. It created the drive to honor father and mother and to seek advice and spiritual support from the elderly. It created an innate respect for moral laws and a natural reverence for the deceased, which is related to the belief that the dead have a continued existence and possess the ability to influence the fortune of the living.

A cult of the ancestors is a component of many religions. The Catholic Church, recognizing the desire of the Religious engene to pray to the deceased and ask for help, provides tangible memorials for the believers in the form of relics (physical remains of a saint or venerated person). Relics are an important aspect of many religions. Reverence for the deceased implies belief in life after death. It's an irrational certainty; whether churchgoer or atheist, we respect the deceased and therefore, in a way, believe in life after death.

How did the Religious engene evolve?

How could the simple expansion of the Brood-care engene evolve into something as complex and formidable as the Religious engene? – The belief that the deceased can still influence our fate in life certainly strengthened the social coherence of people that saw themselves as descendants from a common ancestor, thereby strengthening the group in the struggle for survival.

Posnansky[59] relates the story of the Colla, a kingdom in the region of Lake Titicaca, who used to carry to battle the skull of their powerful ancestor mounted on a pole, which encouraged their fighters and terrified the enemy. The Lupaka, another kingdom in the same region, could only defeat the Colla after they were able to destroy their sacred idol. The use of standards in battle is a universal custom. Roman legions had each their standard with a symbol, like an eagle or other icon, which was carried visibly in battle and revered by the legionaries as a spiritual backing.

Perhaps the Religious engene evolved because it strengthened ethnic definition and enhanced the chance of survival of ethnicities. A shining example is the people of Israel. It may not be an exaggeration to say that the Jewish people survived the Babylonian exile, the defeat when their resistance was crushed by the Romans, and their subsequent dispersal throughout the world, because of their religion. Still today, Indigenous ethnic groups in many parts of the world resist the power of modern civilization and survive by virtue of their religion. And taking away the religion, as the Catholic church did in the conquest of the great empires of the Americas, and as Evangelical missionaries continue to be doing by proselytizing Indigenous people of the Amazon, generally means the end of an ethnicity.

The resilience that religion afforded to the group gave a selective advantage in the competition of groups within Homo sapiens, and perhaps already in the competition of Homo sapiens with other homo species, and this selection gradually strengthened the Religious engene.

Through its laws, religion gives structure to society. The individual obeys, and by accepting the religious rules or commandments she/he accepts a supranatural authority, and this in turn strengthens the feeling of being a member of a large body, the ethnic group, the church, or whatever the name of the religious community. The Religious engene makes people put the interest of the community above their individual interest. The submission under the religious authority has enabled people to sacrifice themselves for the group and to endure suppression, humiliation, torture, and even face death, to a degree that is perhaps impossible for non-religious people. One amazing example is how the Christian religion helped the slaves in America to regain their self-esteem and define a new identity. Although it was the religion of the oppressors, enslaved Africans

---

[59] Arturo Posnansky, *Tihuanacu, the Cradle of American Man, Vols. I - II.* (Translated into English by James F. Sheaver), J. J. Augustin, Publ., New York and Minister of Education, La Paz, Bolivia (1945).

and their descendants easily adopted Christian spirituality and incorporated it into their culture. It certainly gave, and still gives, millions of people spiritual strength and ethnic identity.[60]

The power of the Religious engene

In today's society the power of 'spirituality' is widely recognized. For example, the success of Alcoholics Anonymous, an international fellowship dedicated to helping alcoholics to become sober, has been highly successful in over 80 years since its foundation, more successful than other medically oriented programs. The success is due partly to its peer-to-peer mode of interaction based on voluntary work of its members, and partly to the spirituality of its program. In the words of their founders, members should admit that they are powerless over alcohol and need help from a "higher power." The fellowship induces its members to seek guidance and strength through prayer and meditation from God or a Higher Power of their own understanding. While it is not specifically religious, it is clear that it owes its success (compared to many other attempts to help the addicted) to the power of the Religious engene.

The downside is that the power of the Religious engene can be misused. It is often exploited by individuals or organizations to enforce obedience. For example, Christian communities and faith-based organizations often pressure pregnant teenagers to carry out their pregnancy and then give their baby in adoption. 'Teen Challenge', an organization affiliated with the Pentecostal Assemblies of God church, is made up of centers for adolescents and adults seeking to overcome "life-controlling issues," such as drug use, depression, or sexual promiscuity. Many people are sent there by courts, as an alternative to juvenile detention or jail, but some are simply teenagers whose parents have trouble with their education, parents who feel unable to control their child's behavior according to what they perceive as Christian values, for example, that getting pregnant out of wedlock is a "moral failure" and homosexuality is "a detestable sin." Such parents then decide to get rid of the trouble by turning their child over to one of those centers. In an article in The New Yorker Rachel Aviv reported[61] that Teen Challenge centers pressured pregnant teenagers to give their newborn babies in adoption, telling them phrases like "If you don't give up your child, you are bringing shame on yourself" and "Just like Mary gave up her son,

---

[60] Z.N. Hurston, "Barracoon. The Story of the Last 'Black Cargo'", edited by D.G. Plant. Amistad, New York (2018).

[61] https://www.newyorker.com/magazine/2021/10/18/the-shadow-penal-system-for-struggling-kids

you're making this ultimate sacrifice." Thus the professional caretakers mobilize two social engenes, the first shaming the woman for being pregnant out of wedlock, an engene that evolved to protect the two-parent family (see "Guadalupe" under I.4.6), and second, the Religious engene.

The gripping story of a young woman who did not want to give up her newborn son shows how this concerted effort defeated the most fundamental instinct that tells the mother to have her baby, the nucleus of the Brood-care engene. In the 48 hours that by law had to pass before the mother could sign the adoption document, she was allowed to have her son. But her love was estranged, "I felt unworthy, like I was loving someone who wasn't mine to love," and the director of the center told her, referring to the envisaged adoption family, "Think about your calling. Think about this family. Think about why God chose you to bless them." At a meeting in the conference room of the hospital with two lawyers of an adoption agency, the two directors of the center, and her parents, when the young mother was crying for the entire meeting, she was told, "This is the same pain that God felt when he gave us His son. We are reaping so many rewards from this sacrifice." The experience in the Teen Challenge center left the woman traumatized for life. After she had left the center, got married and had a daughter, she fell into depression: "My daughter was the sweetest, smartest, fieriest little thing, but I didn't feel a bond with her," she told the journalist, "I had gone through this experience of completely extinguishing all my maternal feelings, and I felt like I was incapable of love." But she also remembered, "at Teen Challenge, I had very vivid experiences where I felt I encountered God, and that's been the most complicated part—untangling what I actually believe."

More about the formidable power of the Religious engene, and how it shaped human history, below in section 'Marriage of throne and altar'.

Questions remain unanswered

At the end of this section I want to point out, what is perhaps needless to say, that considering the brain mechanisms that I call 'Religious engene' is all about the human brain. It says nothing about the immortality of the soul and does not speak to the question whether God exists or not.

I.4.9   Strife

Alltid strid	Always strife
ingen frid	no peace
livet är	is life
mennisher strider	mankind strives
världar strider	worlds strive
allting gåta är	everything is enigma

Stone inscription in a park in Stockholm

It has generally been thought that a complex hierarchical society is a feature that distinguishes humans from apes. However, recent studies seem to be changing this view; some primatologists now think that hierarchical societies can also be found in apes and that their social modularity is qualitatively similar to that of humans, suggesting that the difference is not in kind, but in scale. Gorillas, for example, also have a multi-tiered hierarchical society like humans. Tracking the identity of the individuals that regularly meet in a foraging place, researchers found that each individual regularly meets and spends time with various others, and, as in humans, such associations are kin structured.[62] The difference, the study says, is that their circle of acquaintances is no more than a few dozen, whereas humans can recognize and remember details of many more, supposedly over a thousand.

So, is human society qualitatively similar to that of gorillas, just scaled up? I have argued above that evolution took a turn about two million years ago when hominids with superior power emerged, and that from then on it was no longer fitness in foraging and fending off predators what drove evolution, but competition within hominids; and the main reason for that superiority was a new kind of society. What emerged from the long competition were new social engenes that, I argue, differ in quality, not just scale, from all ape societies. One powerful innovation was the two-parent family. Another innovation, perhaps the most fateful, was the strengthening of an engene that distinguishes friend and foe. I call it the 'Strife engene'.

---

[62] Morrison RE, Groenenberg M, Breuer T, Manguette ML, Walsh PD, "Hierarchical social modularity in gorillas." Proc. R. Soc. B 286: 20190681 (2019). http://dx.doi.org/10.1098/rspb.2019.0681

Aggression

Konrad Lorenz[63] pointed out that intra-species aggression can contribute to the fitness of a species, like in territorial animals, where the mutual aggression leads the competing individuals to observe a minimum distance. This behavior discourages crowding of several individuals at one location and thus tends to produce a more even distribution in the environment, thus optimizing the use of the available space. For example, he describes tropical fish that use a cave entrance as their base for preying, and viciously attack conspecific competitors that come too close to their cave. These fish also wear patterns of brilliant colors to warn competitors to keep a distance. Thus, the mechanism of intra-specific aggression here serves the function of distributing the individuals of a species optimally over the available space.[64]

While the evolution of intra-specific aggression may have been driven by this adaptive improvement, it was also strengthened by reflexive evolution. Whether it optimizes spatial distribution or not, aggressiveness generally confers an advantage to the individual in producing offspring. A wren that aggressively defends its territory can secure more resources for feeding its chicks than a less aggressive wren, and thus a genetic code for aggressive behavior will spread across the species. Aggressive humans like Genghis Khan could spread their genes more effectively than other individuals, thus increasing the frequency of aggressive people among the human population. This is reflexive evolution: A behavioral trait that facilitates spreading of its genetic code continues to increase in strength even if, in the course of time, it ceases to provide any survival value. Even when evolution of aggressiveness did not improve fitness of the species, it strengthened over time. In humans reflexive evolution has produced the Strife engene, a special aggressive trait that may have resulted from competition between groups within the species or between closely related hominid species. Different from the Family engene which creates bonding to family and friends, the Strife engene acts across the entire group, producing solidarity and comradery within the group, and also hostility against rivaling groups. Like sexual selection shaped the characteristics of human genders, the Strife engene shaped the structure of human society. It became the most fateful trait of human nature. To see it playing out in modern times is oppressive.

---

[63] Konrad Lorenz (1966) "On Aggression." Methuen & Co Ltd.

[64] Ethologists have pointed out that this mechanism of aggression is physiologically different from the predator kind of aggression. See Lorenz, "On Aggression."

The "us" and "them"

To understand the Strife engene we need to look at the two emotions, love for one's own people and hate against the others. The roots of this dual function may be ancient, the result of reflexive evolution among hominids over millions of years. Because of competition for territory and other resources, genes that facilitated within-group collaboration and protection, and enabled organized defense and aggression against other groups, improved the chance of survival of their carriers. Love, comradery, and solidarity within a group certainly strengthened the group and helped it prevail, both in times of scarce resources and in times of conflict.

Observing children one can easily see that the desire to find one's identity in society is a basic trait of human nature, possibly set up at birth, which then acquires its specifics from the environment. When my son was four, my wife took him to a Karate class which was in another part of town. Although we had lived in Zurich for many years, we were still foreigners; we understood the local dialect more or less, but never managed to speak it. We spoke mostly German at home, and sometimes Spanish. Our son had beautiful curly black hair and a downward bending nose like those of native Americans. In short, he looked quite un-Swiss, as did my wife and our daughter (I could pass for a Swiss as long as I didn't open my mouth). But when she picked him up after the first lesson, trying to find an opportunity for carpooling, she asked him if he had perhaps seen people he knew from our neighborhood, and he replied "There were some that spoke something that sounded like Spanish, I think it was Italian. Then there were several *Tütsche* (the dialect name for Germans). And the others were just normal people, like us." Obviously, children have a natural desire to identify themselves with the ambient, the resident ethnicity, even against the most obvious evidence.

How strong the emotions evoked by the Strive engene are can be seen from the passion that people have for sports teams, like Europeans for soccer, or Americans for football. One does not have to be sporty to be a passionate fan of a team. A young software engineer, who is totally unsporting, craves for college football and enthusiastically follows the games of "his" team. But his wife is unhappy because that team is not the best and loses most of the games (which does not diminish his loyalty at all), and every time when that happens our fan is having a bad day.

It might be thought that competitive traits like the Strife engene have evolved only recently, perhaps in the neolithic when human populations grew, people became sedentary and began to fight for possession of land. But I argued that the Strife engene evolved much earlier (see above, I.2.4 "Group selection"). Migration out of Africa began approximately two million years ago with the early expansions of hominids. The initial migration was followed by other archaic humans, including the likely ancestors of Denisovans, Floresienses, and Neanderthals. Meanwhile, back in Africa, there were more rivaling homo species, and Homo sapiens was one of them. Finally, around 70 thousand years ago, Sapiens also emerged outside Africa and dispersed across Eurasia where they gradually replaced the previous immigrants, including Homo neanderthalensis. Thus, our species is the lone survivor of two million years of competition.

As pointed out, the fundamental condition of life in the paleolithic was that a given area of hunting ground could only support a limited number of hunter-gatherer families. In trying to understand how competition between hunter-gatherers over millions of years created the roots of human social behavior, we must try to imagine how this has shaped human life during the unimaginably long period of two million years. Each of us humans today looks back at some 80,000 generations of human ancestors since Homo erectus emerged, and there were at least eight major climate changes since then, like the cycles of glacial periods and interglacial periods.[65]

And whenever climates changed, or when people migrated, their conditions alternated between periods of starvation and affluence. Imagine hunter-gatherers who had adapted to hunting large animals, like the various mammoth species. These big plant eaters thrived in Eurasia and the Americas during the ice ages when grasslands covered large regions of the continents. But during the interglacial periods, when the grasslands gave way to forests, their populations dwindled. As a result, the different tribes of hunter-gatherers would come into conflict. While herders can defend their flock of sheep, farmers can fence in their land, and cities can build walls, hunter-gatherers cannot protect their resources. When hunters of another tribe intruded into a tribe's hunting ground, it threatened their existence. We can imagine how people felt when after months of fruitless hunting forays, they spotted a column of smoke and found a group feasting on the carcass of a big animal, an animal that they considered theirs, but those were not their people, but others. Also, as hunters, they knew very well that, to preserve the resources, killing calves and cows must be avoided. But calves are the easiest to hunt, certainly much easier than grown bulls. Those who

---

[65] These are cycles within the Quaternary glaciation, which has been in progress since 2.58 million years ago.

practiced restraint on hunting but saw others hunting irresponsibly must have felt intense rage.

This is all psychology of ancient hunter-gatherers in my imagination which might have no relation to how humans feel and act in today's society. Relevant for us today is the genetic code that the competition over hundreds of millennia has helped to proliferate: code that enabled definition of ethnic identity and produced a drive to protect one's own people while being hostile towards others. When the others intruded, they could have just looked on with rage – or could have killed the intruders. And the latter is what drove evolution: the genes of the ones who were quick at killing survived, and the genes of the ones who were more forgiving gradually disappeared. That is how the Strife engene evolved. *Rage* is psychology, *hate* is a product of evolution.

As described above (I.2.4 "Group selection") there is now direct evidence for this process from genetic studies of hunter-gatherers who lived in Europe and Western Asia during the last 35 thousand years. Progress in paleo-genomics has made it possible to register the genomes from bones and teeth that had been found and assigned dates and stowed away in museums over the years. These were all remains from Sapiens (from the time after Neanderthals had been eliminated). The studies show that there was genetic diversity even in this limited region – and there was selection. Correlational analysis revealed geographically separated clusters, the genomes being more similar to each other within clusters than between clusters, corresponding to distinct groups of people that differed in appearance, as evident from the genes coding for skin, hair, and eye colors, and certainly spoke many different languages. The analysis also revealed that certain genetic signatures were present through millennia, but disappeared at some point without leaving a trace in subsequent populations. Apparently, certain people had been 'replaced'.

A hundred thousand years is about as far as paleo-genomics can reach back in time. But the evolution of the genetic code for aggressive group behavior probably started as early as hominid societies formed groups that began to compete with each other. Initially, genetic code for group behavior may have evolved just because of the advantages of group solidarity. Then, competition drove evolution of genetic code for aggression. Initially, individuals had brotherly feelings towards their own; then, they began to hate "the others."

The two faces of the Strife engene may have evolved in tandem during the long age of Homo erectus, combining love for one's own people with hate against "the others." What is remarkable is that, unlike rage, or love, or fear, which are emotions of the individual, those of the Strife engene are collective emotions. With this engene, a society evolved that required its members to distinguish friend and foe. It made the commandment "Thou shalt not kill" conditional on that distinction, creating deadly competitions in the stone age and eventually driving nations into wars. It created xenophobia and racism and justified exclusion which became the basis for oppression and exploitation of "the others:" ethnocentric ideologies sweetened by within-group mutual recognition, affirmation, and support.

Aggressive behavior might be thought of as a regular ingredient of evolution. To grab as much of the available resources as possible is considered the law of the strong, and the use of force his right. The law of the jungle. But it is different in human society. The Strife engene makes people susceptible to the ideology of entitlement which instills the belief that "we" are destined to rule over "them" and are entitled to their property, land, resources, and workforce. We do not know when in prehistoric times human groups first made this claim of supremacy, but it is recorded on the earliest historical documents, such as king Sargon's victory stele showing hand-cuffed prisoners escorted by a soldier (Plate 1). Sargon conquered various cities in Mesopotamia, established his rule and deported people who were then forced to labor on his grandiose projects.

The Strife engene tends to create hierarchical societies rather than the egalitarian society envisioned by the theorists of the French revolution. This means that the modern democracy that we desire, that grants equality and protects the rights of the individual, is continually in conflict with a social engene that we come with when we are born. This conflict needs to be resolved again and again for each generation. Modern democracy is not stable.

Patriotism

The Strife engene generates feelings of love, fairness and responsibility within a group that has a common origin and shared traditions. It makes people willing to sacrifice themselves for the group. But it also produces the corresponding negative feelings of hate and contempt for people that are perceived as outside the group. It makes us feel comfortable in our homeland and care for people of our language and culture, but it also makes us aggressive towards people of other languages and cultures. It instills a sense of commitment and solidarity within the nation, which are pillars of modern nation states, but also hate and envy and the urge to defend the "own values" against the presumed outsiders.

> *Aux armes citoyens!*
> *Formez vos bataillons!*
> *Marchons, marchons,*
> *Qu'un sang impur abreuve nos sillons.*
>
> To arms, citizens!
> Form your battalions!
> Walk, walk,
> May impure blood water our furrows.

No moral issues about shedding the dirty blood of the enemies.[66] When people talk about their own ethnocentrism they often prefer to call it patriotism, which implies positive emotions, like feelings of glory. Note also that the word patriotism reveals a gender bias.

The Strife engene produces ethnocentrism. As explained previously, the function of engenes generally involves three phases, a phase of unrest and longing, a phase in which a specific action is executed, followed by a phase of satisfaction and calm. The emotions in phases 1 and 3, particularly if they are found universally in people of different cultures, are sure indicators of a behavioral engene that is inheritable and thus a product of evolution. In the Strife engene, the phase of unrest may be caused by some crisis spreading fear across people, which leads to actions such as public unrest and mass demonstrations. Calm and satisfaction ensue when a solution to the crisis is apparent, but it could also be simply the satisfaction of finding comfort in being part of the mass and feeling the solidarity of the others. It can be as simple as walking in lockstep, but

---

[66] Perhaps it is unfair to cite the Marseillaise as an example of nationalism; the enemy whose blood it mentions was the ruling feudal class. But it also served French imperialism.

for young men the feeling of comradery in dangerous situations can be a deeply emotional, character forming experience. The Strife engene also creates the desire for a strong leader personality who promises to lead the people out of the crisis and instills loyalty in his followers. And they see him as having supernatural powers. When leaders incite a crowd of people they address this engene. When things do not develop to satisfaction, war may be the ultimate action, leading either to the satisfaction of victory or the calm of defeat and misery.

Racism

I think the specifics of the Strife engene are probably not in the genes, but determined by experience.[67] Just like in the case of language, the genes provide the general mechanism, but its parameters are filled in after birth. I say this because I have seen families in which one partner is White and the other Colored, and if their children are also Colored, then the White person's perception adapts so that she/he perceives color as the norm, and it may happen that when looking in the mirror she/he is surprised how pale she/he looks. Children pick up ethnicity from the environment like birds are imprinted with the image of the parents when they hatch. When I moved with my family from Zurich to Baltimore, my children got scared the first time they saw Black men in the street in front of our house. They reacted like this although one of our best friends in Zurich was a woman from a "Homeland" of South Africa who had children that were pretty dark, and who often played with our children. Perhaps seeing adult Black men on the street they felt was extraordinary and had to get used to it. So, I think, xenophobia, which literally means 'fear of strangers' is a natural response whose specific parameters are filled in by the environment. The Strife engene can later adapt so that the specific xenophobia weakens or disappears.

The brain comes with the Strife engene installed, and only the parameters are picked up after birth. It is then being imprinted with perceptual information in the first years of life. At this stage, the perceptual influence has multiple determinants: People identify themselves by their origin, the place and the landscape where they grew up, by the language and the religion they pick up,

---

[67] But in birds a case has been studied in which both the feather color and the perceptual preference are genetically determined. As mentioned, the European crow has two races, the Carrion crow and the Hooded crow, and although the two races interbreed frequently, the separation remains stable because the genes that determine the feather pattern and the genes that determine the perceptual preference both reside in the same chromosome.

and by the appearance of the people they see around. Thus, a wealth of natural and cultural factors contribute to one's ethnic identification.

The appearance of the people is one factor. It can be quite surprising how children establish a norm, and what is normal is perceived as good and deviations from the norm as bad or dangerous. When my brother visited Cochabamba, a city in South America that had very few tourists at the time, my wife's little nephew said to his mother: "That man must be bad." Why? "Because he has white hair" (my brother was blond). But in the German village where I grew up among local farmers and refugee families from the German East, my little friend, who had black hair was called "*de Schwatte*" by the local people, which means "the black" in Plattdeutsch dialect, and *Schwatte* became his nickname. He was singled out as deviant from the norm and took it as an insult. But he got over it, studied law and became a judge. Still now I find it weird to hear on television a person with 'immigrant background' speak perfect German while her skin color is black. I realize then how much skin and hair color weigh on the scale of ethnicity. Not even the language provides enough counterweight.

It is important to see what education can do. Education talks to the rational mind, but the engenes are deeply irrational. I first came across the great Dr. Seuss' books when I was a graduate student in Zurich and a young American couple invited me to dinner. He was a researcher in biomedical engineering and neuroscience. I listened when he read to his 3-year-old daughter Laura the story of the 'Sneeches'. These were creatures that had a round belly, a small head on a long neck, and long thin arms and legs, and when they were on the beach one could see that some had a star on their belly. Those who had a star looked down on the ones with plain bellies and tried to exclude them from their circles. The plain-belly sneeches got envious and wished they also had stars. A clever entrepreneur noticed that and came with a machine that could print stars on skin. So, the plain-belly sneeches went and paid him to get the star printed on their bellies. This went on for a while until most sneeches did have a star. Only some had refrained, a few that still had plain bellies. And they now thought they were more beautiful and proudly showed their plain bellies on the beach. After a while all the ones who had stars envied the few plain-belly sneeches and some wanted to get rid of the star. And promptly, the clever entrepreneur was there, now with a new machine that could take off stars from bellies, and he made a good fortune again. This went on. I think the sneech society went through another round of changes, but finally they all realized that it was stupid to lose money to that guy and stopped asking for getting stars or getting rid of them, being content each just how they were, and lived happily from then on. – So that was the story.

When the father finished and closed the book, little Laura looked at us with a smile, triumph in her eyes, and said: "I'm a star-belly sneech!" – He looked up to the ceiling for a moment, just pronouncing her name.

The Strife engene plays an important role in supporting social hierarchy and class division. While the us-and-them distinction is usually based on perceived ethnicity, involving origin, race, language and culture, the engene also enables leaders to seize power, and provides the emotional mechanisms required for maintaining a layered structure of society, such as power elite and common subjects, which may be defined by fiefdom and slavery, or by capitalist work relationships. The genetic engene defines the basic mechanisms of perception and behavior in social hierarchy, the specifics being defined by environment and education. That is, the child is born with mechanisms that enable perception of social rank and skills of behaving in a ranked society, while the specific features that define rank, and where it sees itself in that society, are learned after birth. Thus, human social hierarchy is not determined by genes as in Aldous Huxley's fantasy of Brave New World, where a caste system is genetically engineered, but based on the perception of the society in which a child is raised. Of course, some features are defined by genes, such as the colors of skin, hair and eyes, body size etc., perhaps also mental faculties, which will all constrain development. Hence the specification of rank is a complex process that involves feedback interactions. The infant might perceive its rank based on the family it is raised in, say, rank 1, but people outside the family might perceive that differently, for example if the infant's skin color does not match rank 1 but rather rank 2, leading to conflict. Or a child in a low-ranking family might be born with a strong character that makes her/him rebellious against the ranking by the society, and such a child might end up at a higher rank than its family.

Race, class, and ethnicity

Sociologists distinguish race, class, and ethnicity as descriptors of social structure, where race is thought to be biological, class to reflect the economic relationships, and ethnicity the cultural determinant. But it's not that simple. As to race, the biological may seem rather obvious – race is commonly assigned according to appearance. But class assignment and ethnic classification also have their biological roots, although that may be less obvious because the specifics of their assignment depend also on environment and experience.

Class, by definition, identifies the economic relationship, distinguishing owners of the means of production from workers employed by the owners. Ownership is protected by the law. In the U.S., there was a time when owners directly owned the workers (i.e., slaves). Even today, around the world millions of children are trafficked as slaves,[68] and slave ownership is apparently protected by the society. In many parts of the world, skin color also serves to label class. In East Asia, women take pains not to expose their skin to the sun so as to preserve their light tone. In Japan I saw volunteering old ladies tend to the public gardens dressed in hat, long sleeves, and gloves in the heat of the summer. When millions of Africans were traded as slaves by the White, their skin color was a highly convenient marker of their status, and it serves to distinguish class still today, long after the civil rights movement corrected the laws. Also in Latin America, the tone of skin color serves as a convenient marker for social rank. Families that are proud of their Spanish descent cherish their skin color, although that has become more and more difficult because through centuries men of Spanish descent used to impregnate native descendant women. In countries that were built on foundations of the ancient civilizations of Aztecs, Mayas, and Incas, and consequently have a majority of people of Indigenous descent, families of *Criollos* (descendants of the Spanish) find themselves in this dilemma. The circumstance of racial interbreeding leads to comic situations when, in a *Criollo* family which supposedly is White, a baby is born that unexpectedly, but conform with Gregor Mendel's laws, has dark complexion. "*La venganza del Inca* (The revenge of the Inca)," my father-in-law used to remark with a smile. Thus, we see that class distinctions often rely on racial attributes.

Ethnicity is a concept that refers to the origin and culture that people identify themselves with, the main determinants of culture being language and religion. But language serves also as a label for class. Where skin color has lost some of its significance because of the racial mixing, language is used as a more reliable indicator of social class. In the Andean countries, not only *campesinos* (rural farmers), but also the migrants in the big cities often know little Spanish or speak it with an accent (usually from *Quechua*, the most widespread Indigenous language). While they try to assimilate by changing clothing and lifestyle, and often become wealthy, language still identifies them as *Cholos* (a pejorative term for the assimilating). In England, the Cockney accent indicates working class, and when Ms. Thatcher became prime minister, she had to take lessons to improve her accent. A prime minister must be upper class.

Religion defined the ruling class during the conquest of the Americas. But after Catholicism was used to cement the Spanish rule, it could no longer be used

---

[68] https://www.theworldcounts.com/stories/facts-about-child-slavery

to distinguish class, whereas in Brazil, African religions still identify ethnicity and define the oppressed class. Origin, language, religion, tradition, and family names define the castes in India, making its hierarchical socio-economical order durable.

Possession

The object of desire of the Strife engene is generally possession. When wars break out, it is nearly always about acquisition of goods and defending possession of goods. In today's world we take the concept of property for granted and hardly think about its origin. It seems natural that everybody has some property, and that property is protected by law. Not so long ago, when European people settled in the Americas, they found people who gave little importance to private property. Most of what they owned – land, fruit trees, hunting- and fishing grounds – was common property of the group. Possession was communal. But still, as documents of the first contacts with Whites show, indigenous peoples were often in war with each other about territory and dominance. Indeed, the Spanish conquerors of Mexico and Peru took advantage of current situations of war between neighboring peoples. Competition for territory and resources probably has its roots in the long history of hunter-gatherers. Possession of territory and resources of course gained enormous importance in the Neolithic with the transition to agrarian economy. An early written document that defines property rights are the Ten Commandments, one of which says, "Thou shalt not steal" and another, "Thou shalt not covet your neighbor's house; thou shalt not covet thy neighbor's wife, or his slaves, or his animals, or anything of thy neighbor." Thus, Jews had clear property rights at that time. The mentioning of livestock shows that the Commandments addressed an agrarian society. Certainly the transition from a mobile hunter-gatherer society to a sedentary agrarian society had made possession more important than before. So, one might think that property rights are inventions of the agrarian era.

But it seems to me that the desire to possess is deeply ingrained in human nature. I remember when my daughter was three and a visit from her friend was announced, before the little guy arrived she would round up her toys in a corner and sit on them; she literally possessed them (*possedere* in Latin means to sit on something). In today's world disputes about possession arouse deep emotions. In many people the fear of communism, thought to abolish the right to property, is like the fear of the devil. So it seems to me that the concept of possession is much older than the agrarian society. Already for Homo erectus it was important to occupy and defend a favorable territory that provided food and access to clean water. Possession is a feature of the Strife engene. Presumably the transition to agrarian economy strengthened it, but remember that that transition began only ten thousand years ago, an age that makes up only 0.5 percent of the age of Homo erectus; and that was only the beginning of the transition, in most parts of the world it was even later. So, it is unlikely that such a short period substantially changed the genome. The possession genes must be older than the agrarian society.

What might be the evolutionary origin of the emotions regarding possession? In the animal realm, competition is often coupled with taking possession and defending possession. The tropical fish aggressively defends its cave, and the male house wren defends his mate and his territory. Here again we can see three behavioral phases – anguish and searching for the desired object (cave, breeding place, mate) – aggressive taking possession – and calm and satisfaction when it is successfully occupied/defended. In many species, males not only compete for the privilege to inseminate a female, they also strive to possess her. Thus, besides territory and foraging resources, the most important possession has always been the females. The resulting social order is a dominant male with a harem. The male lion defends territory and a group of females together with their offspring. Also gorilla and orangutan societies have this kind of order; a dominant male rules over a group of females with their infants, while young adult males leave the group and live a solitary life, awaiting their chance (see also observations on rhesus monkeys described above). Thus, the alliance of power and possession in the genome is older than the human race.

In human society, which is based on the two-parent family, the situation is different. The two-parent family genes have won. Only few societies today practice the harem family. But the old genes that make men strive for power and possession of women are still with us. As Homer relates in his Iliad, the strife for possessing a woman led to the Trojan war that ended with the destruction of Troy. The war broke out when Paris, prince of the royal family of Ilion, apparently on foray into the Peloponnese, went off with Helen, the most beautiful woman, who was married to Menelaos, king of Sparta. It all began when Zeus failed to invite Eris, the goddess of *strife*, to a wedding party on Mount Olympus (who would want *strife* at a wedding?). For revenge, Eris threw the golden Apple of Discord inscribed with the words "For the most beautiful" into the party. Three goddesses, Hera, Athena, and Aphrodite thought to be the most beautiful and each one claimed the apple. They started a quarrel, so they asked Zeus to choose one of them. Knowing that choosing any of them would bring him trouble, Zeus did not want to take part in the decision, so he appointed Paris to select the most beautiful. And Paris gave the apple to Aphrodite who had promised him the love of the most beautiful woman on Earth. As promised, Aphrodite made Helen fall in love with Paris. So Paris abducted her and took her to Ilion. Tragically, possession of that woman caused a ten-year war that ended with the destruction of Ilion and its kingdom.

All of this is of course mythology, or, if you want, a poetic depiction of an archetype of the human soul. I do not want to imply that the Iliad portrays a picture of an actual human society. Women of course reject being possessed (in fact, the Iliad does not suggest this either; Paris was able to abduct Helen because a goddess made her fall in love with him). But human society is biased. This can be seen in many cultures. For example, the Ten Commandments say, you shall not covet your neighbor's wife, which obviously addresses men. Nothing is said about her coveting her neighbor's husband.

Many societies have norms that demand men to possess, and women to accept being possessed. In most parts of the world, for sure in European countries, the vast majority of women adopt the name of their husband when they get married, indicating that she now belongs to him. In today's Japan, a married woman's legal surname can only be the surname of her husband. An exception I found is Korea, where women traditionally keep their family names after marriage; but even there, their children take the father's surname.

So why does the vast majority of women eagerly accept adopting their husband's family name? It's a wide-spread convention, one might say. But looking at evolution one can see that this convention is not accidental. The power-and-possession conjunction characterized human social order probably as early as the hunter-gatherer societies and drove the evolution of Homo erectus, although the struggle to own a harem was weakened by the new trend towards two-parent family ('new' meaning two million years old).

Conflict about possession

The conflict between autocratic and egalitarian tendencies is inherent in human society. It is the conflict between the demands of the Strife engene and the Family engene, and there is an important difference between the two: The Strife engene demands property rights whereas the Family engene does not. The latter emphasizes *égalité* and *fraternité*, postulating that possessions be common rather than personal. In contrast, the Strife engene responds with aggression whenever a threat to possession is perceived.

The Roman Republic was a rather egalitarian political structure that lasted for hundreds of years. While the power was by the Senate, which represented the aristocratic families, the plebeians were free Roman citizens that lived on public lands and had political rights, represented by the tribunes of the plebs that they elected. However, through the centuries, the aristocratic families used the power of the senate to gain possession of more and more of the public land that had been worked by plebeians, thus converting the land into their farms that were worked by slaves. As a result, in the 2nd century BCE Rome had a large class of landless citizens which led to civil unrest. In 133 BCE, Tiberius Gracchus as the tribune of the plebs attempted a land reform based on an existing law that limited the amount of land that could be owned by a single person. The reform of course met the resistance of the senators, and, although Gracchus had the support of the people and was about to be reelected for a second term, the senators blocked his reelection. In sequel, Gracchus and 300 of his followers were clubbed to death by a squadron organized by the landowner senators. Ten years later, Tiberius' younger brother Gaius Gracchus, also elected tribune of the plebs, made another attempt at reform. Although he had even broader support from both country and urban poor and a growing middle class, his reform tragically failed because, when he planned to extend citizen rights to non-Roman Italians, his support among Roman citizens weakened, and his movement was crushed. When his enemies mobilized a mob to assassinate him, he took his life. Remarkably, even those who lacked property and were at the bottom of the power scale nevertheless tried to defend what they had in privileges against newcomers.

The history of Rome is a mirror that reflects the struggle of egalitarian popular movements against structures of inequality in modern times. Time and again, big landowners crushed attempts of land reform by military power. When Jacobo Arbenz, who promised a land reform, was elected president of Guatemala he was removed by a coup d'état and died in exile. Because the peasants resented the abortion of the reform, a guerrilla movement emerged which was then brutally crushed by the military regime, and 200,000 Mayan peasants were killed in the following; the 'silent genocide' as it has been called.[69] Getúlio Vargas, three times president of Brazil who brought social and economic changes that helped modernize the country, was revered by his followers as the "Father of the Poor" for his battle against big business and large landowners, although he did not even attempt a land reform. When the military tried to force him to retire, he took his life, sharing the fate of Gaius Gracchus. Ten years later another

---

[69] Magda von der Heydt-Coca, "Latin American Development from Populism to Neopopulism." Rowman & Littlefield (2021).

president, João Goulart, tried to follow up on Vargas' reforms. Among others, his plan proposed to expropriate and redistribute only the non-productive properties larger than 600 hectares to the population, which seems like a modest reform. Within 15 months of his presidency he was forced out of the country by a military coup and was later poisoned in exile.[70] Interestingly also, the dwindling support for Gaius Gracchus among Roman citizens when he attempted to extend citizen privileges to other Italians mirrors today's social conflicts in the U.S., where many voters with immigrant background vote for a party that advocates anti-immigration policies. See also Libre Initiative, an organization used by the Republican Party to recruit Latino voters.[71]

The obsession of governments to exterminate leftist movements may be understood as a response of the Strife engene that drives men to hold on to possession. Obsessed with the fear of a communist revolution they mobilized the authority of the state to fight back even at the expense of sacrificing civil rights. After the Russian October revolution, governments all over the globe moved to the right. The fear of communism would lead the German president Hindenburg to push for a right-wing government even at the price of unhinging the constitution, paving the way for Hitler. In the U.S., beginning in the late 1940ies, the 'Red Scare' produced political repression against persons believed to be members of the communist party or Soviet spies, and against leftist intellectuals in general. By instigating fear, this right-wing movement unleashed demagogic attacks on the character or patriotism of citizens, often in violation of the First Amendment of the American constitution. Here again, patriotism produced by the Strife engene was the motor.

Ideology of friend and foe

As said, the Strife engene has a positive and a negative side: the cooperative side that produces love, comradery and solidarity within a group, and the competitive side that produces hate and aggressive behavior against "the others." The Strife engene finds its expression in ethnocentric ideologies where the positive values of within-group mutual recognition, affirmation and support serve to justify and sweeten the institutions of exclusion, oppression and exploitation of "the others," in stunning contradiction to those accepted values. The duality of this engene becomes obvious when a political leader uses conspiracy theories to instigate hate against a supposed enemy, or conjure a fictitious threat, to entice people and

---

[70] ibid

[71] https://thelibreinitiative.com/

mobilize its energies to achieve his sinister objectives that would otherwise not have their support. Or when a class of plantation owners justifies the exploitation of slave work with the ideology of racial supremacy, sweetened with religious values and the prosperity of their own families.

Patterns of peaceful/aggressive behaviors have evolved at various scales of society, strengthening bonds within ethnic groups, and rivalry between; fomenting patriotism, but also aggressive nationalism and chauvinism. The Strife engene enabled oppression of Black people under the rule of slavery and their continued oppression after slavery was abolished. For centuries, it made European countries adopt the predator strategy of colonialism, competing with each other for the best prey, which eventually led to the mobilization of masses and the outbreak of the First World War. The Strife engene fomented the German East-expansion ideology that made the Nazi Regime popular ("People Without Space"[72]) and powered the racial persecution and terror under the Nazi regime – and is still the motor of racial discrimination around the world today. My point is that these disasters of human civilization are not merely historical phenomena, products of traditions, ideologies, and indoctrination. They are the products of a behavioral engene that is part of human inheritance; products that surface again and again, and can only to a limited extent be compensated or redirected by education.

The Strife engene is deeply irrational. It incites patriotism even where patriotism means destruction of the fatherland, and it generates hate even when the hate has no reason. Hitler appealed to the patriotism of people to endure the war, preaching "If the German people cannot win this war, they must perish." Existential threats trigger the irrational response of the Strife engene. The response is hate, and if the hate has no object, the engene creates one. This is the mechanism of conspiracy theories.

The power of rumors and false accusations has long been recognized. Blunt lies have power, and there is little the victims can do to defend themselves. *"Semper aliquid haeret* (slander boldly, something always sticks)." I wonder whether this power of false accusations was the major drive for the evolution of language. Over millions of years, groups that could mobilize hate and hateful action (which has been observed even in chimps) probably had an advantage over others in the competition; and language, more than anything else, enables such mobilization.

---

[72] Hans Grimm, "Volk ohne Raum" (1926)

Plate 4. Conspiracy theory.
A. Paul Weber: Das Gerücht, 1943/1953

The belief in conspiracy theories is almost indestructible. A rather harmless example are the alien invasion theories of our time. A despicable example is the stab-in-the-back theory of the defeat of Germany in World War I. After years of war and continual delusions by the glorifying propaganda of the government, the sudden end with Germany's unconditional surrender was a shock for the people and a mystery that needed to be explained, so a handy theory blamed it on a conspiracy by the Jews within Germany, whereas in fact Jewish Germans served in the German Army and were killed in combat just like other Germans. Hitler would later stir up this irrational belief, adding the theory of the world Jewry conspiring against the German people. Even after the Nazi regime was crushed, this legend lives on. When I was a student in Munich in the 1960ies, I had a landlady who once told me with her Sudeten German accent *"Ich sage Ihnen, das Weltjudentum – das wird uns noch zugrunderichten!* (I am telling you, the world Jewry – that is going to destroy us yet!)" For me, that was so out of the blue that I found it just funny. But, as time went by, that fiction was revived by the Neo-Nazi movement in Germany in the 2010s. Apparently, the post-war remission of the cancer of racism has only been temporary.

The Strife engene invented the myth of the stab-in-the-back conspiracy, focusing the hate on Jews and socialists. To fight the war in Vietnam, the U.S. government conjured the threat of world communism to instigate the Strife engene. When the White working class in the U.S. got squeezed economically in recent decades, the successful presidential candidate of 2016 focused their hate on immigrants. When Putin decided to invade Ukraine in 2022, he claimed that Russia needs to fight a Nazi regime, an absurd fantasy that he could not possibly believe, but conjured up to invoke fears from the historical trauma of the Nazi invasion.

White race supremacy claim

The strength of the behavioral engenes varies between individuals, and I believe that the average differences between races are small compared to the large individual variations within races, perhaps with one exception. The Strife engene might be a case where behavioral traits differ between races because of genetic differences, just like in Aldous Huxley's fantasy of 'Brave New World' where a caste hierarchy is created by genetic engineering. It seems to me that, if there is any specific character trait that comes with race, then history indicates that it is the aggressiveness of the White (Indo-European) race. White people have come to dominate the world and used their racial specifics to claim supremacy of Whites over people of Color. Studies in mixed race kindergarten classes have documented that instances of aggressive behavior are more frequent among White than Colored children. The history of the modern world seems overwhelming evidence for the aggressiveness of the White race. When the Portuguese under Prince Henry the Navigator developed the science of navigation and learned to build ocean-going ships, they soon put cannons on their ships, seized Malacca, the main hub of the Southeast Asian trade, and from then on monopolized the Asian-European spice trade. After the fateful discovery of America, the Spanish conquered two huge empires within a few decades, established feudal serfdom across the country and forced labor in the silver mines, empowering the small White ruling class to brutally exploit the work force of millions of Indigenous Americans. When the English discovered the lucrative triangular trade sailing from Liverpool with cheap industrial merchandise to West Africa, crossing the Atlantic with loads of slaves, and sailing back to England with sugar, tobacco, and other colonial products, they cold-bloodedly enslaved and traded millions of Black people.

It may be hard to separate the racial from cultural and geographic factors in the expansion of White world dominance, but recent racial conflicts, where a dominant racial majority tries to disparage and oppress a vulnerable racial minority, again indicate a predisposition of White people to claim supremacy over Colored people. Struggles for social dominance occur in any society, and it seems natural that underprivileged rise up to claim their rights. There have been uprisings of the oppressed, like the slave revolt in Santo Domingo. But how do we explain that in today's Germany groups of the *dominant* White majority feel they have the right to threaten immigrants that are a small, vulnerable minority? How come that groups of White Americans feel they can claim their country as a White country? These are instances where people who are in a racial *majority* feel entitled to privileges, claiming their perceived rights aggressively. It is hard to find examples of similar supremacy claims by colored people over White people.

The cultural dominance of the White race is overwhelming. One only needs to turn on the television set in a South American country, or in Japan, or China, to see how fashion is advertised by whitish models. When a baby is born in South America it is immediately judged according to its degree of whiteness: "What a beautiful baby!" if its skin happens to be light. Many women become blond with age (perhaps there are technical reasons – it might be easier to maintain a light color).

Art historians remarked that ancient Egyptian artists depicted the spouses of the Pharaoh light skinned in contrast to the Pharaoh himself. In middle age Europe, the princesses had white skin, and the name of the young woman the prince awakens with a kiss is Snow-white. Perhaps in Europe white skin became an attribute of nobility because it distinguished the people who lived protected from the sun from those who worked on the fields and thus got tanned. To be white appears as an attribute of female beauty in many cultures today, from Turkey to China to the Americas.

Dominance of the White race might be a case of reflexive evolution. If inheritances of genes for Strife engene and skin color were correlated, the aggressive nature of the Strife engene might have helped to spread light skin color, and light skin color would have become an attractive feature because it meant strong Strife engene.

Blemish on the leftist movements

It may seem ridiculous, or even offensive, to compare human political conflicts with the mating conflicts of rhesus monkeys. But politically Left generally means challenging possession and patriarchal rule. Looking back at the evolution of primates we see that the primordial possession is the females, and the primordial patriarchy is the rule of the dominant male over his females and their offspring. Adolescent males generally leave the group and live independent lives until they have a chance to replace the dominating male, or to found their own group. The evolutionary measure of value is procreation of genes, and thus females are the capital. The leftist movement of 1968 was primarily a protest of the young generation against the ongoing war in Vietnam, a war intended to fight communism. In West Germany the young generation protested also against the rule of the self-complacent post-war generation who indulged in the economic boom, ignoring the inconvenient past of Nazi Germany. The young people perceived the Vietnam war as a campaign to defend possession and political power against the challenge of communism, and in West Germany, which was not involved in that war, they perceived the thriving capitalist economy as oppressive because in a capitalist society possession means power, and they saw possessions and power in the hands of the old-generation leaders.

What is interesting considering the primate roots of human society is that the 1968 movement, and in fact all leftist movements, also had a sexual undertone. In West German universities the walls of student dormitories were sprayed with slogans like "*Nieder mit den Bullen* (down with the bulls)", referring to the police and the oppressive authority, a designation implying big testicles and macho behavior. The students converted the dormitories into autonomous territories defying state authority. And just like in the flock of rhesus monkeys, the young male students claimed possession of the women students, proclaiming free love. Rejection of the oppressive political norms included rejection of the perceived-oppressive sexual norms. Although the female students felt they were equal partners in the protest, the sad truth was that they gave in to the possessive claims of the male students and accepted their own sexual exploitation. Interestingly, in the DDR, the eastern part of post-war Germany, where communism was imposed by the Russian occupation, the political change also brought sexual liberalization, despite the regime being de-facto authoritarian. Together with the realization of equal opportunity (and equal duty) for women at the workplace, this put more responsibility and burden on women in the East than in West Germany.

I.4.10   Marriage of Throne and Altar

While Strife and Religious engenes have obviously different evolutionary origins—the former focused on defending the homeland and being loyal to its leader, the latter looking up to the supranatural—the history of the rules of power shows that they generally cooperate, but sometimes they are in conflict.

Harmony

Religion generally serves to strengthen the political rule. Most ancient leaders were regarded not only as the ultimate authority of the state, but also as descendant from gods, or having a divine nature; the Pharaohs and the Inca were revered as descendants from the Sun god, and kings of Europe ascended to the throne as "king by the grace of God." The crowning of a king is generally a religious ceremony, in the United Kingdom held in Westminster Abbey.

Religion helped ethnicities to keep their identity and survive as minorities surrounded by people of different ethnicity. Their faith helped Jewish people to preserve their identity in the diaspora. In the Balkans under Turkish rule, the Greek orthodox religion was the lifeline for Greeks, Bulgarians and Serbs under an Islamic government. Because of its importance in supporting ethnicity, conquerors have always tried to suppress the religion of the conquered. The Spanish conquerors of the Americas used Catholicism to crush the native resistance, largely succeeding in replacing native deities with Catholic saints.

History also shows the reverse: political power can strengthen a religious community; for example, when the Roman Caesar declared Christianity the official religion of the empire; when Queen Isabel of Castile initiated the Spanish Inquisition; or when Mussolini made Catholicism the state religion, made divorce impossible and religious education obligatory and declared anticlerical propaganda illegal.

The combination of Strife and Religious engenes has always been particularly powerful. Joan of Arc heard the voice of God giving her the instruction to defend France and crown the young king in Reims. The fascists in Italy endowed the pope with unlimited power in the Vatican, and the pope in return declared, "Mussolini has been sent to us by providence." Also Hitler often invoked in his speeches *"die Vorsehung"* (providence) to justify his leadership and the Nazi ideology. After the end of the Nazi tyranny the Vatican helped high-ranking Nazi criminals to escape to South America.[73] More recently, Putin broke with the 70-year-old atheist tradition of the Soviet Union, allying himself with the Russian Orthodox church. The words 'In God we trust' are printed on U.S. money.

Conflict

When the Pharaoh is Sun-God-descendant, and the kings have God's blessing, being loyal to the worldly leader conforms with the religious vocation. Conflict arises only under certain political constellations when the subjects are confronted with the dilemma of whom to obey. The Pharisees tried to trick Jesus asking the hostile question if he thought Jews should pay taxes to the Caesar or not. They knew that Jews rejected it and there had been riots when the Romans imposed the tax. In response Jesus asked bystanders for a Roman coin and had them read the inscription, which said "Caesar Augustus Tiberius, son of the Divine Augustus." He then asked them "whose is this?" and when they replied, "it's Caesar's" Jesus said to them "So give back to Caesar what is Caesar's, and to God what is God's."[74] Conflict arose also in the Middle Ages when people in central Europe did not know whether to obey the Pope or be loyal to the Kaiser (the investiture contest). In this dilemma the desire to win eternal life generally prevails.

These and other examples of historical conflicts are additional indications that the powerful mechanisms of social organization that I subsumed under the terms Strife and Religious, which appear similar in that both have broad appeal, and both demand unconditional obedience, are indeed different engenes that have evolved separately.

Many people in modern democracies may not even be aware that there is a conflict. Especially when growing up in the U.S. where "In God we trust" is embossed on the coins and Presidents always conclude their state-of-the-union address with "God bless America", many people are not aware that some of their religious tenets are in conflict with basic principles of their democracy, where the state does not have an official religion and supports neither religion nor irreligion; principles that give equal rights to people of all races, and to men and women, give everybody the right to define their sexual identity, and grant woman a say in matters concerning their body. The presidential election of 2016 was

---

[73]   https://www.dw.com/en/the-ratlines-what-did-the-vatican-know-about-nazi-escape-routes/a-52555068, accessed 1/11/2022

[74] Matthew 22:21

decided to a large extent by evangelical Christian voters who opted for an undemocratic and racist candidate who hypocritically asserted that he would defend their 'Christian values' against those of the opponent party. And when that candidate four years later lost the election but did not concede the defeat, it became clear that millions of Americans really do not want their secular egalitarian democracy, but rather an authoritarian rule of racism and religious intolerance.

I.4.11 Short- and Long-Range Engenes

There is a difference between friendship and comradery. The basis of friendship is the Family engene which promotes equality, responsibility, and mutual care, whereas comradery is a product of the Strife engine; it's the positive behavioral side of the Strife engene. Comradery flourishes in combat, in war as well as in sports in which one team fights another team. Friendship is universal, man and women are equally capable of friendship, but comradery tends to be a male virtue. J.B.S. Haldane and Ernst Jünger enthusiastically described their frontline experiences in the First World War (the former on the British, the latter on the German side) and how they loved it. They thought that war is a primordial experience in the life of a man that he should not miss.

Because the Strife engene evolved from competition, it has features that are characteristic of games as we know them from sports in which two individuals, or two teams, compete with each other. The outcome is uncertain: either victory or defeat. Thus, every such game has an element of gamble. The Strife engene rewards gamble with pleasure. But gamble is also inherent in fights that are a matter of life and death. They are an ingredient of wars, producing the 'primordial experience' praised by Haldane and Jünger. The Strife engene makes the uncertainty of the fight attractive.

Because they are based on two different engenes, the social bondings produced by friendship and comradery differ. Friendship has a limited range, the manifest family and other members of society that someone knows well personally. Its largest extent is the clan. Friendship does not polarize, that is, friendship is neutral towards people that are not among those known face to face, it does not produce hate against "the others." In contrast, comradery implies an enemy, and the stronger the enemy, the stronger the bond between comrades.

These two forms of bonding have wide-reaching consequences in our society and our moral judgments. The Family engene, which derives from the brood care instincts, is deeply rooted and almost universally present in all people. So strong is this engene that brutal repressive regimes can use its power to extort confessions from prisoners and to subjugate dissidents by torturing their relatives. Even politically right-wing people who declare themselves anti-socialist, love their children and care for others in their family who might be in need, right down to their pets. When a relative or friend is in need, the Family engene can drive people strongly, to the point of self-sacrifice. But it has that short range of force. Humanitarian organizations know this when they do their fundraising: moral feelings cannot be aroused merely by telling the audience about others in need, it requires moving pictures of children, or a mother with a child, or young animals, pictures that can activate the Family engene.

In contrast, the sympathetic range of the Strife engene is the entire ethnic group, while any conflicting group is the enemy. The Strife engene calls for a military organization with a strong leader and a clear command structure – law and order. Although the Family engene may be older and more deeply rooted in the human soul, the Strife engene has also been strengthened by millions of years of struggle between hominid groups.

Clearly, the slogan of the French Revolution, *"liberté, égalité, fraternité"* appealed to the Family engene. It called for freedom from the tyranny of kings and nobility and proposed brotherly bonding between equal members of society. The French Revolution broke down the laws and order of the establishment. But the Revolution was short-lived. Soon the society reverted to the hierarchical prototype with military organization and an emperor at the top.

This is not just old history; the conflict between Family engene and Strife engene lives on in today's politics in the form of the Left and Right visions of society. Left and Right are commonly perceived as symmetric, as the two ends of the political spectrum, like a seesaw. But the evolutionary aspect shows that the left-right struggle in society is lopsided; the fight for equal rights and social justice is an uphill battle.

The reason for the bias, as explained above, is that the Family engene has a short range and therefore less power in moving the masses, and less traction in democratic elections, than the long-range engenes. The factory owner and the worker, the landowner and the peasant, they all share the Strife engene, but there is no such thing as a 'Class-struggle engene'. When people unite in the struggle for more justice, labor rights, equal pay for women etc., they are usually in a

	Family engene	**Strife engene**
Character of relationships	Personal	Anonymous
Range of force	Limited, declining with distance	Entire ethnic, religious, or racial group
Mobilization of masses	Transient	Persistent
Response to risk	Seeking security	Gamble
Positive relationships	Reciprocity within group, brotherhood, friendship	Solidarity within group, comradery, loyalty to leader
Negative relationships	None	Competition between groups, hostility
Type of possession	Common good	Private property

Table 2. Family and Strife engenes compared

minority; large popular movements only form in situations of crisis, when the burden of injustice becomes unbearable. The masses have momentum for a short time, as long as the common pain induces solidarity, but as soon as the worst is over, the momentum diminishes . Labor movements fought hard for the right to unionize, but after they achieved better conditions for the workers, the solidarity fractured and the unions lost ground. The emancipation movement fought for women's suffrage and equal standing of women and men, and, as long as they were a unified front, they were successful, but in the next generation, when the strong feeling of solidarity faded, they lost ground again. Because the Family engene lacks emotional long-range force in society, these movements must rely on a feeling of solidarity that is ephemeral, depending on the momentary pressing needs. Once the situation relaxes, the feelings of solidarity ebb and the momentum stalls.

In contrast, the Strife engene has emotional long-range forces: Comradeship works across an entire ethnic group, and a political leader can kindle nationalism and incite hate against the proclaimed adversaries across the country. Workers that face dwindling wages and the prospect of unemployment can easily be called to the polls by portraying the competition of a foreign country as the source of all problems. Both comradeship and hate work well across the entire population. The leader can also portray a domestic subgroup, an ethnic or religious minority, as the source of the problems and incite hate in his followers against that subgroup, be it immigrants, or a minority that is an integral part of the society.

Hitler, who deceptively named his party "National Socialist Laborer's Party", did not have any socialist ideas in mind, but clearly appealed to law and order, where, by order he meant that one *Führer* must have the absolute power: "*Ein Volk, ein Reich, ein Führer* (One people, one Reich, one leader)." A year before he became chancellor he expressed that view in a speech to CEOs of the big industry, comparing the state with an industrial enterprise; like a capitalist enterprise is based on competition and requires strong leadership, the state in his view requires dictatorship.[75] This of course appealed to the leaders of the industry; the German workers fell for the trick because he promised them jobs and pay and later arranged for state-organized recreation and entertainment that made them forget any class solidarity with workers in other countries and even with the forced laborers in the country.

This is one of many examples in history showing that the Left loses against the Right when the Strife engene rules. It is not because people don't have good moral judgments, but because these judgments become worthless in the distance. They work well in the social vicinity of the individual, in the face-to-face society, but lose power when it comes to showing solidarity with anonymous masses of society. In contrast, the Strife engene naturally includes the entire ethnic group as comrades in the fight against the enemy (which is often fictitious). A mere call to the arms is sufficient.

The mismatch in range of force between the two engenes is a persistent danger in democratic elections, because it makes it easy for the Right to mobilize voters, while the Left struggles. I will say more about how the Strife engenes endangers democracy in Parts II and III.

---

[75] Hitler's speech of Jan 1, 1932, before the Düsseldorf Industry Club. Cited in Reinhard Kühnl „Formen Bürgerlicher Herrschaft." Hamburg, Rowohlt (1971), p. 88.

Recognizing the superior long-range force of the Strife engene and its potential danger for an egalitarian society, one should not ignore that the Family engene can also inflict damage to society. While other engenes rule at the distance, the Family engene outstrips all of them at short range. When it comes to the family, people ignore concerns of fairness and sense of justice, and even honesty. Because of its strong short-range force the Family engene can damage society by producing nepotism and corruption.

Interestingly, people who have lived under the communist rule of the DDR (former East Germany) agree that, despite the pain of the oppressive and unlawful authoritarian regime, they enjoyed friendships, and many still cherish their old friends 30 years after the communist regime has been abolished, and complain that such deep friendships are not possible in the free democratic society they now live in. This is interesting because it shows that communism, even in the ugly, distorted form of the DDR, allowed the Family engene to thrive, in contrast to the new democratic society that brought justice and freedom (under capitalism). Apparently, friendship flourishes under communism, but freedom stifles it.

While the Family engene is not suitable to command masses because its force is short-range, the *Religious engene* does have long-range force. Just like the Strife engene acts across the entire ethnicity, the Religious engene acts across the entire religious community. Much like the Strife engene, the Religious engene also discriminates "us" and "them," those within their own religious community from those outside. But I'm not sure whether agape, the love of the Religious engene, has also a negative counterpart, producing hate (cf. *Negative relationships* in Table 2). Of course, there have been religious wars, but they might have been the result of the Strife engene trying to harness the Religious engene for its own goals. There is no shortage of examples in history of leaders trying to grab power by means of the Religious engene. In the investiture conflict of medieval Europe mentioned above, the pope challenged the power of the German king as Holy Roman Emperor, leading to 50 years of civil war after which the kings backed down and made concessions that left the institution of the Emperor weakened. But that was a power struggle between Strife engenes on both sides, and the side that harnessed the Religious engene more effectively, won. In 8th-century Japan, the emperor moved his residence from Nara to Kyoto to escape the growing power of the Buddhist clergy, another example of how the Strife engene gained power by harnessing the Religious engene. Thus, hate against "the others" might be the unique product of the Strife engene.

I.4.12   Ethics

I have emphasized above the evolutionary origin of brain mechanisms that might underlie human behavior and society formation. Looking closely at human behavior and how it is motivated, we saw a surprising variety of patterns that suggest an influence of evolution and thus a genetic basis, from family to group dynamics to aspects of human culture. The reader may have noticed also that I discussed these 'engenes' not in a neutral way like the rules of science would demand; an ethologist would be more careful. Rather, I put value tags, explicitly or implicitly, to the various engenes according to common sense: Love and friendship are 'good', aggression and racism 'bad'. Ethologists are reluctant to associate mechanisms of brood care or intra-species aggression with moral values. But the terms of the language I use are already loaded with emotions, and it would have been hard to avoid the common perception in this essay; it would have rendered the text difficult to read or even incomprehensible.

But it is important to realize that our system of values that we take as the norm is also anchored in evolutionary grounds. Indeed, ethical behavior shows the three-phase structure that is characteristic of the regimes of other behavioral engenes: (1) a phase of discontent and unrest when we see that someone needs help, or witness cruelty or injustice, (2) a phase of action like helping or defending the afflicted person, and finally (3) the pleasure or relief after successful completion of the action (and even after an unsuccessful action). The 'someone' can also be a non-human being, an animal, a plant etc. Similarly, dishonesty is associated with unpleasant feelings of shame and gilt, and establishing truthfulness with satisfaction. Thus, perhaps, we can also identify Ethical engenes and trace them back to the ancient conditions of human life.

Some readers might object to the following treatise as it seems to put some items into perspective that are generally perceived as part of "Our Christian values," "The values our country stands for," or "Unalienable human rights" – taking away their absolute authority and making them appear as relative. But, as we will see, adopting the evolutionary perspective does not mean that we treat values as relative and arbitrary. On the contrary, considering the evolutionary origin makes us see that much of our values are actually grounded in human biological nature and anything but arbitrary. If we want to understand human behavior we must look at the origin of our values. Taking them out from the holy shrine of tradition may feel disturbing at first, but we must get used to it, it is what understanding means. Understanding the evolutionary origin of our moral feelings is only the first step towards a rational view of the human condition. It does not mean to accept what evolution has produced, on the contrary, it makes us critical and alerts us to the fact that we are not embedded in a given moral system but have responsible choices to make.

Compassion, fairness, sense of justice

The feeling of compassion develops during childhood. But I'm sure, human children develop a sense for protecting friends from danger quite early. When my daughter was two, the Zurich government decided to change the landing flight corridor of the airport because the Germans no longer tolerated it over their territory. So, from that day on, planes thundered over our house from morning to night, and my daughter got concerned about the safety of the birds. When she heard a plane coming, she ran out into the yard shouting *"pajaros, didado aviones!"* to warn them of the danger (*didado* being short for *cuidado*; "birds, watch out airplanes!"). The urge to adopt and protect the vulnerable seems to be innate in the human. Infants already love to adopt and shelter little creatures, or toys, with a passion that is astounding.

Compassion evolved because it increased the chance of weak members of the group, like women and children, and the sick and the injured, to survive and pass on valuable genes. Compassion is probably a feature of the Brood-care engene that evolution expanded to include unrelated children and other members of the group. It involves love and the drive to protect and has an element of taking into custody or domination. In today's people this engene is amazingly strong. It often includes dogs, especially puppies, cats and other pets, and even plants. In their long history as companions of men, dogs and cats have also acquired specific behaviors of their own to latch on to the perceptual mechanism of the human Compassion engene, cats imitating baby cries, and dogs imitating the whining of infants, and both have amplified other child-like behaviors like playing.

Humans value fairness and justice. How much of this is learned, and how much simply develops spontaneously according to the inherited plan, is often hard to tell (remember Lorenz' experiment on pigeons starting to fly). Recent studies indeed suggest that sense of fairness might be innate.[76] Thus, its origin must go back long ago. But where this strong feeling originated in evolution is mysterious. Perhaps the origin is mother love. Mothers are generally fair, extending love evenly among their offspring. But the sense of fairness is exquisitely human – I'm not sure if there is anything comparable in the animal

---

[76] S Sloane, R Baillargeon, and D Premack. Do infants have a sense of fairness? Psychol Sci. 2012 Feb;23(2):196-204

kingdom. And it is very common, the basis of sports. Many people may be unfair, but there are few who do not know what it means to be fair. My guess is that sense of fairness might have evolved through the long struggle of hunter-gatherers. The continual pressure through millions of years to secure sufficient food and other resources and share them may have honed the sense of fairness because it served the survival of the group and thus procreation of its genes, in contrast to other character traits that merely helped to pass on genes of the individual. Most likely, it created strong bonding between the individuals of a group; and groups that were bonded together by the fairness principle had a better chance to survive as a whole in times of stress and in competition with other groups. They were more resilient in defense and stronger in attack. Most people today have a strong sense of fairness; that everybody has the right to have what is necessary to live and the right to live without fear and pain; that nobody should be condemned to digging for food in garbage or drinking contaminated water. Sense of justice might be a cultural derivative of the sense of fairness.

The way we apply compassion and sense of justice to the people around us is typically human. I am not sure about apes, but monkeys don't seem to have that. When observing rhesus monkeys in captivity, I was struck by their lack of these faculties. One can give the monkey in one cage a banana, an apple, and an orange, while the monkey in the neighboring cage has nothing and is obviously thirsty; then monkey 1 will eat the banana with one hand, holding the apple in the other hand and the orange with his foot. He will eat all three without compassion, being watched by monkey 2 smacking his lips. In most mammals, compassion and fairness are limited to the mother-child relationship.

Rejection

Just like love and friendship are part of human nature, so are dismay and rejection, we cannot ignore that. Perhaps negative feelings also have a root in evolution. Most people have sentiments of rejection of the mentally ill. In the antique and until fairly recently epileptic people were thought to be possessed by an evil spirit. In modern societies such feelings have largely been overcome by education, but only recently, in the course of progress in medicine in the 19th century. The original emotional reaction is strong and widespread, as one can see in children and uneducated people. The aversion against the abnormal might be an ancient behavioral pattern, comparable to the fear of spiders and snakes, which led to rejection of the afflicted individual from the group, and hence to predictable death, thus serving to maintain a healthy genome through the ages.

Taboos

Innate moral judgments are often reinforced by the society as we saw above in the case of Guadalupe. It lies in the nature of evolution that it rewards reproductive behaviors with pleasure and fences off any behaviors that could compromise reproduction with negative emotions. Often society also erects corresponding taboos. For example, masturbation produces feelings of shame and guilt in itself, and is additionally outlawed by the religious community; and similar double barriers are erected against homosexual behaviors. The Catholic church explicitly lists both as sins and requests them to be confessed – but also extends absolution to the repentant defendant, for a certain price to be paid, e.g., in prayers or good deeds.

Love and hate

While love (that is, *agape*) is part of the Family engene and includes relatives, friends, and the people we know well, love is also an expression of the Strife engene, where origin, language, tradition, and race determine who is friend and who is foe; people love their fatherland and hate its enemies. And love and hate figure also in the Religious engene, distinguishing the faithful from the infidel. This proximity of love and hate in the human soul makes me wonder if there are mechanisms that can invert the value of the underlying engene – not in the individual, as when Saul converted to Paul – but during evolution by modification of genetic code.

Moral intuition

Religions generally claim moral values as their domain and many religious people think that when others are not religious, or reject their religion, that they would then lose their moral values. But that is not the case; I think that irreligious people have moral values as good as religious people on average. We do not need commandments to be moral. Religious people refer to their scriptures for moral laws, but these codifications are ultimately based on inherited feelings about right and wrong. Moral rules, and laws in general, are based on the natural ethical judgment of people and determined by consensus. These include the rejection of murder, lying, and stealing. Even the first three of the commandments of Moses which refer to God, as well as many other religious rules, are ultimately based on feelings produced by the Religious engene and thus part of human nature, and not merely tradition.

Choices

Given these biological roots of moral behavior, one might think we should just listen to our inner voice when deciding what is moral. But that is not easy because there is not just one inner voice. Our soul is a complex system and even the ethical engenes are several, and may contradict each other. Like in Heine's poem of the two French grenadiers of Napoleon's Grand Army who, returning from Russia, hear the story of Napoleon's defeat (see below). They get depressed and consider ending their lives. While one remembers he has family, the other just wants to die and be buried in French soil to wait until he would hear his Emperor's army returning and riding over his grave, when he will rise from the grave to protect him. They had to decide; one was drawn to his family, but for the other patriotism and loyalty to the leader were stronger; one listened to the Family engene the other to the Strife engene.

> *Der eine sprach: „Wie weh wird mir,*
> *Wie brennt meine alte Wunde!"*
> *Der andre sprach: „Das Lied ist aus,*
> *Auch ich möcht mit dir sterben,*
> *Doch hab' ich Weib und Kind zu Haus,*
> *Die ohne mich verderben."*
> *„Was schert mich Weib, was schert mich Kind,*
> *Ich trage weit bess'res Verlangen;*
> *Lass sie betteln gehn, wenn sie hungrig sind—*
> *Mein Kaiser, mein Kaiser gefangen!*
>
> The first said: 'Ah, the agony;
> How my old wound is burning!'
> The second said: 'This is the end;
> If only we could die together.
> But I've a wife and child at home,
> And they would perish without me.'
> 'To hell with wife, to hell with child,
> My aims are for far higher things;
> Let them beg, if they've nothing to eat—
> My Emperor, my Emperor captured!

Excerpt from Heinrich Heine's poem "Die beiden Grenadiere." (Translation by Richard Stokes).

Evolution has produced various kinds of engenes, like the Family, Strife, and Religious engenes, each of which has been perfectly useful to enhance the chance of their proper genes to get passed on. In terms of the evolution these different developments are consistent, but in the individual human being they often produce sharp conflicts. A mother loves her son, but accepts that he goes defend their country, and when he dies in combat, she implores her countrymen to continue to fight so that her son's blood has not been shed in vain. Siblings love each other, but religion may compel a young man to kill his sister after she has been raped. And in existential border situations people may have to choose between their moral consciousness and their will to live. There is no accepted standard that tells us the right choice in each situation.

The contradictory commands of the different engenes produce conflicts in society. The demands of Family and Religious engenes are trumped by the commandment from God, suddenly go to war and kill their neighbors. Lying is shameful in the family context, and honesty a virtue, "Thou shalt not bear false witness against thy neighbour." But in politics slandering the opponent is applauded by the partisans. The one who deceits the enemy is a hero, whereas the one who lies to his own people is a traitor and must be punished harshly. When in conflict, many people obey the Strife engene because it can motivate behaviors that are regarded as high virtues, like love for one's homeland, patriotism, and self-sacrificing service for one's country.

Because of the ambivalence of the evolutionary inheritance we must be careful not to accept what is natural as good. It is very common in our modern society to justify behavior by saying "That is natural." In the supermarket the label "all natural" signals quality. "Natural" is the magic word. Knowing that salt is not good for our health we buy sea salt because it is "natural", although it contains as much sodium chloride as any other salt. To accept as good the way evolution made us is a horrible mistake. We would accept that if unmarried women have children, they are bad, and their children must be expelled because they have bad blood. We would accept violence of men against women, or that a woman who lost her virginity before being married is worthless and must be killed. We would accept that it is moral to destroy enemies like vermin. We would accept that one race is better than the other and destined to dominate, and that there are races that are detrimental to society and must be exterminated; that America belongs to the White Christians and all others could be expelled if they do not gratefully accept being just tolerated. Accepting what is natural as good is the fundamental error of the new libertarian ideology.[77] Nevertheless, most

---

[77] The original libertarian movement correctly viewed private property as a barrier to freedom and liberty, but, in a bizarre twist, U.S. libertarian ideologies turned this upside down, advocating laissez-faire capitalism and strong private property rights in land,

people have a good sense of what is right and what is wrong, and how to make the voice of the good be heard in society is a political problem. We will get to this below under "What Can We Learn".

I.4.13   Summary. Two Sides of Reflexive Evolution: The Divine and the Evil

When a child is born it comes with an amazing genetic program for developing a human brain. We do not fully understand how this program unfolds from the limited genetic code, but the above discussion of the evolutionary roots of behavioral traits throws some light on this mystery. While we are not born with a language, we inherit a sophisticated setup mechanism that launches the acquisition of a language and the corresponding language processing tools. The process is probably similar in the case of religion. We may be born with a basic set of values, or we absorb them with the mother milk, and there is a program that makes the child receptive for religious behavior of the person(s) of reference, and subsequently sets up the specific religious beliefs and ritualized behaviors according to the given social context. Just like in the case of language, general inherited brain mechanisms enable the acquisition of a specific pattern. The result are brain circuits for certain behaviors that I call engenes, and those that affect social behaviors underlie the formation of human society.

In part, these social engenes have been important in the struggle for survival of the Homo species as hunter-gatherers. But to a large part they do not reflect survival of the fittest. Sexual selection is the most obvious of the exceptions, which Darwin already realized, one example of what I have termed 'reflexive evolution'. Reflexive evolution has given us beauty and love, the smile of the child, the fun of humor and the pleasure of music. It created the roots of human culture. But it also created aggressive behaviors. Ethnocentrism, xenophobia, racism, claiming supremacy, addiction to power and complacency of obedience, are clearly the results of reflexive evolution: they provide advantage in proliferation of genes within the species rather than strengthening fitness in confronting the challenges of nature and competition with different species.

---

infrastructure and natural resources. Originally, libertarians sought to abolish capitalism and private ownership of the means of production in favor of cooperative ownership and management. But the new ideology, following the call of the Strife engene, emphasizes civil liberties and free-market capitalism, seeking a major reversal of the modern welfare state. Basically, they want the role of the state stripped down to the protection of private property.

Everybody has a different set of social engenes

I have given many examples of behavioral traits that can be traced back to hominid evolution and thus must have a genetic basis. This was to stress that we come to this world with a bag of tools for life, but in no way do I want to diminish all the influences an individual is exposed to during development, from the womb of the mother to graduation from school. These are powerful and individually different, so that one cannot predict from the genetic makeup what character a child will develop. Acknowledging the importance of both the genetic makeup and extra genetic factors might seem like walking a fine line. But it is not. In this case, the path of truth is broad and clear. Each brain develops according to an evolutionary plan under the influence of the specific environment, and therefore we cannot understand human society if we ignore the evolutionary roots of human behavior. And the claim that genetic brain mechanisms move us around does not mean that our mind is preprogrammed and our behavior genetically determined.

That the character of a child cannot be predicted from the characters of its parents is obvious, just consider the different characters of brothers, or the differences between father and son. This is the crux of dynasties; between generations, character traits get lost more often than not. The continuity of dynasties rests more on cultural continuity – the power of the royal institution and the people's reverence for the royal family – than the reliability of genetic inheritance. Every child has two parents, four grandparents, and generally eight great grandparents, and each child comes with an unpredictable individual mixture of genes from all of them. Even in the case of the Bach family that I mentioned, which is certainly a clear example of inheritance of an artistic talent, the pedigree would not allow us to predict the musical talent of J.S. Bach's individual children.

Many factors influence the development of the brain after the fertilization of the egg. As the anatomical gender differences develop in the womb under the influence of hormones, the brains also develop differently. Male and female brains are visibly different in their gross anatomical appearance, and they differ grossly also in their behavioral engenes. This is the effect of the sexual hormones (which are genetic). But there are other hormones that also influence the development of the brain, and these depend on many factors, like whether the mother is happy or unhappy during pregnancy, whether she is stressed or at peace. Nutritional factors also influence the development before and after birth. After birth, a wealth of new influences modulate brain function during infancy, childhood and adolescence. As a result of all these factors, the development of the personality of the individual cannot be predicted from the genetic makeup which is already an unpredictable combination of those of the parents.

Because of these multiple factors that each has its variation, the behavioral engenes are expressed to varying degrees in the individual person. A simple example might help to see the consequences of this. If we gave a hundred people a set of vocabulary of a new language and measured the time it takes each to learn them, we would find a large variation, perhaps between 5 and 20 days. Thus, although all people have the ability to learn a foreign language, the power of this faculty varies among people. If we plotted for each amount of days x the number of people who learned the words in x days, we would find a broad distribution. Nobody could do it in less than 5 days, and nobody needed more than 20 days; the most common might have been 11 days. Thus, the distribution would peak at 11 and show similar numbers at 10 and 12, but very few counts for 5 and 20, perhaps one or two each. These are the fringes of the distribution. If we measured a thousand people instead of hundred, we might have found someone who could learn the words in 4 days or someone who needed 25 days, and there would of course be more counts in the 5- and 20-day bins. The more people we test, the larger the counts in the fringes. All character traits and behavioral engenes come with their distributions. Thus, we will always find individuals in which one engene is expressed to an unusual degree, for better or worse, and we might also encounter individuals who seem to lack that engene entirely.

Humans are not cattle

When accepting the facts of human evolution, we must not fall into the mentality of cattle breeders. Evolution is the combined product of mutation and selection. Primates evolved over many millions of years, and what distinguishes us from our chimp-like ancestors is a chain of mutations that have been tested, and corrected by selection, over 6 million years. This process cannot be imitated by breeding. It's a matter of mutation and selection over millions of years, not just selection over a few breeding cycles. Humans are not cattle. The idea of improving human nature by manipulating the genome is not only immoral but also wrong.

Even an eminent scientist like Konrad Lorenz got entangled in the confusion of eugenics. Fascinated by his observations on animal behavior he admired evolution, and comparing wild animals with their domesticated relatives, like the greylag goose and the domestic goose, he saw the degenerating effect of domestication. And he thought that similarly in humans civilization had a domesticating effect which would endanger the beautiful, noble, and heroic in Man. He believed that this needs to be reversed, and that the government should take measures to protect racial purity. Worrying about human genes he did not realize that it was the Strife engene that entangled his thoughts. How could ugly racism protect the beautiful, noble, and heroic?

Πολλά τὰ *δεινὰ* κοὐδὲν ἀνθρώπου δεινότερον πέλει

(Many things are dreadful on earth, but nothing more
dreadful than man)

Sophokles, Antigone 332

The entertainment industry has created all kinds of monsters to give people the thrill they crave for, but the most thrilling is not a confrontation with a dinosaur or some fantasy dragon, but feeling the presence of a man that one cannot see. The 1949 thriller movie "The Third Man" has a scene that shows the entrance of a house in a dimly lit street and one can see nothing but the tips of the shoes of a man. The thought, there must be someone, is scary. Biking through a park in the dark, it struck me how the sight of some upright standing structure drove up my pulse rate. Sophokles is certainly right that man is man's worst enemy, and it has probably been like this for the last two million years.

The long period in which Homo competed with Homo has left its trace in the genome of our social engenes. Aggressive individuals have a reproductive advantage in society, and, as a result, the human genome has been enriched with genes of aggressive behavior. The more aggressive people subjugated other people and impregnated or abducted their women. Under Genghis Khan and his sons, the Mongols conquered dozens of kingdoms all over Asia, spreading their genes. They devastated entire cities in Iran, killing most of their population, and wiped out the people of Western Xia entirely, destroying a thriving civilization including their architecture, technology, and literature.

The most fateful aspect is not individual aggressiveness, but aggressiveness of entire peoples. Competition between different peoples created psychological mechanisms that mellow internal aggression, while boosting external aggression. Mechanisms that foment solidarity and cooperativity within a

169

people, and hostility between peoples. The Strife engene not only produces autocratic leaders, but also loyal, patriotic followers. The collusion between leaders and followers results in a power structure of demonic strength.

But evolution has also endowed humans with ethical engenes. Feelings of aggression are generally counteracted by feelings of compassion, guilt, and sense of fairness. However, like all genetically coded traits, the engenes producing moral behavior, as well as the Strife engene producing aggression, are expressed to various degrees in each individual.

Recently I came across a book titled *"Räume der Gewalt* (Spaces of Violence)"* in which the author compiled eyewitness reports of violence by the SS and troops of Nazi Germany.[78] After reading only a few passages I felt sick for days. I just could not get rid of the images painted in my mind, they haunted me day and night. Many people may have felt such nausea when reading Elie Wiesel's "Night."[79]

Most people certainly react like this, but not all. We must realize that there are people among us who are quite normal in all respects except that they lack this kind of emotion. Take the example of Radovan Karadžić, the Bosnian Serb who was responsible for horrific war crimes against Bosnian civilians. He grew up in a good family and his grandmother described him as a nice and caring young man. He studied psychiatry, worked in hospitals, and received additional medical training at Columbia University in New York. Karadžić was also a poet, published eight volumes of poetry before and after the Bosnian war, and has been awarded a Knights' Order by the Greek Orthodox Church. Together with Ratko Mladić he cold-bloodedly ordered the killing of thousands of unarmed defenseless civilians in the Srebrenica massacre. I don't think his childhood and the environment he grew up in can be blamed for his cruelty. Or take Bashar al-Assad, who graduated from medical school, was a doctor for four years and then attended postgraduate studies in a hospital in London. Because of his education he was seen as a potential reformer and more amenable to human rights concerns than his father, but he became the most ruthless and cruel despot his country has ever seen. Striving to hold on to power he massacred, incarcerated, and tortured his own people, that is, people of the country he ruled but did not belong to his specific religious caste and ruling clan.

---

[78] Jörg Baberowski, „*Räume der Gewalt.*" Frankfurt am Main: S. Fischer, 2015
[79] Elie Wiesel, *"La Nuit."* Paris: Les Éditions de Minuit (1958); "Night" (translated by Stella Rodway). New York: Hill and Wang (1960)

It is important to realize that ethical behavior is a brain function, just like the ability to learn to read. To care for the weak is a passion, an elementary feeling that strongly motivates, and this passion cannot be learned if the corresponding brain mechanisms are defective. Just like there is dyslexia which affects reading, there is a deficit that affects the Compassion engene. Compassion is often confused with empathy. Empathy is a concept in psychology, suggesting a mental act of identifying oneself with someone else, so to speak slipping into someone else's mind with the result that one can feel what the other person feels. It's a psychological theory, a popular theory. In a TV broadcast the guest speaks about a person who seemed to lack empathy and quickly the moderator interrupts: "surely, empathy can be learned!" – "and *should* be learned" seemed to be the implication. This is generally assumed. But I think caring for the vulnerable is a spontaneous elementary feeling that does not require learning or the mental acrobatic suggested by the empathy theory. I use the term 'Compassion engene' for lack of a better choice, although the term 'compassion' (*Mitleid* in German) also suggests that one suffers with the other's suffering. In fact, I think it is a basic emotion, an atom of the human psyche. Imagine watching an 11-year-old boy jump from a train that transports Jewish people from Belgium to a concentration camp in the East, as his mother pushed him, because she wanted him to live.[80] This scene evokes a strong feeling much like love, including the desire to protect and defend the boy and his mother, as well as hate, disgust and aggression against the powerful. People in the resistance against the Nazi regime, like the members of the White Rose, have documented this response. They felt not only compassion, but also reacted with disgust and rage. I have the greatest admiration for people who honored their moral feelings and resisted, although they had no chance against the minions of a brutal regime and were executed.

And we must also acknowledge the obvious, that not all people feel like this, and this is not because of lack of education or the result of a childhood trauma. Reinhard Heydrich, the SS official who planned and organized the mass murder of millions of Jews, was from a family in good social standing and had a good education. His father, a composer and opera singer founded the Halle Conservatory of Music, Theatre, and Teaching, and his mother taught piano there. Heydrich developed a passion for the violin, and still as an adult he impressed listeners with his musical talent. His father was a nationalist (not a

---

[80] The boy was Simon Gronowski. He survived, became a Doctor of Law and a jazz pianist. https://unric.org/en/holocaust-survivor-lifts-lockdown-spirits-with-jazz/, 29 Apr. 2021, accessed 14 Sept. 2021

member of the Nazi party), but most people were nationalists. Most had also been exposed to antisemitism, but would have been horrified had they known of Heydrich's projects. Even Hitler was impressed by Heydrich's lack of compassion and feeling of guilt, "This is a man with an iron heart." Something was missing in his personality that we take for granted, a stunning defect of moral judgment. For reasons that I think are largely genetic, some people lack the Compassion engene.

When Hannah Arendt observed the trial of Adolf Eichman, she too was stunned by Eichman's responses at the trial in Jerusalem in 1963.[81] Often they were not even intelligent and suitable for his defense; he simply had no moral insight, a defect of personality.

II.1 THE ERROR OF IGNORING THE INHERITABLE COMPONENT

Although the inheritable component of the human mind is quite obvious, ignoring it has a long tradition in sociology and political science. It is as if our mind shies away from looking at itself. Education is thought to be omnipotent.

In that tradition the most fateful case, perhaps, is the communist ideology: the idea that there must be a transitional stage of socialism before society can arrive at communism. As a schoolteacher in a socialist country explains, even though the revolution has brought down the capitalist dictatorship and given power to the workers, the class struggle is not over because the people who had once been rich and had lost their privileges and property are plotting to undermine the rule of the workers. Therefore, after the capitalist dictatorship, the ensuing stage of socialism requires the dictatorship of the proletariat. "But when people grow up in a humane system and children are educated in the right ideas", the teacher says, "they internalize them. The class struggle then softens and finally disappears. That is when communism really starts: it does not need laws to punish anyone, and it liberates people once and for all."[82] – Thus, according to this theory, creating the ideal society all depends on educating the children in the right ideas. But, despite 40 years of socialist education in East Germany and other socialist countries (70 years in the case of the Soviet Union), internalization

---

[81] Hannah Arendt, "Eichmann in Jerusalem. A report on the banality of evil." Viking (1963).

[82] Words of teacher Nora in: Lea Ypi, "Free : a child and a country at the end of history." Norton (2022).

of "the right ideas" apparently did not happen. Still today, China is brutally trying to 're-educate' millions of people in Xinjiang from Islam to communism.

Notably, I do not doubt the importance of education in shaping our feelings and behavior. But if ethical feelings were entirely the product of environment and education, and given the world as it is, we would have to conclude that the kind of education our society offers is fundamentally flawed (which has actually been said, unjustly, of 19th century Prussian education).

A modern way of dealing with disturbing behaviors in society is psychology. It embitters me to hear after every school mass shooting the chorus "psychologists have yet to analyze the background of the shooter" (in case he is still alive). That's wasted time and wasted resources. It has also been suggested, again and again, to examine the psychology of any person that someone suspects of being capable of mass shooting in order to prevent them from doing it. As if scattered psychological tests would have predictive power of significance, compared to restricting gun ownership, which is much simpler and definitely has predictable and significant effects.

No doubt, education and the environment shape a person's character through learning. There may also be epigenetic mechanisms that affect behavior. There might even be acquired behaviors that can be inherited. Arthur Koestler[83] believes that a behavior that is often repeated becomes a habit, and habits are "somehow transformed into inheritable genetic code," as in the case of giraffes that are continuously trying to stretch their neck to reach the remaining leaves of trees until their neck grows longer, and its extra length is somehow encoded in genes and passed on to the next generation. But the question here is not: are there epigenetic influences, but: are there genetic influences. Is ethical behavior *entirely* a question of education and environment, or is it anchored in the ancient ground of evolution. My claim in this book is: there are inherited foundations of ethical behavior, and we can see their footprint almost everywhere in human society. Whether epigenetic influences also exist is irrelevant.

Fortunately, people with deficiencies of the ethical engenes are in a minority. Still, as history has shown, in a society of 80 million people it is easy to find thousands that are perfectly capable of running concentration camps and performing mass murder. Ethical feelings are not a matter of perspective, as Nietzsche's scholars think, but a function of behavioral engenes deeply rooted in the social brain. They are not arbitrary. The fact that they can be deficient in

---

[83] A Koestler "Janus. A Summing Up" London, Hutchinson (1978)

marginal populations is typical of any kind of brain faculty and does not detract from the fact that the vast majority of people shares them. Most people have a powerful Face-recognition engene that enables them to recognize hundreds of faces quickly and without effort, a faculty envied by machine vision engineers. Nevertheless, there is a brain deficit called prosopagnosia, the inability to recognize faces, even of close relatives, and this has been found to run in families. To repeat what I said earlier, the notion that a faculty has a genetic basis does not mean that everybody has that faculty. On the contrary, variations in the genome are the raw material for evolution; without variation there can be no evolution.

Philosophers who lectured on moral values, like Socrates and Kant, knew that morality is rooted in human nature and therefore, our judgments of good and evil are *not* arbitrary choices. Nietzsche lacks this insight; he accepts that humans have evolved from apes and sees them in a state of transition to overman, but he does not see that human moral values have also evolved, and therefore we are not free to define what is good and what is evil.

II.2 GENOCIDE

The monstrous genocide of the Holocaust shook up the world's consciousness. But genocides still happen. The massacre of Srebrenica is only one of 18 genocides that happened after the Holocaust. Genocide has been practiced at least 38 times in the 20th century and 3 times in the first 19 years of this century, and an estimated 20,867,079 (lowest estimates) to 50,288,123 (highest estimates) people were killed.[84] The list of genocides does not include ordinary war crimes and crimes against humanity. Numbers do not speak to us; whether it's 50,288,123 or 50,288,124 makes no difference, it is the individual suffering that moves us.

To historians who claim that the world is actually getting better if we look at the proportion of murders per capita, I say, be that as it may, it is little comfort and may not be more than just a quirk of unpredictable trends. By analogy, someone wrote a thesis in which he calculated the average percentage of carbon content in fuels from the beginning of the industrial age until recently, and found that the percentage decreased continuously over the last two hundred years (fuel

---

[84] From https://en.wikipedia.org/wiki/List_of_genocides_by_death_toll. The list only considers mass killings recognized as genocides by the UN Genocide Convention. It excludes other mass killings, variously called mass murder, crimes against humanity, politicide, classicide, or war crimes.

being initially mostly coal, later oil and gas). He concluded that we don't have to worry about carbon emissions, the trend shows that they will disappear. The trend in percentage of cruel behavior may be equally treacherous. Who knows what the world will look like in the near future?

II.3 THE GERMAN DISASTER

For those who put hope in the progress of civilization since the Enlightenment, the German disaster (including the Holocaust) must be worrying, as Germany has been regarded as one of the most civilized countries. So, it is important to look at the German disaster more closely. Genghis Khan and the Mongols devastated countries and slaughtered populations in the twelfth century, but Hitler Germany did it in the 20th century. The text to the "Ode to Joy", now the anthem of the European Union, was written by a German poet, Friedrich Schiller, and the music by a German composer, Ludwig van Beethoven. German people are also highly religious, partly Catholic, and partly Lutheran, following a religious reformation that put the gospel of Jesus back in the center of worship, Jesus, who preached love and humility. – It is clear that the progress of civilization does not protect us from sudden total breakdowns of civilization. Of course, there were historical conditions, like the First World War and the chaotic years after it that shook up society; the revanchist treaty of Versailles and its enforcement that enraged the German people who were already stressed socially and economically. But how is it possible that civilized and religious people helped a leader to power who would trash all German civilization within 12 years?

There has been a movement in Germany during the last 3 decades to come to grips with this disaster, and lots of efforts all over the world to not forget what had happened. Indeed, forgetting is becoming a problem 75 years after waking up from a nightmare. We have to remember. But I think remembering is not enough, as Hannah Arendt said: I want to understand.[85]

Understanding has been decried, "understanding is forgiving!" – but that is not the kind of understanding we are talking about here. True understanding means being able to make predictions and to prepare for the future. And my hope is that analyzing the evolution of the human mind will contribute to the understanding. Knowing about the behavioral engenes that we are born with, and

---

[85] Hannah Arendt, "*Ich will verstehen. Selbstauskünfte zu Leben und Werk*", ed. Ursula Ludz, Munich, Zurich (1996). Arendt was a political theorist. The evolutionary theory of the present book is not related to her work.

where they come from, makes a big difference. But if we think it is all just education and environment that forms the mind, we will certainly be surprised to see the Neo-Nazi movement strengthening in Germany, just at a time when historical insight and political education in radio, television and schools are better than ever. Of course, education and explanation are important, if not just to alert the rest of society of the danger. But certainly, remembering is not enough. We need to understand the past, how could it happen?

The German disaster is most instructive. In November 1923, Hitler and his Nazi party, a small right-wing extremist group, conspired to overthrow the German government and, in coalition with other groups, attempted an insurrection (Beer Hall Putsch). The Putsch was put down by the Munich police and Hitler was arrested, convicted, and sentenced to five years of jail (of which he served only eight months). In the 1920ies his movement grew only slowly, and his book "*Mein Kampf*" was read only by few. In fact, it sold in large numbers only after he came to power and people were obliged to buy it. Although it contains the infamous program that Hitler later carried out, it was overall boring and dumb. His movement picked up strength with the economic crisis in the early 1930ies. The fertile ground was the German defeat in the First World War and the frustration people felt with the treaty of Versailles and its enforcement by the Allied. Germany had been stripped of territories all around, territories that had historically belonged to Germany, despite their populations voting for Germany in polls ordered by the League of the Nations. The treaty allowed Germany only a small army; and the Rhineland, first occupied by French troops, was demilitarized, a situation that was perceived as humiliating. For ten years after the war, Germany was treated as a pariah, blaming it alone for the war, and the post-war political constellation was designed to isolate it.

Another important factor was the feeble democratic order. The German people had been ruled by autocratic regimes until 1918 and only reluctantly accepted a republican constitution that many felt was imposed by the victorious powers. They were not used to political parties, except perhaps the Social Democrats, the only party that had a tradition and was recognized, because it had forced the Bismarck government to cede ground to the workers and their unions. Although the Social Democrats had governed since the foundation of the new republic, and in 1930 were still the largest party, Hindenburg, the president,[86] and many Germans disliked them as leftists. Hindenburg, an 86-year-old former general, was revered as a war hero because he had defeated the Russians in East

---

[86] In the Weimar Republic the president was the highest authority, but the head of the government was the chancellor.

Prussia. Himself a big landowner, and surrounded by other big landowners and military leaders, he tried to establish a conservative government without the Social Democrats, although such a government lacked support in the parliament. Unfortunately, when the parliament could not agree on a government backed by a majority, the constitution allowed the president to name the chancellor, Heinrich Brüning, who would then rule by emergency decrees (*Notverordnungen*), that is, bypassing the parliament. After two years of this authoritarian government trying to solve the economic and financial problems by imposing austerity, the economy collapsed and the number of unemployed rose to 6 million, compared to only 12 million that were still working. Instead of responding to the dire situation of the people, the president still tried to move the government to the right, dissolving the parliament and calling for new elections.

The elections of November 1932 resulted in four blocs, from left to right: the Communists, the Social Democrats, the Centrist bloc, and Hitler's NSDAP (National Socialist German Workers Party). In these last free and fair elections, Hitler's party won 33.1 percent of the votes (196 of the 585 seats in the Reichstag, the parliament), which means, because the situation was highly polarized, that 66.9 percent of the people voted against Hitler. Significantly, the voters of the Centrist parties, which included the royalists and the nobility, detested Hitler. They perceived him as a disgrace. They could not vote for the Social Democrats, the "socialists," because of fear of communism. The Communist Party had won 16.9 percent, which in itself may not seem much, but after the victory of communism in Russia, many Germans perceived the weakness of Germany in political and military power and were terrified. The people who gave their votes to Hitler did so because he promised to be the strong man who would vindicate the German nation. On January 30, 1933, because his party had the largest number of seats in parliament, Hindenburg named Hitler chancellor with the task to form a cabinet. A senile patriarch gave Adolf Hitler the blessing.

After Hitler had thus seized power, Nazi storm troopers unleashed a widespread campaign of violence against the Communist Party, left-wingers, trade unionists, the Social Democratic Party and the Catholic Centre Party. Because Hitler's NSDAP controlled only 196 seats in the parliament, far short of the 293 required for a majority, and no other party was willing to form a coalition government, he called for new elections. These were no longer fair elections since his brown shirts and SS (Hitler's protection squadron) wielded terror, repression and propaganda across the land, and Nazi organizations 'monitored' the voting process. The new elections, held on March 5, 1933, brought the NSDAP 288 seats (43.9 percent of the votes), still short of the majority. The German National People's Party had won 52 seats with the votes of people who abhorred Hitler, among them my grandfather, but their leader betrayed those voters, helping Hitler to pass the Enabling Act only a few weeks after the election. The Enabling Act effectively gave Hitler dictatorial powers. Within months, the Nazis banned all other parties and turned the Reichstag into a rubber stamp legislature.

What is significant is that an aggressive minority group was able to seize absolute power because the democratic institutions failed. Hitler should have been barred from running for office because he openly vowed to overturn the Republic and had already been convicted for attempted insurrection. But his party grew, and in 1930, when the governing coalition formed by Social Democrats and two centrist parties broke over the debate of how to deal with the burden of growing unemployment, it became impossible to form a government supported by a majority in parliament because the two extreme parties, Hitler's NSDAP and the Communists, together held more than half of the seats. Both were openly against the republic rule and neither of them could find a coalition partner. In this dead-end situation, according to the constitution, it was the president's power to name the chancellor or call for new elections. The president could also invoke Article 48, the so-called *Notverordnung* (emergency decree) provision, which gave the president broad powers to suspend civil liberties. Any new legislations were generally blocked by the two extreme parties who were not interested in supporting the government. Thus, henceforth the president chose the government, and the government ruled by emergency decrees. In effect, the country was under a dictatorial regime already before Hitler ascended to power. Hindenburg and his advisors were trying to establish a conservative regime, a 'cabinet of the barons'. Hindenburg cherished the idea of Germany returning to a monarchy. They disliked the Social Democrats (who had ruled since the Weimar constitution was established) and feared the Communists who flexed muscles in street demonstrations, and when chancellor Brüning outlawed Hitler's storm trooper organizations SS and SA by decree, Hindenburg reversed that. Hindenburg was dreaming of monarchy, but out came not a monarch, but the *Führer*.

Sebastian Haffner, a German journalist and author, gave a vivid account of the collapse of the rule-of-law institutions after the Enabling Act was passed.[87]

---

[87] Sebastian Haffner, Oliver Pretzel (Translator) "Defying Hitler: A Memoir" Picador (2003), translated from "*Geschichte eines Deutschen. Die Erinnerungen 1914–1933.*"

Haffner, who studied law in Berlin at the time, wrote his important documentation in exile after emigrating to England in 1938. His intent was to inform the public in Britain about what was happening in Germany. The switch to terror happened virtually overnight. Hitler had built up his SA and SS for years before he seized power, and Nazi activists had already subverted the police in great numbers long before he came to power, so that his henchmen could operate largely without restraints, entering houses at 3am and arresting whomever they wanted, communist leaders, politicians of the opposition in general, independent writers and Jews, threatening officers who tried to oppose the illegal actions. Hannah Arendt was among those who were arrested, for her activity in an organization that helped displaced Jewish children; she was lucky and could escape. Haffner describes the oppressive atmosphere in the Berlin Palace of Justice, the prestigious place of Prussian law tradition, when people suddenly stopped talking in the corridors, and judges and attorneys disappeared one by one, being replaced by party functionaries who had no qualification but their political alignment.

A peculiar function of the Strife engene is the one that gives people pleasure in mass gatherings that demonstrate to the individual the power of their people. After the Nazis seized power, they arranged triumphant, well organized folk festivals that made people forget their worries. And Hitler's government knew how to mesmerize the millions, thanks to new radio and loudspeaker technologies. Almost the whole world applauded the 1936 Olympic games in Berlin. Many Germans, blinded by nationalism, accepted the conspiracy theory blaming the Jews for the defeat in the First World War (the stab-in-the-back legend), a shameless lie considering that an estimated 100,000 Jewish Germans served in the German Army during the First World War, of whom 12,000 were killed in action, and 18,000 Jewish Germans were awarded the Iron Cross.[88] Educated people knew the truth but did not speak out. People applauded to Hitler's hate sermons in which he declared the World Jewry as the primary enemy of the German people. (As in other countries, it was obvious that Jews were overrepresented in banking and control of newspapers until 1933.) Used to antisemitism, most Jews did not see the danger. They could not believe that the institutions of justice that they were used to would soon be eliminated.

It is hard to believe how many people accepted injustice and obvious violations of civil rights, throwing overboard their moral judgments in exchange

---

(Written about 1938, manuscript discovered and published posthumously by his son in 2000) ISBN 3-423-30848-6. 'Sebastian Haffner' is a pseudonym he adopted in the exile.

[88] https://en.wikipedia.org/wiki/German_Jewish_military_personnel_of_World_War_I

for their ethnocentric emotions. Few people cared about the race theories that were plainly ridiculous (except to the Jews and Gypsies), but even intellectuals discovered their dislike of Heine's poetry and Mendelssohn's music, two highlights of German culture. Just like with love, one can say nationalism makes blind. The Nazi race ideology was a collection of stupid assertions that no intelligent person could take seriously, except opportunists. And there were numbers. Of course people noticed that Jewish families left the country and housing in Berlin became more affordable after 1933, but the Religious engene squelched feelings of guilt, instilling its poison: wasn't it the Jews who murdered Christ our savior, the son of God?

II.3.1   Resistance

One could argue that the German people were historically not prepared for a parliamentary democracy, or that they had authoritarian character by nature, but the simple fact is that from the moment the parliament passed the Enabling Act on March 24, 1933, Germany ceased to be a lawful state and it would have been impossible, even for any people who were well prepared and of the best character, to change the course of events. In fact, there were Germans who had the insight and the courage to oppose the regime. One example is the *White Rose*, a small loosely organized group of students and faculty in the University of Munich who decided to follow their consciousness and get active. They were informed to some extent because they kept their eyes open. In the summer of 1942 two of the young men, Hans Scholl and Alexander Schmorell, had seen at the Eastern front how emaciated Jewish women were driven to forced labor, and they had also heard of mass executions of innocent people. In Munich, Hans' sister Sophie Scholl heard from a friend that mentally handicapped children of a sanatorium had been picked up by SS men and disappeared.[89, 90] In the following,

---

[89] The White Rose, like the German people in general then, did not know about the mass killings in the death camps. The plan for the mass exterminations was laid out in the Wannsee Conference, a meeting of senior government officials of Nazi Germany and Schutzstaffel (SS) leaders, held in the Berlin suburb of Wannsee on 20 January 1942, when *SS-Obergruppenführer* Reinhard Heydrich outlined how European Jews would be rounded up and sent to extermination camps in the General Government (the occupied part of Poland), where they would be killed.

[90] The Nazi regime kept these operations a tight secret. The German historian Joachim Fest (arguably the best expert on Nazi Germany) whose father regularly listened to BBC (for which, if discovered, he could have been shot) recalls that the BBC first reported about mass killing of Jews in fall 1943. But researchers from the University of Münster, who went to Rome for the historic opening of the Pope Pius XII's wartime papers of the Vatican

the group produced leaflets in which they informed about the lawlessness and monstrous cruelty of the regime, appealing to the consciousness of the readers. They distributed the leaflets in the University and then also among friends and in other cities.

Between the summer of 1942 and February 1943 the group edited and distributed six leaflets; the 5th of them appeared in an estimated total of 6,000 to 9,000 copies in several cities of southern Germany and Austria. Used to copying machines we can hardly imagine the mere technical difficulty of this task. The text of each leaflet had to be typed by hand over and over again with as many carbons as possible (perhaps three?), with the instruction to the reader at the bottom of the leaflet to repeat this her/himself and distribute the copies. By comparison, Hitler's propaganda department could use millions of *Volksempfänger* ('people's receiver', in the Berliner jargon known as "*Goebbels-Schnauze* – Goebbels snout", Goebbels being Hitler's propaganda minister) to indoctrinate people; 7 million were produced between 1933 and 1939, and by 1941 65% of German households owned one. Listening to foreign broadcasts was declared a crime punishable by a sentence in a concentration camp, and at the time of the White Rose the *Gestapo* was instructed to execute anyone discovered listening to enemy radio stations on the spot. It was not allowed to discuss even the slightest hint that Germany was losing the war, even as late as 1944 when Germany was being hammered by air raids and the Allied were attacking the Reich on both sides.

The White Rose started their leaflet campaign after the bombardment of Cologne that destroyed the city, hoping that after this tragedy people would start to think whether Hitler's war was really worth that sacrifice. They had the same desperate hope after the battle of Stalingrad in which the German 6th Army and several other brigades were wiped out entirely.

But the Strife engene is weird. I called it irrational, which is to belittle its demonic power. The feeling of solidarity and brotherhood grows stronger the

---

Archives in 2020, found out (or confirmed) that the pope learned of the mass slaughter of Jews already in fall 1942. The files also indicate that, following an advisor who dismissed the reports (Jews "easily exaggerate"), the pope told the United States government that the Vatican was unable to confirm news of Nazi crimes. - Die Zeit, April 22, 2020. "*Der Papst, der wusste und schwieg* (The Pope who knew but said nothing)." https://www.zeit.de/2020/18/papst-pius-xii-holocaust-akten-information?utm_referrer=https%3A%2F%2Fwww.google.com%2F; https://www.washingtonpost.com/history/2020/04/29/vatican-pope-pius-records-holocaust/; both accessed 1/14/2022.

more desperate the situation. This always happens in a war. In a victorious situation, most people will be conforming, but threatened by defeat, they all come together. In their 5th leaflet the White Rose wrote:

> But what are the German people doing? They will not see and will not listen. Blindly they follow their seducers into ruin. Victory at any price! is inscribed on their banner. "I will fight to the last man," says Hitler – but in the meantime the war has already been lost.[91]

In a situation when people felt their existence threatened, a fear systematically fueled by the Nazi propaganda, they lost any reason. The large-scale bombing of German cities was the best way to strengthen Hitler's grip. If there were misgivings about the Nazi regime, or any political opposition to it, it all vanished in 1943, after the defeat in Stalingrad. Virtually everybody said, "even if we don't agree with Hitler, we cannot betray our soldiers at the front." I admit that when I heard this from my mother years after the war, I found this a reasonable argument (my father was killed in action on the Eastern front). But thinking about what it meant to the German soldiers to be encouraged by the *Führer* and his generals in the secret, well-guarded *Wolfsschanze* (the *Führer* Headquarters) and by Goebbels giving his hate speeches at home, and how much this helped them against the Red Army tanks, one can see the absurdity of this argument. As if the front would collapse the moment the *Führer* died.

II.3.2   Insanity Of A Christian Society

The White Rose appealed to the religious values of Christianity, and they were clearly aware of the demonic power of their enemy:

> Every word that comes from Hitler's mouth is a lie. When he says peace, he means war, and when he blasphemously uses the name of the Almighty, he means the power of evil, the fallen angel, Satan. His mouth is the foul-smelling maw of Hell, and his might is at bottom accursed. True, we must conduct a struggle against the National Socialist terrorist state with rational means; but whoever today still doubts the reality, the existence of demonic powers, has failed by a wide margin to understand the metaphysical background of this war. Behind the concrete, the visible events, behind all

---

[91] Translated from the 5th leaflet, https://www.weisse-rose-stiftung.de/widerstandsgruppe-weisse-rose/flugblaetter/v-flugblatt-der-weissen-rose/

objective, logical considerations, we find the irrational element: The struggle against the demon, against the servants of the Antichrist.

…

> I ask you, you as a Christian wrestling for the preservation of your greatest treasure, whether you hesitate, whether you incline toward intrigue, calculation, or procrastination in the hope that someone else will raise his arm in your defence? Has God not given you the strength, the will to fight? We must attack evil where it is strongest, and it is strongest in the power of Hitler.[92]

But unfortunately, the Religious engene generally cooperates with the Strife engene boosting its power, and it does so especially in critical times. Hitler masqueraded as the savior sent by providence to the German people in the time of tribulation. Almost all Germans are Christians, but "they would not see and would not listen." How could Christians not see the contradiction between Jesus Christ preaching love, and the *Führer* preaching hate? The White Rose had the insight and the courage to call for resistance. They were motivated by their consciousness and belief in justice and felt the obligation to denounce the lawlessness and cruelty of the regime. They also denounced the catastrophic military defeats; not because that was their main concern, but hoping it would convince more of the public. Their growing concern to end the horrendous crimes of the regime that the German people would be guilty for, led them to risk their lives. When distributing the sixth leaflet in the court of the University, Hans and Sophie Scholl were trapped by a Janitor and handed over to the *Gestapo*. Four days later they were sentenced to death by a *Volksgerichtshof* and guillotined on the same day, together with a third member, Christoph Probst. Hans' friend Alexander Schmorell and two other members of the group were arrested subsequently and also executed. In the following months the *Gestapo* arrested more friends and supporters of the White Rose in Hamburg who were also sentenced to death or long prison terms by the *Volksgerichtshof*. A monstrous injustice. What for us is the constitutional right to Freedom of Speech becomes High Treason under the rule of the demonic Strife engene. Death sentence for telling the truth.

As in previous times, the Religious engene potentiated the force of the Strife engene. Once the war had started, and even more when the luck of war turned,

---

[92] Translated from the 4th leaflet, https://www.weisse-rose-stiftung.de/widerstandsgruppe-weisse-rose/flugblaetter/iv-flugblatt-der-weissen-rose/

many Germans who disliked Hitler would nevertheless feel obliged to be loyal to the troops and the military leadership. My father was deeply religious, son of a Lutheran minister who had been field chaplain in the First World War. He was not a Nazi,[93] but he believed that defending his country was fighting for the right cause. In one of his first actions in the military he had suffered a skull base fracture when driving over a mine and woke up from coma in a hospital weeks later. But after recovering and having a young family, he was not happy until he succeeded in getting a doctor to attest him '*kriegsverwendungsfähig*' – fit for war. I doubt that he was, but in 1943, after the disastrous defeat of Stalingrad, I guess they admitted about anybody. He firmly believed that fighting for the sacred cause of defending his people God would hold his hand over him. Around Christmas of 1943 he was ordered to the Eastern front. He was happy, and seven weeks later my mother opened the door to a Party official who said something she did not hear nor remember, handing her an A5 format (about a half letter size) sheet of war quality paper stamped with Eagle and Swastika that stated my father's death in action.[94] She had not expected this outcome at all. Later, looking at her wedding picture – she holding his right arm, he in uniform, his left holding the steel helmet – and remembering the wedding guests, her in-laws and the colonel and his wife whom they had befriended; the colonel who had persuaded my father, the young conscript, to continue service for another year to become a lieutenant in reserve, which he did, and then the war started; and thinking he could have returned to the university and continued his studies of literature and become a regisseur – he had written a script for a film "The Downfall of Carthage" – she felt bitterness. But then they said, the Lord calls early the ones He loves most.

The German people knew that their troops were fighting deep in Russian territory, thousands of miles away from their home. How could they think their troops were defending Germany? How could they not see the difference between betraying their soldiers and ending an aggressive war? One cannot avoid concluding that fear and bad consciousness were behind the resolve to support the war, fear of the brutal revenge and fear of being punished for all the horrendous crimes of the regime. It was the irrationality of the Strife engene that

---

[93] In the many letters he wrote to my mother after he returned to service, he never mentioned the *Führer*. My mother recalled that one night in Stettin they went out with his friend, a lieutenant Oster (son of General major Hans Oster, a key figure in the resistance), and on the way home out on the street Oster gave a mock Hitler speech while my mother was scared half to death.

[94] I was born three months after that and celebrated my first anniversary on the day the war in Europe ended.

made them accomplices to Hitler's crimes, and it was the irrationality of the Religious engene that entrusted God with the sequel, hoping for forgiveness. As said before, from the moment the parliament passed the Enabling Act on March 24, 1933, Germany ceased to be a lawful state and the way the Nazis seized power made it impossible later to change the course of events. Resistance was almost sure death, and members of the various resistance groups knew that. Some resigned while others followed the voice of their consciousness and accepted being executed, and these are our heroes.

Assuming that people would be able to reason and judge rationally, it would be hard to understand why so many Germans held on to their wrong convictions even years after the Nazi regime was abolished. In 1951, when asked about the coup of July 20, 1944, and Stauffenberg's failed assassination attempt, only 43% of men and 38% of women in West Germany judged the men of the plot positively. Recent documentations have revealed how the surviving relatives of the victims of Nazi terror were widely discredited as survivors of traitors, and widows of men of the resistance had to fight for indemnity or pension. In July 1951, the chief finance department in Munich decided to discontinue support in the amount of 160 Deutsche Mark for the widow of a colonel tried and executed by the *Volksgerichtshof* after July 20, 1944, because "former *Wehrmacht* members who were sentenced for high treason" had no right to any pension or social security. Another widow of an officer involved in that failed resistance plot who subsequently committed suicide was denied pension payment with the explanation "Your husband did not suffer any national-socialist injustice; he rather shot himself and did not await a finalizing national-socialist injustice." These examples could be interpreted as showing how deeply the minds of people were poisoned by the 12 years of Nazi rule and propaganda, but the reason why the propaganda was so successful is the irrational nature of the human mind.

As the White Rose phrased it in their 5th leaflet, "…behind all objective, logical considerations, we find the irrational element: The struggle against the demon, against the servants of the Antichrist." This is a remarkable insight. It describes the demonic aspect of the Nazi rule in the view of a religious person. In my view, what is demonic is the power of the Strife engene. It was not Hitler who had demonic powers – he was an ordinary person of mediocre intelligence who proclaimed common, simplistic ideologies of his time –, it was the irrational, machine-like collusion of leader and followers that was fateful. The threat of "being surrounded by enemies" makes the masses cheer the leader who promises to defend them, the cheering gives them pleasure, and for the one who ascends into the role of the leader the cheering of the masses is the ultimate pleasure; it enhances his leadership, incites him to compete with rivals, which are always plenty, and once successful in defeating the rivals he will establish his tyranny. For someone like Hitler the cheering of the millions was intoxicating.

Not all cheered him out of the fear of being surrounded by enemies; some cheered because he promised victory and profit from the occupation of the defeated. The Strife engene not only cares about defense, but also seeks expansion and acquisition of resources. Indeed, both in Germany and Italy, fascism owed its political success in large part to the promise of expansion. Both explicitly considered imperialism as a natural and necessary goal of the nation. In a speech to the military leadership a few days after he had been named chancellor, Hitler proposed the conquest of new *Lebensraum* in the East and its ruthless Germanization. The objective included Germany's Eastern neighbors as well as large parts of Russia. In Italy the proclaimed imperialism led the Mussolini regime to occupy Tunisia and Libya and invade the practically defenseless Ethiopia with bombs and poison gas.

The fear of being surrounded by enemies incited the Bolsheviks after the October Revolution when they were threatened for years by an international coalition and had to fight left- and right-wing armies in a bloody civil war. After the Bolsheviks defeated their enemies on Russian territory, the young Soviet Union was threatened by Nazi Germany and eventually invaded. Certainly, the threat of existence was a factor supporting Stalin's ascent and tyranny. Nevertheless, despite Lenin's efforts to mobilize the worker and peasant class against the worldwide imperialism of the capitalist class, the Soviet Union also embraced imperialism. Following the footsteps of the Czar, the Soviet Union metamorphosed into a Soviet Russian Empire. Thus, here again, people's motivation to defend their existence merged with the appetite to expand their rule and dominate others.

II.4 GROWTH OF XENOPHOBIC NATIONALISM

I have argued that we must understand, because if we understand what happened and why, we will be able to make predictions and prepare for the future. Of course, education and explanation are important, if not just to alert the rest of society of the danger, but today's world makes us worry that education and remembering are not enough. Today, historical insight and political education in the media are certainly better than ever. But still, we find similar xenophobic nationalist groups all over Europe (see Table 3), and yes, even in the

United States, the greatest immigrant society in the world.[95] The fact is that the seeds of ugly nationalism seem to sprout in all Western countries, appealing to about 15 percent of the population. Only a much smaller percentage is aggressive and prone to violence, the others are sympathizers. For several decades after the Second World War, this cohort did not have much visibility in Germany, partly because of shame, and partly because of legal actions against a Neo-Nazi political party, but recently it has picked up steam and recovered, becoming equally strong as in other European countries Second World War, this cohort did Thus, despite all the historical insight and political education we have today, we

Country	%	Country	%
Hungary	68	France	13
Austria	26	Netherlands	13
Switzerland	26	Germany	13
Denmark	21	Czech Republic	11
Belgium	20	Bulgaria	9
Estonia	18	Slovakia	8
Finland	18	Poland	7
Sweden	18	Greece	4
Italy	17	Cyprus	4
Spain	15		
		Median	15

Table 3. Percent of votes won by nationalist parties in recent elections (as of May 2019) in Europe[1]

cannot get rid of the problem of ugly xenophobic nationalism. Considering the evolutionary roots of the human mind we can understand this paradox. The core of those nationalist movements, and perhaps its followers too, are not amenable to education or rational reasoning: too strong is the ugly Strife engene. The core

---

[95] Polls in 2013 estimated that slightly over 10 percent of Americans identified as part of the tea party movement, the right wing of the Republican Party. A Reuters/Ipsos poll in May 17-19, 2021, found that more than six months after the 2020 election and four months after Joe Biden's victory was confirmed by Congress, 25% of Americans (53% of Republicans) say Trump is still the "true president," Trump, the ostentatiously xenophobic nationalist president who in his last days in office incited a violent mob to storm the capitol to block the confirmation of the election results   .
https://www.usatoday.com/story/news/politics/2021/05/25/poll-quarter-americans-surveyed-say-trump-true-president/7426714002/

corresponds to the top fringe of its distribution. This inheritance is the reason why civilization does not make as much progress as might be expected. We need to understand the behavioral engenes that we are born with and where they come from.

II.5 RACIAL DISCRIMINATION IN SERVITUDE AND SLAVERY

What we learn in school about society is often tainted. Before I moved to the U.S. for good I had been there several times, but only for conferences and short visits. These experiences did not really change my high-school picture of America, the great melting pot of nations. Sure, with a history of slavery. But it was hundred years since the slaves were freed by Lincoln, and recently the civil rights movement has succeeded in giving them the same rights as the Whites, ending racial segregation. So, when I arrived and settled with my family in Baltimore, I remember, we went to a shopping mall and entered a restaurant

there. I was stunned by the graceful view of dignified old Black people with white hair. It was new to me: brown skin with white hair – in Europe it had all been white skin with brown hair. The picture of Uncle Tom flashed through my mind. But then I realized that my family, we were the only Whites in the room. That was when I noticed that Baltimore is a segregated city. Education is special; reading "Uncle Tom s Cabin"[96] you get one picture, but reading "Ways of White Folks"[97] gives you a different picture.

Racism is strange. Apart from the brief surprise and fear when a child from a white family first sees a Black man, or the reverse, no negative feelings remain that would not be dispelled by the first personal encounter. But racial difference has always been a convenient condition for profiteering. Slavery has a long tradition, but it has been said that in Africa a slave was traditionally much like a servant for a wealthy owner, and owning one was an ostensive sign of prestige. I don't know about that, but I know it really went bad when the Europeans discovered their craving for sweet. To supply enough sugar for their continent, the Portuguese built sugar cane plantations on an island off the West coast of Africa, probably the first plantations in history. Worked by slaves, the plantations were hugely profitable to the owners who lived in Portugal, a safe distance from the malaria-infested island. To satisfy the enormous demand for sugar in Europe, plantations sprang up in the following all over the Caribbean

---

[96] Harriet Beecher Stowe, "Uncle Tom's Cabin, or, Life Among the Lowly." John P. Jewett: Boston (1852).

[97] Langston Hughes, "The Ways of White Folks." A.A. Knopf: New York (1934).

islands, Brazil, and the southeast of the British North American colonies, with slaves shipped over from Africa. The scheme that worked so well with sugar was then repeated with tobacco, another addiction of the European countries, and then once more with cotton, which supplied the textile industries producing enormous wealth in England and the New England states of the U.S.

These are well-known historical facts that have been analyzed by sociologists who pointed out the capitalist nature of the plantation industry, plantations as means of production, and how their owners systematically optimized their gain on the backs of slave workers, extending work hours and reducing the costs of living (of the slaves of course).

Racism and economic profiteering are both children of the Strife engene. Because the evolution of the Strife engene was driven by the pressure of the economic situation, the strife for dominance and oppression of "them" is primarily motivated by the prospect of acquiring resources and expanding possession. In a great article in the New York Times Magazine Nicole Hannah Jones explains how, even after slavery was officially abolished, racism still served exploitation:

> Though our high school history books seldom make this plain: Slavery and the 100-year period of racial apartheid and racial terrorism known as Jim Crow were, above all else, systems of economic exploitation. [98]

The Strife engene did the same in Latin America, not only where the economy was built on slavery, like the Caribbean and Brazil, but in all countries that inherited colonialism, which includes all of Latin America. This heritage is alive everywhere where an Indigenous population exists. It's not black and white, but bronze and white, one might say. The features of the *Indios*, who are descendants of the original immigrants who arrived 15,000 years ago, are distinct from those of the *Criollos*, the people of Spanish and Portuguese origin. Different from the U.S. and Canada, the populations of the Andean countries as well as of Mexico and Mesoamerica are heavily mixed because these regions were colonized by conquering existing high civilizations, by White men who fathered children with indigenous concubines. Nevertheless, the *Criollos* established the ruling class and exploited the work force of the Indigenous from the beginning, the Spanish Crown using forced labor in the silver mines of *Alto Peru* (today's Bolivia) and Mexico, and the *Criollo* landowners using servitude

---

[98] https://www.nytimes.com/interactive/2020/06/24/magazine/reparations-slavery.html

in the *Hacienda* system. Just as Blacks in the regions of slavery, the indigenous people were, and are to date, economically exploited and socially oppressed.

What is hard to understand is how Christian societies can reconcile the injustice with their Christian values. The White *Criollo* upper class in Latin America claims racial supremacy and God-given political power, which was, and still is, explicitly supported by the Catholic Church. Does oppression and exploiting the poor not contradict the Christian values? How could deeply religious Christians in the Southern states of the U.S. accept the heinous injustice and cruelty of the slave economy and the White terror that continued for decades even after the institution of slavery was abolished, with the lynching of an estimated 6,500 Black people (there might have been more). How could they watch the lynchings and be entertained?

The short answer is that people's values originate from a sense of righteousness that is part of the Strife engene, not from Christian faith. The Strife engene seeks those values for its people. Establishing equal rights and justice satisfies its moral demands and makes people feel good. Of course, making someone work as a slave violates these moral demands, which is worrying, sinful, unpleasant. But the worries are easily dispelled if there is a racial marker. Then, the moral demands can easily be appeased by an ideology that proclaims that the own race is superior and therefore destined (supposedly by God) to rule and set the conditions for the society and a prosperous economy. Thus, it is the complacency of emotions produced by the Strife engene that makes the injustice acceptable. The double-faced Strife engene makes it easy to create a double standard of values, one for "us" and another for "them." Living the pleasant life of a White European it took the experience of Baltimore for me to see this.

We see that racism is just one way of discriminating between "us" and "them" when both live in the same geographic location. Other criteria commonly used for discrimination are language, tradition and culture, religion, and origin of migration.

II.6 POVERTY

The Strife engene defends possession and produces the sense of entitlement, and this implies depriving "the others," which to them means poverty. After the Civil War, the slaves cheered the day in 1865 when they were freed. Oluale Kossola, one of the last Africans to be brutally kidnapped, sold into slavery, and shipped to America remembers the day in Mobile, Alabama, when Yankee soldiers came and told him that he was now free and should leave the boat he was working on for his master. He and the other Africans who had come with the last slave ship rejoiced and celebrated the day with drumming and singing. The following days, talking about what to do now, they all said to go back to their hometown on African soil. They thought, now, after working hard five years and six months as slaves for Tim Meaher, the owner of the ship that had brought them, that he ought to take them back home. Now that they were paid for work, they would save money to buy the tickets. They worked hard and tried to save money, men and women, but soon realized that it was impossible – the tickets were too expensive – and decided to stay. But they had no homes, and no land to build houses. They knew that Meaher owned a lot of land in Mobile (in fact, Timothy Meaher owned many thousands of acres). So, they delegated Kossola, who worked on Meaher's sawmill, to approach his master. The next occasion when Kossola saw his master, he took the plunge and asked him:

> "Capt'n Tim, you brought us from our country where we had land. You made us slaves. Now they made us free, but we have got no country and we have got no land. Why don't you give us a piece of this land so we can build ourselves a home?"

But Meaher got angry, called him a fool, and said:

> "I took good care of my slaves and therefore owe you nothing. You don't belong to me now, why must I give you my land?" [99]

The result was that the newly freed remained poor. They first rented land from the Meahers and worked hard for years, men and women, until they had saved enough to buy it. And their families remained poor for many generations. In fact, today in the U.S., "the land of unlimited opportunities," the average White person holds seven times more wealth than the average Black person.[100] You read it right: SEVEN times more. Virtually unlimited opportunities were offered to the White settlers. The Homestead Act of 1862 made it possible for any adult male U.S. citizen, or intended citizen, to gain title to 160 acres of undeveloped land by living on it for five years and paying eighteen dollars in fees.

---

[99] From Zora Neal Hurston, "Barracoon: The Story of the Last 'Black Cargo.'" Ed. Deborah G. Plant, Amistad (2018). Kossola was interviewed by the anthropologist Hurston in 1927. Her text was published only posthumously. Hurston recorded Kossola's narrative in his dialect. I reproduced it here in ordinary English.

[100] N Bhutta, A C Chang, L J Dettling, & J W Hsu, with assistance from Julia Hewitt "Disparities in Wealth by Race and Ethnicity in the 2019 Survey of Consumer Finances" FEDS Notes, Sept 28, 2020

One fundamental condition of happiness is being relieved from poverty and the stress of starvation, and being able to provide one's family with what they need. Poverty is one of the big problems of our time, a problem that does not seem to go away soon. When a mayor of a West African fisher village was asked by a journalist what he thought of the new development that would bring electricity to the village, he responded "with the development comes poverty." Poverty is the dark side of inequality, and the roots of inequality, it seems to me, lie in human nature.

How does the world deal with poverty? The creed that the free-market economy is the best way to satisfy the needs of the people is now widely accepted. Especially in the U.S. we find a quasi-religious belief in the free market. When people from Europe migrated to the New World many came to escape poverty, a life that did not offer any opportunities to build one's future because there was not enough land for the growing population, most everything was already someone's property and protected by law. Pursuing happiness was denied. When the British colonies declared their independence, the founders of the new states explicitly recognized that every human has the right to "life, liberty and the pursuit of happiness."

People are now giving this phrase a narrow, materialistic interpretation. They believe they have the unrestricted right to pursue their personal business, rejecting state intervention as much as possible, in particular rejecting that the government collects taxes for social welfare, or that it interferes with their exploitation of natural resources. Ideally, they think, the role of the government should be restricted to protecting property rights and providing safety; the capitalist free-market economy will satisfy our desires.

II.6.1   Evolutionary Roots Of Human Economic Behavior

What are the evolutionary roots of human economic behavior? First of all, people are consumers. To be happy we feel that we need to satisfy our desires, and that's what the free-market economy does. It strives to satisfy the desires of the individual consumers, whereby the desires are weighted by the purchasing power of the respective group of consumers. But our desires are the desires of our engenes. So, if the government of the country has other concerns, like fair distribution of wealth, or the health of the planet, it has to come up against the formidable force of the engenes in millions of consumers.

Since we are descendants of hunter-gatherers it is no surprise that the corresponding engenes influence us in our daily activities. Today's supermarkets and shopping malls cater to the ancient Gathering engene. Buying something makes happy. For some people shopping (or buying shares of stocks for that matter) can become addictive. It works as an antidepressant. Not surprisingly, women tend to have more pleasure in shopping as they were the main gatherers in the paleolithic society. Some women with bipolar disease find relief in shopping sprees. For men, malls are less effective as antidepressants, but car dealerships work well.

The hunting part has also left its trace. Where people have the opportunities, like in the U.S., hunting and fishing are popular leisure activities, and mainly so among men. Hunting is implicit in many sports, and men love shooting. The National Rifle Association with its millions of members takes care of that passion, and a billion-dollar gun industry thrives from it. No surprise that in a country that champions freedom of enterprise and free-market capitalism, the Hunting engene wields its power. The gun industry there currently produces and sells 10 million guns per year, mostly pistols and rifles. (That is *one every year* for every 30 inhabitants, including babies, children and old ladies!) And because shooting is the activity that the Hunting engine rewards with pleasure, automatic weapons are the most popular (the more rounds per minute, the more pleasure?). As a side effect, 40,000 people die every year from the misuse of guns in the U.S., while the sporting arms, ammunition, and related industries rake in 60 billion dollars (as of 2019). From the economic point of view, 60 billion dollars divided into 40,000 deaths = 1.5 million dollars per death might seem like a bargain. Are the deaths an accepted side effect? Is killing a human passion? If we can trust the economic rationale of the designers of computer games (and I think we can) there is no doubt that men enjoy killing.

Emotions of the consumers drive the market economy. It is fascinating – and scary – to see how the desires and pleasures produced by ancient evolutionary engenes are propelling modern technology. One is the urge to listen and talk (we might call it the Gossip engene, borrowing from Yuval Harari) which led to the meteoric rise of the cell phone becoming the most popular device on earth. The other is the Strife engene which creates the thrill of the gamble of a fight, and rewards destruction and killing with pleasure.

The pleasure of computer games has driven economies and sciences. Until the 1960ies, computers were 'mainframes' housed in large halls filled with the roar of dozens of fans. To learn computer programming, physics students were given a few seconds on a mainframe to test their programs. Soon, 'minicomputers' became available, and well-funded laboratories would have one, housed in two head-high 19-inch racks, that still needed a separate room with air conditioning. Vision research, the science that tries to understand how the brain sees, and to find ways to give vision to the blind, initially used 'tachistoscopes' to present precisely timed visual stimuli: the subject looked into a box in which the researcher inserted cards with letters or drawings on them, which were then illuminated with a flash. But slowly computers came into use to generate dynamic visual displays on a computer screen, pioneered by the almighty Bell Labs. But they were more expensive than tachistoscopes, a minicomputer was about $30,000. The computer age really began in 1977 with the introduction of mass-produced home computers, little machines that were affordable because millions of users bought them for playing games. Soon, all scientific laboratories used these little machines (also called personal computers, or PCs) for computation and control of devices. The innovation was dramatic in vision science where researchers must be able to present synthetic images in controlled rapid sequence. The home computer architecture was ideal because computer games require exactly this, controlled rapid sequences of synthetic images. By the 1990ies they had become the backbone of all vision laboratories. So, the sciences owe it to the games.

Why did computer games become so popular? It's because of the pleasure produced by the Strife engene. This engene strives to distinguish "us" and "them", where "they" are nasty and dangerous, and "we" (the player and his comrades) must defend ourselves and wipe them out. One of the first successful computer games (which I got to know through my son in the 1990ies) was Duke Nukem. "Nuke them" means to wipe them out, alluding to the nuclear strike. The thrill of the fight whose outcome is uncertain, the pleasure of killing, and the reward of the final victory (defeats don't matter because you can restart the game) are so powerful that today five-year-old boys spend much of their waking hours playing.

When driven by the Strife engene humans become competitive and strive for possession. The result is that people in the U.S. are driving around in bigger and bigger cars, cars with engines of 400 horse power, usually one person per car. (Occasionally I see a second little head next to the driver's head; that's the time when the schools open or close.) And people need ever more space and bigger houses. The credit card is an incredibly easy way to satisfy the desires of the engenes, and people suffer under the ever-growing burden of debt.

Wealthy people feel entitled to their wealth, and so do wealthy nations. They generally feel that it is the result of their virtues, although wealth is usually based on historical conditions, inheritance, or mere luck. The sense of entitlement also implies that "the others" are poor because they lack those virtues. That's the behavioral pattern of the Strife engene. Indeed, the influence of evolutionary engenes shapes the capitalist society in various ways.

II.6.2   Engenes Shape The World Economic System

The engenes are not only driving the economy as consumers, they have also shaped the world's economic system. The free-market economy is the pillar of the capitalist system which is so efficient in driving the economy. The capitalist system provides mechanisms by which people invest some of their wealth in the productive apparatus of a society and are rewarded for it by a share in the profit from the production. It is so efficient because, by rewarding individual investment decisions proportionally to their success (the profit from the investment), it sets up positive feedback loops that amplify production. The crucial point is that investment decisions are only successful if they correctly anticipate the future demand for a product. Predicting the future is generally difficult, and that is why the capitalist economy is superior because it relies on the investment decisions of a large number of investors, in contrast to a planned economy which relies on the investment decisions of a small group of people in government.[101] As explained above, decisions that amplify production of a good that is in demand optimally satisfy the desires of the people (because that is where the demand comes from). Thus, the 'invisible hand' of the markets will make everybody happy, according to the free-market ideology that is now widely accepted.

Why is it then that the invisible hand, that is supposed to make everybody happy, creates so much unhappiness? In fact, the invisible hand steals the fish from African fishermen who return from the sea with empty nets, and the quinoa from Andean farmers who can no longer afford to eat their own produce. No question, the invisible hand exploits the poor and serves the rich, takes from the workers and gives to the shareholders. And not-so-invisible hands drive Indigenous people in the Amazon at gunpoint from their land to make space for industrial-scale cattle farming.

At the heart of the capitalist economy is the legal construct of the shareholder society; it is what makes that kind of economy so highly efficient. It originated when Portugal and Spain developed ocean-going ships which enabled them to

---

[101] Beside the advantage of their big number, the decisions of individual investors are also generally better (in economic terms) because they are purely based on predicting the future profit of an economic enterprise, whereas government decisions can also have political reasons.

trade with remote places on the globe, bypassing the traditional trans-continental trade routes. To build fleets of those ships and equip them for a trip around the world was costly, but the expected profit when the fleet would return was big. So, people with money founded shareholder societies that enabled them to invest their money in such an enterprise, providing legal security for reaping the future profit. The shareholders could then invest some of the profit in other enterprises, thus giving this new economy a dynamic that the world had not seen before. This is the concept of capital. Capital was first provided by banks in Northern Italy and in the following the Spanish Crown was continually in debt, first with the Genoese, and later, under Charles V, with the Fuggers in Germany. The new ocean-going fleets initially brought those two countries enormous wealth, but in the following also enormous debts, and much of the wealth flowed into the accounts of the new banks.

It is obvious that this new economic system from the beginning was not purely economic, but much above all political, a matter of power.[102] The profit came from trade – within a decade Portugal usurped the South Asian coastal trade run until those days by the Arabs – but also from wars of colonization. Both Portugal and Spain equipped their fleets with cannons and soldiers to subdue existing trade centers, to conquer empires in the Americas, and then to protect their precious cargo of spices, silk and silver on their way back to the mother country. The birth of capitalism was also the beginning of colonialism. Thus, capitalism from its origin was based on military power and imperial politics. Rather than the king, the one who ruled was now the investor. The East India Company, a joint-stock company founded in London in 1600 that seized control of large parts of the Indian subcontinent and colonized parts of Southeast Asia and owned trading posts and colonies in the Persian Gulf, maintained its own army (until the company was dissolved in 1874).

Power and possession have always been intimately related in society. While in the paleolithic, power was originally the physical power of a dominant male, or of a gang, and possession was possession of women, hunting grounds etc., the nature of power and possession adapted through the ages; power became rank in a hierarchical society, and possession came to encompass all kinds of material goods, land, resources, and eventually, after the invention of money and the ensuing capitalist economy, capital. And in society the two become one and the same: power means possession and possession means power. The rich can easily spend millions of dollars on political lobbying, thus tweaking laws so as to boost

---

[102] Magda von der Heydt-Coca, "Andean silver and the rise of the Western world" *Critical Sociology* 31, 481-513, 2005.

their wealth; they can afford the best lawyers to defend their wealth and power; they can acquire TV channels and social media to manipulate voters, thus undermining the foundations of democratic responsible government.

A capitalist enterprise has an authoritarian command-chain structure. This is the signature of the Strife engene: it calls for a strong leader and loyal subjects, and its objective is expanding power and possession. The force of the Strife engene acts across the entire group, be it an enterprise or the nation; it's a far-field engene. It divides "us" and "them" and gives "us" the sense of entitlement; it says, we are successful because we work hard, the others are poor because they are lazy; and: don't give to the poor, it makes them lazy; if they don't feel the need, they won't work hard.

The Family engene also governs power and possession, but it acts only in the near field, the family. The Family engene caters to the family business, the Strife engene to the shareholder society. One is personal, the other is anonymous (Société Anonyme, S.A.).

In what might seem like a democratic structure, the CEO of a capitalist enterprise, who is at the top of the command chain, is also responsible to the shareholders. But the shareholders do not represent the subjects the CEO rules over, as it would be in a democracy, where a government responds to representatives of the people. The CEO is like the vizier in a kingdom, where the vizier responds to the royal family. The shareholders are the royal family, the true rulers.

As noted above, the Strife engene, which originated from the drive to fight in the Paleolithic, has the ingredient of gamble. The outcome of a fight is uncertain, victory or defeat, and naturally the Strife engene inherited the genes of the victor, not those of the loser. That is why gambling is so popular, even addictive. The same engene drives the investor, and the billionaire who pursues his investments up until the grave; investing is also a gamble, and it's addictive.

The modern invention of the nation state has made the Strife engene enormously powerful; the well-developed power structure of territorial states has allowed this engene to create nationalism, making people believe that they *are* a nation, "the greatest nation on earth" as politicians in the U.S. tirelessly assert. But this is an illusion, because, what the Strife engene means is a group of people defined by wealth, race, and ethnicity. Thus, the Strife engene drives one group to seize power in the state, trying to marginalize or subdue other groups living in the same state.

The nation state is unfortunate in two ways. For one, it foments chauvinism and supremacy claims of subgroups *within* a nation and enables discrimination and suppression of others under the mantle of national sovereignty, undeterred by international laws. It permits governments to expel Indigenous people from their land to make space for large-scale farming and the construction of megaprojects like hydro-electric dams[103] and highways,[104] ignoring their constitutionally guaranteed rights. National sovereignty enables the most horrific human rights violations in many countries all over the world.

And second, the concept of nation states allows the Strife engene to exert its power internationally, creating competition *between nations* and fomenting hegemony claims, be they based on military force or on economic power. Just as the Strife engene divides "us" and "them" within a society, it divides nations into "us" and "them." It creates nationalism: we are successful because we are good and work hard, they are poor because they are bad and lazy.

The evil influence of the Strife engene affects autocratic states and democracies alike. In fact, the governments of democratic states are helpless because they are responsible to their voters, which are compelled by the Strife, Religious, and Family engenes. In the affluent democratic countries, voters feel like shareholders and want the state to be run like an enterprise; they want the government to maximize profit. Although many people also embrace other values, like social justice, protection of the environment, fight against climate change etc., the election results invariably show that the recent economic performance of the country has the biggest influence. Everybody appreciates a salary increase and affordable housing. This is the crux of democratically elected governments: voters are to a large extent motivated by selfish interest. People always want more. Under the rule of a wise king, people might be happy with less.

As pointed out before, people are driven by both Family and Strife engenes, but the force of the Family engene, the strongest in the near field, has only short range, while the Strife engene reaches the whole group, be it defined by ethnic, economic, or political standards. The power of the Family engene stretches out to the people only in crises, when conditions become unbearable; then it

---

[103]   https://www.reuters.com/article/us-brazil-indigenous-mining/brazils-bolsonaro-moves-to-free-mining-hydro-dams-on-indigenous-lands-idUSKBN1ZZ2TG,   accessed 1/5/2022

[104]   https://news.mongabay.com/2019/05/bolivia-nature-rights-tribunal-condemns-tipnis-project/, accessed 1/5/2022

mobilizes mass demonstrations or leads to a revolution, but its power does not last. By contrast, the power of the Strife engene is unremitting.

The result is that the Strife engene rules the world, despite the United Nations, its World Food Program, and other humanitarian Programs. The Family engene does promote its social values to some extent, keeping alive the United Nations Children's Fund (UNICEF) and other programs. The Family engene powers the UN, one might say, but the Strife engene controls the nations. As a result, the percentage of what rich nations spend on international development aid is tiny; only a few nations reach the UN official development assistance target of 0.7% of the gross national income. Most citizens of the wealthy nations are probably not aware of their country's dismal fraction of development aid but only see the absolute amounts which are perceived large by those irrational engenes.

Once it was hoped, and some people still hope, that the expansion of industrial production would be able to rid the world of poverty. But in fact, the expansion of industrial production is the direct or indirect cause of vast impoverishment on earth. The *direct* cause, where people are driven away from inhabitable lands because of the forced expansion of industrial-type agriculture and for the exploitation of raw materials. The expansion of hi-tech fishing into the traditional fishing waters of defenseless people also directly causes starvation. Expansion of the industrial society is the *indirect* cause when industrially advanced countries dominate the economy of 'developing' countries, forcing them to give up their traditional ways of production in exchange for importing products of the advanced countries. Previously, clothes were sewn by thousands of tailors and were expensive. Then, the global free-market economy let investors build factories in countries where women would sew clothes 12 hours each day for a 'minimum wage', the minimum to allow survival and reproduction,[105] and for ordinary people in the wealthy countries clothes became so cheap that they could buy a new wardrobe every year and donate their used clothes, which were then sold with profit in countries where clothes were still sewn by tailors, preparing them for the 12-hour shift work in newly built factories.

---

[105] In Bangladesh $96 per month is the legal minimum wage, but 85% of workers are paid less.

https://www.openaccessgovernment.org/bangladeshi-garment-workers/89939/, accessed 8/6/2021.

These expansions into territories of defenseless people and exploitation of their resources, including their labor, happen all over the world, despite United Nations, international organizations, and nice words and promises of national governments. Indeed, the democratic governments are helpless because they must respond to voters compelled by their Strife engenes.

II.7 JUSTICE

Notwithstanding its emanations of ugly nationalism, racism, genocide, aggressive wars and greed, human nature shows traits that one cannot help but call divine. I have mentioned some above under "Whence it Came," such as the faculties of love and friendship, the ability to feel compassion, and the aptitude to create culture. But one should be explained here under "What it Did": the passion for justice. One might think that sense of justice is acquired by education or from a role model, and to some extent that is certainly true, but its wide distribution across cultures and its character as a passion, I think, show its genetic nature. Sense of justice also shows the three-phase structure that is characteristic of other engenes: discomfort when witnessing injustice and the urge to right it or punish the offender, then the corresponding action, and finally relief and satisfaction if one's action succeeded, or, if one neglected to act, the feeling of guilt. No education can teach those emotions. They are miraculous achievements of evolution. Sense of justice is the condition for a lawful society.

As Kant noted, common sense generally gives people good ethical judgments, but, referring to the virtue of moral intuition, he cautions that "her innocence cannot be preserved well and gets easily seduced." As recounted above, the power of the Strife engene has often overruled Christian and humanitarian values, paving the way for genocide, slavery, and exploitation of the poor. Many people witnessed injustice but did not speak out. But some were repulsed by the lawlessness they saw and stood their ground, like the group of The White Rose who stood up against Hitler. It would be wrong to see these as rare exceptions, white roses bloom all over the world. The tragedy is that those who defend justice are generally left alone by the society; small circles of friends struggling against the force of armies driven by the Strife engene. Sadly also, appealing to their faithful Christian contemporaries did not help; the churches generally failed to defend them, either letting their sense of justice become corrupted, or resorting to Luther's doctrine of the two kingdoms, the worldly and the eternal, deferring justice to the latter. But occasionally, passion for justice did change the course of history.

II.7.1   John Brown

The abolitionist John Brown, who was deeply religious, perceived his mission to free the enslaved as a mandate according to the 'Golden Rule', the principle of treating others as one wants to be treated. Since decades of peaceful efforts to end American slavery had failed, he believed that violence was necessary. After years of covert campaigning for the anti-slavery movement in the North he led a small armed force, including three of his sons, to attack the U.S. Armory at Harpers Ferry, a complex of water-powered hammer works on the Shenandoah River not far from Washington. Muskets and rifles were stored in huge numbers in the complex. His idea was to distribute the arms to the slaves in the surrounding plantations and encourage an uprising which, without much bloodshed, would cause a collapse of the institution of slavery in Virginia, a process that would then gradually spread through the other pro-slavery states. But the plot failed because, instead of slaves joining Brown to be freed, local farmers, shopkeepers and militia pinned down the raiders in the armory by firing from the heights behind the town until U.S. Marines arrived the next day. In the fighting, Brown's men killed four people and wounded nine. Ten of Brown's men were killed, including two of his sons. Seven were captured along with Brown and were quickly tried and hanged. But Brown was content; his trial got a lot of publicity. He was given the opportunity to speak in the courtroom, which was packed, and there were many journalists both from the North and the South. As he wrote to his wife, he thought that his "blood will do vastly more towards advancing the cause I have earnestly endeavored to promote, than all I have done in my life before"[106] and "I am worth inconceivably more to hang than for any other purpose."

Brown and his sons fought for justice, but they were sentenced for treason against the state of Virginia, a state to which they owed no loyalty and of which they were not residents. The court wanted them to be hanged in public to give a sign to the people that this is what you get when you try to free the slaves; to people who were Christians and pretended to follow the word of Jesus "Love your neighbor as yourself."[107] They did not put the epitaph on Brown's grave that he wanted:

---

[106] John Brown, "Brown's letter to his wife." United States Police Gazette. 2 (82). p. 2. (November 8, 1859/ December 10, 1859).
[107] Mark 12:31

> I have fought a good fight.
> I have finished my course.
> I have kept the faith. [2 Timothy 4:7]

Indeed, the abolitionists were a minority even in the North and their activity was largely clandestine. Brown's attack triggered the Civil War, but ironically, the war broke out not to vindicate justice, but because the Slave holder states perceived their rights threatened and proclaimed secession from the federation, which then caused the war.

II.7.2   Christian Churches

One might think that the Christian churches would support justice, but tragically those members who show passion for justice often find themselves left alone. Because of the power of the Religious engene, which for many people embodies the ultimate reason, and because this engene rules the entire religious community, political leaders have always been eager to appeal to people's religious feelings. That is, the Strife engene tries to recruit the Religious engene for its purposes, and it generally succeeds. This leads to the incredible distortions of people's religious values, as recounted above. How else can we explain that Catholic Christians embraced Mussolini's colonial war against Ethiopia, that both Catholic and Protestant Christians accepted Hitler's aggressive wars? How could people reconcile the brutal slave owner society with their Christian values, and how can church-going Catholics wage wars against the Indigenous poor in El Salvador, Guatemala and Honduras?

Apparently, the Strife engene can easily supplant its values for those of the Religious engene, and people are either not disturbed by this, or they resign and live with the inner conflict. And yet, some have that miraculous passion for justice and resist their values being consumed by the Strife engene. They feel compelled to act when they witness injustice, or feel guilt if they don't.

Some of Germany's Protestants opposed the request of the Nazi regime to submit the churches under state control (*Gleichschaltung*). They would not let the Nazi regime control the appointment of church officials and dictate what a pastor can say in Sunday's sermon, and what he cannot. Thus Protestant clerics founded the organization *Bekennende Kirche* (Confessing Church), which defended the autonomy of the consciousness of the individual and their right to help and give shelter to people who were threatened by the regime. Many thought that Christian-converted Jews deserved protection, but then they were paralyzed by theological arguments that the worldly should not intrude into matters of the eternal and that politics should be kept out of matters of faith. It has been estimated that only about 20% of the protestant clerics joined the Confessing Church. Ultimately the church did not speak out for the Jewish Christians, let alone for the Jews. The theologian Martin Niemöller, one of those who defended the freedom of Christian conscience against the Nazi dictate, for which he was imprisoned seven years in concentration camps and only narrowly escaped execution, later reasoned:

> When they came for the communists, I did not speak out—
>   I was not a communist.
> When they came for the trade unionists, I did not speak
>   out—I was not a trade unionist.
> When they came for the Jews, I did not speak out—I was
>   not a Jew.
> When they came for me—there was no one left to speak
>   for me.

II.7.3   Dietrich Bonhoeffer

And yet, some did speak out, and these inevitably paid with their lives. Dietrich Bonhoeffer believed that the Incarnation of God in flesh made it unacceptable to speak of God and the world in terms of two kingdoms. Christians should not retreat from the world but act within it. He believed that two elements were constitutive of faith: the implementation of justice and the acceptance of divine suffering. He was one of the clerics who opposed the Nazification of the church and a founder of the Confessing Church.

Bonhoeffer had studied theology, and during postdoctoral studies in the U.S. he was introduced by a friend to Abyssinian Baptist Church in Harlem and taught Sunday school there. While he did not advance in theology ("there is no theology here"), he began to see things in a different way, from the perspective of those who suffer oppression. He later remembered this experience as "the point at which I turned from phraseology to reality."[108]

Bonhoeffer opposed the Nazi regime from the beginning and was the first to raise his voice for church resistance to Hitler's persecution of Jews, declaring that the church must not simply "bandage the victims under the wheel, but jam a spoke in the wheel itself."[109] Bonhoeffer spent years teaching an underground seminary for training pastors of the Confessing Church, but in 1937 the regime declared the training of ministers for Confessing Church illegal, and the Gestapo

---

[108] David Ford, "The Modern Theologians: An Introduction to Christian Theology Since 1918," 3rd Edition, Wiley-Blackwell, 2005, p. 45

[109] Ditto, p. 38

closed the seminary and arrested 27 pastors and former students. Bonhoeffer was forbidden to speak in public and his activities were controlled by the police. An opportunity to act according to his conviction came when his friend Hans von Dohnányi introduced him to members of the German resistance movement and a group within *Abwehr* (the German military intelligence service) that sought to overthrow Hitler. Bonhoeffer was able to join the service on the claim that his wide ecumenical contacts would be of use to Germany. In the face of Nazi atrocities, the full scale of which Bonhoeffer learned through the *Abwehr*, he concluded that "the ultimate question for a responsible man to ask is not how he is to extricate himself heroically from the affair, but how the coming generation shall continue to live."[110]

As an agent of the *Abwehr*, Bonhoeffer was able to contact and inform the Western Allies about the existence of the resistance movement. His visits to Norway, Sweden, Denmark, and Switzerland were camouflaged as legitimate intelligence activities for the *Abwehr*. Dohnányi and Bonhoeffer also took part in *Abwehr* operations to help Jewish Germans escape to Switzerland. But their activities raised suspicions and in April 1943 Bonhoeffer and Dohnányi were arrested and imprisoned.

For a year and a half, Bonhoeffer was imprisoned at Tegel Prison awaiting trial. There he continued his work in religious outreach among his fellow prisoners and guards, some of whom helped him to smuggle letters out of prison. A sympathetic guard even offered to help him escape, but Bonhoeffer declined it, fearing Nazi retribution against his family, especially his brother Klaus, and Dohnányi, who were also imprisoned. But after the failed attempt to assassinate Hitler on the 20th of July 1944, when the secret *Abwehr* documents relating to the conspiracy were discovered, Bonhoeffer was accused of association with the conspirators and transferred to a concentration camp.[111] On April 8, 1945, Bonhoeffer was sentenced to death by an SS drumhead court-martial without witnesses, records of proceedings or a defense, and on April 9 (29 days before the end of the war) he was executed with six other members of the resistance. They were not hanged, as John Brown was, but, on Hitler's personal request, slowly strangled to death with piano wire (most likely, there are no reliable witness reports).

---

[110] Dietrich Bonhoeffer, "Letters and Papers from Prison." New York: Touchstone (1997). p. 7.

[111] In total, an estimated 7,000 people were arrested and approximately 4,980 were executed

Bonhoeffer's consciousness was anchored in his Christian faith which dominated all his thinking – he was a theologian – and apparently guided and supported him through the horrible days and hours up to his death. But, in participating in plots to assassinate Hitler he consciously crossed a border that for many Christians is the limit. He certainly knew about those plots; in one instance his friend Dohnányi personally smuggled a time bomb to Smolensk (Belarus) that another officer of the resistance managed to activate and deposit aboard Hitler's plane – an incredible achievement (it did not go off; apparently the ignition failed because of low temperature). Like John Brown, Bonhoeffer accepted killing if it was for a good cause.

One would think that parliamentarians should have a passion for justice because they are the ones who make the laws. But none of the thousands of judges who had sentenced tens of thousands of innocent people to death or years in concentration camps, was ever held accountable after the end of the Nazi rule. They were protected by the legalistic argument that they had judged according to laws that were then in force; laws whose legitimacy rested solely on the one primordial sin of the 1933 Enabling Act. The parliament of the German Federal Republic, while exempting Nazi crimes from statute of limitations, did not legalize an exemption for the Nazi judges. I guess they had their law experts, and one crow does not peck the other's eyes out. Although the laws are ultimately based on the human sense of justice, injustice is often justified by the letter of the law.

II.7.4   When I Feed The Hungry, They Call Me A Saint. When I Ask Why They Have No Food, They Call Me A Communist[112]

To understand what fighting for justice means in our time we need to understand the multi-level power structure precipitated by the Strife engene. As we have seen, the "us" and "them" can be one nation striving to dominate other nations, as in the case of Nazi Germany, but the "us" and "them" can also be two political parties within a democracy; or the military and the civilian population, as in many Third World countries; or the wealthy ruling class and the class of landless peasants, as in Latin America. The distinction of "us" and "them" is the vehicle in the strife for power and possession, the prototype of a structure that repeats itself at multiple levels. In one country, like Honduras, the winning party creates a government that controls police and military and protects "us," those who own the land, in the fight against "them", the poor peasants and some 'leftist

---

[112] Words of Archbishop Helder Camara

intellectuals'.[113] But the rulers of that country are controlled in turn by a more powerful country, like America, that defends its privileges and the property of its citizens, defending "us," the Americans, against "them," the Communists; and also defending "us," America, against "them," the underdog countries.

II.7.5   Berta Cáceres

In modern times, people who call for justice are simply eliminated by death squadrons under the auspices of the state. Berta Cáceres spoke out against the destructive intrusion of energy companies into the land of the Indigenous Lenca people in Honduras.[114] The police had arrested Lenca protesters en masse, and in 2013, at a demonstration of residents in front of the local headquarters of the Honduran energy company DESA, soldiers opened fire on a crowd of residents, killing one Indigenous leader and seriously injuring several others. Cáceres, who had founded a group that had organized much of the opposition, denounced the countless murders of her fellow activists (in a country in which murderers can count on impunity with 98% certainty). She received multiple death threats. "They follow me. They threaten to kill me, to kidnap me; they threaten my family. That is what we face," she said.

In 2016, gunmen stormed into her home and shot her dead. A longtime friend of Cáceres and a fellow human-rights advocate, the Jesuit priest Ismael Moreno Coto remembered when he met Cáceres who was then a twenty-year-old schoolteacher obsessed with social justice. "She had a special way of making us uncomfortable," he said. "She wouldn't leave us in peace until we were all part of the fight."[115]

Perhaps the country does need cheap electricity; the Honduran Congress had passed a law that awarded contracts to a group of private companies like DESA to realize dozens of hydroelectric dams, some on territory inhabited by the Indigenous Lenca people. But the dams were to be built by the Chinese engineering and construction company Sinohydro with backing of the World Bank. Sure, the country needs electricity, but who knows how much money was channeled to those who passed that law and to those who awarded the contracts.

But to understand what happens in Honduras we must understand the multi-level power structure precipitated by the Strife engene. Hondurans are not a

---

[113] The term used by The New York Times to characterize the six Jesuits murdered by the military in El Salvador in 1989

[114] https://www.newyorker.com/news/news-desk/the-death-of-berta-caceres

[115] Ditto

bunch of crooks and rapists, as the 45th U.S. president would have it, and the problem of Honduras is not simply corruption of government, or the inability of the Honduran people to form a legitimate democracy with a responsible government, nor is it the refusal to embrace the blessings of the free-market economy (as The Economist might argue).

In 2005, Manuel Zelaya, the candidate of the Liberal Party of Honduras, was elected president. He had been a deputy in the National Congress between 1985 and 1998 and had held many positions within the party including a Minister in a previous government. Although Zelaya was from a wealthy business family and had been elected on a conservative platform, he surprised his supporters and opponents with a center-left agenda. During the few years of his government (2006-2009) Honduras made remarkable social progress. Free education for all children was introduced, subsidies to small farmers were provided, the minimum wage was increased by 80%, school meals were guaranteed for more than 1.6 million children from poor families, domestic employees were integrated into the social security system, poverty was reduced by almost 10% during two years of government, and direct state help was provided for 200,000 families in extreme poverty, with free electricity supplied to those Hondurans most in need.

But his political opponents, particularly business elites, did not like the turn from conservative to left-of-center politics and fiercely opposed Honduras joining ALBA, an international cooperation organization based on the idea of social, political, and economic integration between the countries of Latin America and the Caribbean, which was founded by Cuba and Venezuela. Yet Zelaya was legitimately elected president and his achievements made him popular. Whenever elections do not produce the desired result, the courts commonly serve as a last resort to rescue the conservative cause. When Zelaya proposed to hold a (non-binding) referendum asking voters whether to convene a National Constituent Assembly for the purpose of writing a new constitution, the opposition appealed to the supreme court who ruled that such a referendum would be unconstitutional, and when Zelaya went ahead with the planning, he was removed by military coup on 28 June 2009. He said, soldiers assaulted his guards and pulled him out of bed. They brought him to an air force base and flew him into exile in Costa Rica.

While the constitutionality of the planned referendum was disputable, the coup was clearly against the constitution. U.S. President Barack Obama stated: "We believe that the coup was not legal and that President Zelaya remains the president of Honduras, the democratically elected president there" and: "It would be a terrible precedent if we start moving backwards into the era in which we are seeing military coups as a means of political transition, rather than democratic elections." Also a classified cable sent by the U.S. Ambassador to Honduras a few weeks after the incident that was later published, stated that the removal of President Zelaya was a coup. But the U.S. never formally declared that a coup had occurred, and after a while, in a 180-degree turn that surprised the world, Secretary of State Hillary Clinton accepted the new Honduran government as legal, and the U.S. continued its military aid (from 2009 to mid-2016, the U.S. provided about $200 million in military and police aid to Honduras, despite the coup, the violence and the government's human rights violations).[116]

After an interim presidency, the next general elections in 2013 brought Hernández Alvaro to power, the candidate of the National Party. According to documents filed in U.S. district court, Hernández Alvaro was identified as a co-conspirator in a drug trafficking and money laundering case against his brother. Prosecutors say $1.5 million in drug proceeds was used to help elect him in 2013. In 2017, he had himself reelected (against the constitution), winning by a narrow margin after a fraudulent reelection campaign. But the United States swiftly recognized him as the official winner.

How can we understand those decisions by the U.S. administration? Do they not contradict the values our country stands for? What was the rationale behind sacrificing a modest reformer president like Zelaya for the drug lord Hernández? All U.S. governments in recent decades tried to avert the flow of illegal immigrants across the Southern border. But after the coup of 2009, with ensuing corruption and police impunity, with persecution of opponents, peasants, and indigenous protesters by the state security forces, the crime rate increased massively and more than 13,000 Honduran children crossed the U.S. borders from October 2013 until May 2014, a more than tenfold increase compared to 2009.[117] I know one of them, the son of a peasant farmer who himself had tried to flee poverty and violence but lost his legs when he fell from a train while crossing Mexico. After the father returned home mutilated, the son decided to make it to the North. At the age of 15 he crossed the Rio Grande using plastic bottles strapped to his arms, and then helped others cross the river, going back and forth, to make some money. Once in the U.S., he earned money as an undocumented worker of which he sent some back home to his family to help

---

[116] Jonathan Blitzer, "Should the U.S. Still Be Sending Military Aid to Honduras?" The New Yorker, 17 August 2016.

[117] Dan Beeton, "The legacy children of the Honduran coup." Al Jazeera, 28 June 2014, http://america.aljazeera.com/opinions/2014/6/violence-in-hondurasunaccompaniedminorsimmigrationtous.html

them plant coffee trees on their land. But a few years later, before they brought fruit, a disease wiped them out. Now son and father and other family members live undocumented in the U.S.

Immigration across the Southern border is a problem U.S. governments have tried to address for decades. It began with the civil war of El Salvador that drove millions out of the country; between 1980 and 2015 about 1.1 million Salvadoreans migrated to the U.S. The U.S. administration sided more or less openly with the military-led junta in the fight against the leftist guerilla organization FMLN. That was during the time of the Cold War. But when Zelaya became president, the Cold War had ended long ago. It was 16 years after the collapse of the Soviet Union, so the threat of world communism was gone. Accepting Zelaya's illegal removal from office paved the way for a drug lord as president of Honduras with the predictable rise of corruption and violence and an avalanche of people fleeing the country trying to reach the U.S. Did the Obama administration not remember the flood of refugees when the Reagan and Bush administrations backed the military regime in El Salvador?

Of course they knew. As Obama said: "It would be a terrible precedent," but it happened. Political transition by military coup, rather than democratic elections. The decision of the U.S. to recognize the coup as a legal transition is remarkable in two ways. First, the coup against Zelaya was a slap in the face of anybody who has a sense of justice, not just because it violated the letter of the constitution, but because it predictably led to an unlawful regime and widespread human rights violations across the country. Second, it was rationally against the interest of the U.S. because Zelaya established a responsible government, perhaps the first Honduras has ever seen, initiating social reforms that had the chance to heal the country from the cycle of violence and gave people hope that their country will provide them with a livable future. When people have that hope, they do not leave their homes; the avalanche of refugees is the result of hopelessness. The decision was neither just nor prudent.

So, why does an American government go down that path, against the cause of justice, and against rational pondering? The reason, I think, is that even a president like Obama, who had shown passion for justice in his previous life, had to make concessions to members of his government and members of congress that were strongly dominated by the Strife engene: nationalist, xenophobic, racist, and authoritarian. Members who, despite their oaths of office, do not really respect their constitution; members who insist that the U.S. must dominate the countries beyond its Southern border and continue to exploit their resources as it has done for the past hundred years. Once again, the voice of justice was drowned in the roar of nationalism.

The Strife engene makes the Honduran elites strive to control their country, defending "their" privileges against "them," the peasants and 'leftist intellectuals'. But the elites in turn are controlled by the more powerful United States which defend their privileges and the property of their citizens, defending "us," America, against "them," the Latin American countries. A powerful country obsessed with the mission of defending the sacred order of free-market capitalism against the threat of Socialism. Many Americans probably perceived the new president of Honduras Manuel Zelaya as a danger; could he not become another Hugo Chavez? Honduras another Venezuela? Sure, Honduras is not sitting on the world's biggest oil reserves as Venezuela does, but Honduras has bananas! When the Strife engene compels people to make decisions, their decisions are not rational. They act according to their gut feelings. The urge and the desires created by the social engenes (whether good or evil) are principally short sighted. The Strife and Family engenes react to the present situation; they care for the immediate family and the contemporary people. Engenes are mechanisms, they provide only a foggy idea of the future. To realize the consequences in ten years and for the next generation, today's decisions must be based on reasoning, not gut feelings.

PART THREE

WHAT CAN WE LEARN?

III.1 WE NEED TO UNDERSTAND

The facts that I recounted above in "What it did" are well known. Fortunately there are now many documentations about the Nazi terror and the Holocaust, and efforts to keep the memory of the victims alive. This is absolutely necessary because societies have a short memory, especially if it is shameful. But just remembering and hoping it will never happen again is not sufficient. I feel with Hannah Arendt: We need to understand. Understanding means using the power of our rational mind to come to grips with the historical facts. Perhaps seeing these events on the background of evolution gives us a new perspective; being aware of the fundamental conditions that drove the evolution of hominids makes us see the recent history in a different light.

III.1.1 The Roots of Fascism

Given the historical facts described above, it is hard to understand how people could act as they did, why they did not see what was going on, and why so many Germans held on to their wrong convictions even years after the Nazi regime was abolished. If human behavior were entirely a matter of education, it would be hard to understand all this. When growing up, Hans and Sophie Scholl had both been in the *Hitler Jugend*, the Nazi youth organization, and were enthusiastic about that experience. But that did not keep them from seeing the truth about the Nazi regime. Thus, their ethical judgments were resistant to indoctrination and environment. And conversely, people growing up after the war in East Germany (the DDR) did learn the truth about the Nazi terror and the Holocaust; in contrast to post-war West Germany, schools in the DDR taught the history of the diverse resistance movements, portraying (some of) their victims as heroes. But the recent Neo-Nazi movement is strong among the people who were taught in those schools. Why did education not immunize them against Hitler's ideas? How can we understand these paradoxical results?

The reason why the Nazi rule had such strong and lasting effects is that it appealed to the people's Strife engene. The Strife engene calls for the nation to be united behind a leader, it considers political compromise a weakness and the democratic order a sign of decadence. In the aftermath of the defeat in the First World War this engene was depressed in German people; they were humiliated and craved for national resurrection and revenge, and, perhaps most importantly, they were scared by loss of their income, the economic breakdown, and the threat of a communist revolution. Hitler promised the German people everything they wanted. The racism and the lawlessness had only a marginal presence in people's consciousness. As we saw in the discussion of the evolutionary roots of Left and Right, Right means both autocratic rule and protection of property. The election of Hindenburg, the war hero, for president in 1925 already forebode the turn of the political climate from democratic to autocratic. Hindenburg not only sympathized with the idea of returning to royal rule, but he was also a big landowner in East Prussia. In 1931, when the government was going to expand a program in which the state was buying indebted large land properties to resettle landless farmers as a way to alleviate unemployment during the economic crisis, this measure was decried as "agrarian Bolshevism" in the circle of landowners, and Hindenburg blocked the program, leaving the landless farmers on their own. Paul von Hindenburg, the noble war hero, the president and father of the nation, was also father of a son, the heir of his property. Having defended the nation, he defended the rights of his class, the landowners. How right was Kant when he cautioned that common moral judgment is easily corrupted by interest. Unfortunately, the nationalism produced by the Strife engene combines strife for subjugation of the supposed enemy with material interest.

Likewise, it would be hard to understand how a Christian society could accept as normal the slave economy, which produced wealth for a class of slave owners at the expense of denying the enslaved their human rights, indeed, in complete negation of the Christian values. Unfortunately, the Religious engene regularly ties with the Strife engene, giving the blatant injustice the pious blessing. The "national interest" easily overwrites any moral concerns. Indeed, Christian societies had no issues with the subjugation of the conquered when they established their colonies. When the fascist Italy attacked Ethiopia, the archbishop of Milan blessed the departing troupes with the words, "We are working with God's help in this national and catholic mission of the good, especially in this moment when on the battlefields of Ethiopia the banner of Italy triumphantly advances the holy cross of Jesus Christ."[118] To understand means to be aware of, and prepared to control, the irrational influence of those engenes.

III.1.2 Blaming Hitler

In a manner that is common among historians, some authors now portray Hitler as the key figure in the German disaster, claiming that without Hitler there would have been no Holocaust. It is always tempting to find explanations after the fact. So, Hitler would be the cause. But to blame Hitler's extreme antisemitism for the Holocaust would be a grave error. Given the statistical nature of the expression of engenes, extremely hateful and racist individuals are not unusual, and that a man gets intoxicated by feeling power is quite common. The truth is, there was nothing exceptional or demonic about Hitler. There were many candidate advocates of hate, and one was successful – in a roulette, one is always successful – and that one happened to be Adolf Hitler. It could have been someone else as well, and a Holocaust would have happened in some form, perhaps not exactly the same, but similar. The historical situation of the young Weimar Republic and its constitutional flaws were the fertile ground for the seeds of fascism. It is true that the *Führer* played a central role, naturally. He commanded the institutions of power, the police, the *Gestapo*, and the military. He came to direct the war, which is not surprising; generals are not famous for their high IQ. They took his word for the voice of destiny. All this does not mean that it could not have happened without Adolf Hitler.

Also, the special circumstances that helped him to power were not unique in world history. They were unfortunate, and we should learn from history to make sure such circumstances will not concur again. The disaster occurred because it was so easy for Hitler to entice the masses and obtain the blessing of the people for his purposes. It was so easy because he appealed to the Strife engene in millions of people, insinuating that their lives and possessions were threatened by powerful enemies, those surrounding the country as well as those secretly lurking within the country, among them the Socialists and the Jews. Simply invoking the two powerful stimulants of the Strife engene, comradery with their countrymen, and aggression against "the others," he poisoned the people with a mix of sweet *völkisch* dreams and bitter xenophobic hate. The oppressing insight is that it does not need a powerful figure to do this; the power is in the nature of that engene. It can easily be done again.

---

[118] Cited after K.H. Deschner, „*Mit Gott und den Faschisten.*" Stuttgart, Günther (1965).

Aging autocrats are often suspected of undergoing pathological mental alterations. Developing mental problems have been invoked to underly the increasing cruelty and irrationality of Hitler, Stalin, and Mao Zedong, and recently to explain Donald Trump's behavior when he incited a mob in an attempt to reverse the election result instead of accepting his defeat, as well as Wladimir Putin's decision to invade Ukraine. I think this is a misinterpretation. First, the idea of pathological versus normal behavior is mistaken because the strength of expression of behavioral engenes varies continuously, and what appears pathological are individuals in the fringes of distributions. Second, what really happens may not be an alteration of their brains, but a change in their environments. Once in power, autocrats succeed in surrounding themselves with obedients and sycophants, which enhances the dominance of their Strife engene. The mental isolation caused by the environment brings out the irrationality of this engene which already controlled their life when they were younger; the Strife engene in its purest form. This interpretation is supported by psychological studies showing that the influence of genes tends to increase with age, one of the surprising results of behavioral genetics.[119] It is based on correlating psychological measures between identical and fraternal twins, and between siblings raised in different families and siblings raised in the same family. The reason is thought to be the effects of environment and education which level out genetic differences in young people, but weaken later in life, resulting a stronger influence of the genetic factor.

III.1.3 Understanding the Evolutionary Roots of Evil Behavior

Being aware of the inherited roots of evil behavior does not mean to demonize human inheritance. The problem is not the 'dark side' of human nature in general. Like other brain engenes, the Strife engene and its components vary in strength of expression between individuals. Only few are endowed with an extreme drive to rule, and not many may be prone to absolute obedience to the leader. But the fraction of such people in a society does not measure the power of the Strife engene. Its real power comes from the interaction between leader and followers. The tragedy of a democratic society is that some political activists or leaders, people who shape the political climate, intuitively understand this side of human nature and deliberately exploit it to their personal advantage. I have tried above (I.4.9.8 "Ideologies of oppression") to explain the Strife engene with the dry words of science, but political leaders understand its mechanisms intuitively. Effective demagogues know intuitively how to pull its strings. They

---

[119] R Plomin, "Blueprint: How DNA makes us who we are." Cambridge, MIT Press (2018).

know that it needs no education or indoctrination to get people to respond; the Strife engene is there, it's there from birth. They know how to incite passion, fear, and hate, and they know how the Strife engene makes people susceptible to conspiracy theories. They realize that a large part of the people of the country – and a large part of the voters – do not really want democracy. The ones who respond may be a minority, but many others are impressed by the demonstrations of power, by masses chanting slogans in unison, by hundreds walking in lockstep, they feel the comfort of companionship – and follow. And those who are just standing by are surprised by the outbreak of hate.

History shows the fundamental difference between the Strife- and Family engenes. While the Strife engene has unbounded power across the group, the power of the Family engene is only strong between people that are close, but declines with distance. As pointed out in Part I (I.4.11 "Short- and long-range engenes"), the Family engene, which stimulates brotherly feelings of sense of fairness, can only incite large popular movements in situations of crisis, when the burden of injustice becomes unbearable. The masses then have momentum for a short time, as long as the common pain induces solidarity. With the slogan "*Liberté, égalité, fraternité*" the fathers and mothers of the French revolution tried to engage the Family engene for their cause, but the success was short lived; after a few years, brotherly feelings gave way to loyalty to the emperor, and what drove history was not the strife for the ideals of the revolution, but the strife for the glory of the fatherland. Also in the Russian October Revolution the socialists tried to engage brotherly feelings by addressing people as comrades (*товарищ; Genosse* in communist Germany). It stimulated feelings of solidarity among subjects under the tyranny of the Czar, but did not help the revolution. For the revolution to win and survive, its leaders had to appeal to the Strife engene. Only the call to defend "us" (the revolution) against "them" (the counterrevolution) moved the masses. When the Weimar Republic tumbled, many Germans were happy to trade parliamentary discourses for the word of the one *Führer* and change their identity from equal and brotherly to obedient and *völkisch*. Mao Zedong understood the transience of the revolutionary impetus generated by the Family engene and therefore proclaimed from time to time the threat of a fictitious new enemy of the revolution, thus instigating hate responses in the millions. In the resulting crusades millions lost their lives. He was keenly aware that the Family engene, which had initiated the revolution that brought him to power, could not sustain it, and only the Strife engene could.

It is trying to hear politicians in the U.S. appeal to "our family values," pretending that empathy and sense of justice will move the people, while the tallies of votes show that in fact their choices are dictated by Strife engene and Religious engene: economic status and political power according to ethnic, racial, and religious identity. Often the appeal to "family values" is used as a disguised call for religious intolerance regarding sexual orientation. The endless repetitions of phrases like "this country that I love so much" and "the greatest nation on earth" during presidential campaigns and inaugurations in the U.S. reveal the truth: igniting the Strife engene is a more effective way to move people than appealing to reason, compassion, and sense of justice.

Systematic defamation of the opponent, lying to the public and spreading false rumors are ancient tools of demagogy. They are effective, and the victim has virtually no defense; even proof of the truth cannot repair the damage (*semper aliquid haeret* – some of it always sticks). Unfortunately, the old tools were magnified enormously with the advent of modern mass media in combination with psychological methodology.

According to historians it was the First World War when governments started to use the newly available mass communication media systematically to influence public opinion towards accepting the war and their specific goals. Hitler and his propaganda minister Joseph Goebbels took lessons from the American propaganda under Woodrow Wilson and perfected the method. Here is what Demm and Sterling write in their article "Propaganda":

Propaganda could be used to arouse hatred of the foe, warn of the consequences of defeat, and idealize one's own war aims in order to mobilize a nation, maintain its morale, and make it fight to the end. It could explain setbacks by blaming scapegoats such as war profiteers, hoarders, defeatists, dissenters, pacifists, left-wing socialists, spies, shirkers, strikers, and sometimes enemy aliens so that the public would not question the war itself or the existing social and political system.[120]

What is missing from this description is the reason why propaganda works. It is not simply a method cleverly devised by the respective leader to achieve his goals. It comes from the intuitive insight of how to appeal to the Strife engenes of the millions. The leader may lie, but the people do not check whether his words are true or false. The response does not depend on the truth value of the word, but only on how it fits the receptors of the Strife engene. The leader knows he must tell them what they want to hear. Goebbels knew this when Hitler rose

---

[120] E Demm and CH Sterling, "Propaganda" in SC Tucker and P Roberts, eds. *The Encyclopedia of World War I: A Political, Social, and Military History.* ABC-CLIO (2005) 3:941.

to power, and Tucker Carlson (a successful cable TV anchor in the U.S.) knew it when Trump rose to power, and the leaders of today's right-wing parties in Europe know it, waiting for their turn. Their sermons always paint the threat of a powerful enemy, of "them" who are about to crush "us;" in Hitler's time, the alleged conspiracy of the communists and the world Jewry; today, socialism and the immigrants and refugees, and the demographic growth of minorities supposedly instrumentalized by the opponent party in the elections. Like the Nazis hailed "German culture" which they claimed to be under the threat from "degenerate art," Carlson and colleagues warn of "the collapse of Western civilization."

The sermons target not only receptors of the Strife engene, inciting hate against the alleged enemy, but typically also the Religious engene (which likewise appeals to the masses). The Nazis propagated "German Christianity" and "German values," Carlson portrays Christianity under threat from Islam and other religions. Mechanisms of moral intolerance, characteristic of the Religious engene, are particularly effective in inciting hate. Goebbels preached hate against homosexuals. Carlson incites hate against proponents of gay rights and same-sex marriage. He also attacks advocates of equal rights for women, portraying feminism as "harmful to masculinity," insinuating that it would cause birthrates to drop (meaning: among Whites). One of the most effective slanders in recent U.S. history claims that leaders of the Democratic Party are pedophiles and run a secret child trafficking business, an insinuation that arouses one of the most powerful sexual taboos. Today's unsupervised social media provide unlimited power of communication for both the truth and the lies, but the lies overwhelm the truth.

Any rational argument is trumped by the power of the irrational engenes. What convinces people is not the objective truth, but the irrational 'truth'. In 2012, after the school shooting at Sandy Hook in which 20 children and 6 staff members lost their lives, the irrationality went so far that, when a television anchor suggested that the news of the school shooting might have been "staged" by the government to push for stricter gun control laws, and there had been no shooting at all, polls showed that 30 percent of the people asked had doubts that a shooting had in fact occurred. These people were unconvinced despite having seen extensive reports of the tragedy and live coverage of the grieving parents on television.

Political lies can be simple and the truth easily verifiable, but still effective. The day before a mob stormed the U.S. Capitol on January 6, 2021, an observant congresswoman noticed a group of visitors with a guide giving them a tour around the extensive complex. It called her attention because someone had apparently given those people access despite the Capitol being closed to visitors for the COVID-19 pandemic. When she reported this shortly after the riot, the presumed 'guide' and other Republican congressmen denied that there had been any visitors, claiming that they had scrutinized the recordings of the security cameras and found no evidence of a tour. They went so far as to denounce the congresswoman as a liar and to file ethical claims against her to make her shut up. But later, when a congressional committee inspected the recordings and apparently found footage showing a tour guided by that congressman, he conceded that he had "given his family a private tour." And when it then became apparent that it had been a larger group of adults, he conceded he had shown around about a dozen people. So, it became clear that he had broken the prohibition to let visitors enter the Capitol and then repeatedly lied about it.

One might think "how stupid" of that congressman to deny what would inevitably come out. But his political calculation was not stupid at all. His continued denial of any tour through the Capitol was applauded by his partisan colleagues and their leaders who were trying to cast the well-planned storming of the capitol as a spontaneous riot of angry voters, and none of them felt shame when it finally turned out to be a lie. It was a successful scheme. All the time while the lie was out there, it was received as the truth by millions of Republican voters, and the Democrat congresswoman's report as a scheme to hurt their party, and few of them would later pay attention when the truth came out. The lies overwhelm the truth because the Strife engene magnifies the power of the lies.

The power of this kind of political scheme has never been clearer in my lifetime than in the weeks after the 2020 U.S. presidential election. Mr. Trump, the incumbent president who lost, tried to overturn the result by forcing his vice president to refuse the formal certification of the electoral counts on January 6, 2021. Plenty of legal advisors explained to him that this would be both unconstitutional and unprecedented in U.S. history, which he well understood. But he proceeded with his plan, using the legal discussions in the mass media as a smoke screen that gave the public the impression that there was indeed a constitutional ambiguity, although the Electoral Count Act of 1887 was simple and clear, saying that the vice president has the duty to certify the counts, and nothing else. Trump's demagogic intuition told him that he could convince millions of his voters simply by appealing to their Strife engenes, and that their emotional responses would easily overwhelm the legal considerations. Any thinking American could understand that it was not in the spirit of the American Constitution to give one man, vice president or other, the power to choose the president. If it were, Al Gore, who narrowly lost the 2000 elections while being vice president, could have simply decided to be the new president.

Using this scheme, Mr. Trump almost succeeded in staging a coup d'état, which other dictators only achieved by using the power of the military. The strategy is simple: Speak to the masses following your gut feelings, and don't worry about legal issues or political correctness. It is much easier to mobilize the irrational engenes than to build on rational insights. Once you do away with the distinction between true and false, the rule of self-consistency, have no moral constraints, and no fear of legal liability because you are the president, or a candidate backed by millions of voters, political acting becomes very easy. – One man of mediocre intelligence confronted an army of law professors and truthful politicians, and almost won.

III.1.4 Understanding the Roots of Moral Judgment

As explained in my introduction to the concept of engenes, I think that not only our behavior, but also our perception of values builds on a number of fundamental social faculties that are genetically preprogrammed, like the ability to feel and give love, to feel compassion, the values of honesty and fairness, the desire to feel joy in a group, and the need to be accepted as a member of the group (and each faculty is expressed to varying degrees in the individual – engenes have statistical distributions).

We are born with a set of values that may be strengthened or weakened by education and upbringing. Values are often associated with religion, but they are basically innate and only the specifics of a religion are taken up from the environment. Religious people often see this the other way round: they think religion gives us the values that determine our social behavior. And consequently they feel these values threatened by people of another religion or by a progressively secular society. Thus, for religious people, it should be a comfort to learn that the basic values are innate and will be reproduced by every new generation, even without the specific religious environment. They can relax. They don't need to get stressed out watching over the values that would otherwise get lost. They are not responsible for enforcing moral laws.

On the other hand, people who are all too convinced of the progress of civilization and the power of Enlightenment should watch out. Knowing that human nature comes with a powerful Strife engene will make us see Enlightenment and the efforts of education in a different light. The making of this engene during evolution implies that under certain circumstances it will produce eruptions of hate, like poisonous gas eruptions of a volcano. Here also, many people are in error, believing that such negative behaviors must be caused by the wrong education or by a childhood psychic trauma etc., and these people are generally surprised when they witness evil behaviors.

That human nature has good and bad sides is, of course, not a new insight. Many religions acknowledge that; one side is divine, the image of God, the other is evil, in popular wisdom incorporated by the devil. Although Christian theology does not recognize a devil, it acknowledges the primordial sin: all humans are guilty of their sins and the sins of their fathers and ancestors, and they cannot ever free themselves of that sin, and that is why God sent his son who saves humans by making atonement through his painful death. This kind of theology might subsume the Holocaust and other Nazi crimes under the primordial sin.

This theological interpretation contrasts with the rational view taken by many historians. They see the German disaster as a result of circumstances, a historical constellation, perhaps including German military tradition, their authoritarian heritage, and the lopsided peace treaty of Versailles.

The ideas put forward in this book share neither of these views. Considering evolution we can see the roots of a number of human traits, corresponding to both the 'divine' and the 'evil' sides of human nature. The German disaster and other genocides of history are not historical accidents, disasters that just happen under certain circumstances that we must try to avoid. No, they are the direct consequence of inherited structures and behavioral programs of the brain that every human shares to some degree, larger or smaller. Recognizing these fateful inheritances also does not mean to accept the concept of the primordial sin. Understanding the horrible crimes that some of us committed as a result of an outbreak of hate-exuding engenes does not mean that everybody is capable of such crimes, and that everybody should examine their soul for such evil components. Hannah Arendt pointed out this kind of attitude among the post-war generation of West Germany, young intellectuals saying that "everyone has a small Eichmann in themselves," which she found annoying: "I don't have a small Eichmann in me."

The expression of each engene varies between people. Only a small fraction of people have an unusually strong disposition for developing reprehensible nationalism and racism and at the same time lack the mechanisms that in other people control the drive of those hateful motivations. A father who is a ruthless hard-core Nazi can have a son who is caring and righteous. Hans Frank, a lawyer who after the German invasion of Poland in 1939 became Governor-General of the occupied Polish territories, instituted a reign of terror against the civilian population. He lived in a castle like a king, while overseeing the use of forced labor and the extermination camps, being directly involved in the mass murder of Jews. But his son Niklas, who grew up in Cracow where his mother posed as the "Queen of Poland," recognized the lawlessness and cruelty of his father. The son suffered under the burden of his father's monstrous guilt and as a journalist and writer later fomented awareness of the past among Germans.[121] His education and childhood experience did not make him like his father. Another striking example showing that inheritance can outweigh education and environment are the sons of Frederick Trump, an American real estate developer and businessman, the father of Donald Trump, the 45th U.S. president. Fred Trump was an ambitious, ruthless and bigot entrepreneur whose principle was to always fight back when attacked, and to sue back when sued, even when sued by the state for illegal racial discrimination. He wanted his oldest son, Fred Trump Jr. to take over his business, but the son had a different character and other plans, he wanted to become a pilot. The father wanted his son to be "invulnerable" in personality so he could take over the family business, but Fred Jr. was the opposite. Trump instead elevated Donald to become his business heir, teaching him to "be a killer", and telling him, "You are a king."[122] As it turned out, Donald became what his father wanted, a "killer" and – president of the U.S. But the elder son, Fred Trump Jr., the pilot, whom he constantly attacked, denigrated, and ridiculed, became an alcoholic and committed suicide at age 48. This family drama shows that even the strongest pressure of education and the power of material inheritance are powerless against the genetic inheritance.

I do not want to downplay the power of education and environment in developing our moral judgments and how we perceive friend and foe. Having had my children attend public schools of Baltimore City, I know the importance of family and environment, and what it does being raised by a single mother in a broken society in a run-down neighborhood. And the Baltimore School for the Arts showed me what a wonderful antidote arts education can be.

Education does make a difference. When I was a little boy, my brother and I played war with armies of toy soldiers that we had cast from old lead pipes. We had German troops, painted gray, and Russian troops, painted khaki. We knew about the German defeat – there was a steady trickle of people in worn clothes walking through the village where I grew up, people coming from the Russian

---

[121] Niklas Frank, "In the Shadow of the Reich." Knopf (1991).

[122] Mary L. Trump, "Too Much and Never Enough." New York, Simon & Schuster (2020).

occupied zone who had crossed the green border that was only a couple of miles away (before the 'iron curtain' was fortified with fences, watch towers, and mines, Russian troops guarded the crossings). In our war games, the German army was outnumbered by the Russian army and would have been defeated, had there not been the Bearish army who came to their rescue, in blue uniforms, commanded by Emperor Pooh, and together the Bears and Germans crushed the Russians. But my mother was passionate about literature and fond of 'the Russian soul' (which was not uncommon among Germans, see the circle of Lou Andreas Salomé). She read us Tolstoy and Dostoyevsky with the effect that, in high school, my brother took evening classes in Russian language (which was not regularly taught in West Germany) until he could read Dostoyevsky's novels in the original. Certainly, education does more than giving us knowledge and skills, it also teaches us who we are and how we feel about "the others."

Still, I cannot help thinking that someone like colonel Dyer – who commanded his troops to shoot at a crowd of unarmed civilians, including children, gathered for an important Sikh festival; people who ignored or did not know about the curfew, thousands in an enclosed public garden from which they could not escape; and then commended his soldiers for having done a good job, – I cannot help thinking that someone like Dyer is born with a defective compassion engene that education cannot repair.[123]

III.1.5 The Impact of the Extremes

The strength of expression of the social engenes varies between individuals – each engene has a statistical distribution that has fringes of extreme overexpression and extreme underexpression. I have argued above that extreme strength and extreme weakness of certain engenes can have fateful consequences. I discussed four topics: genocide – racial discrimination – poverty – passion for justice; arguing that in the case of the former three the evolutionary root is an overexpression of the Strife engene, or of a combination of Strife- and

---

[123] The massacre happened on 13 April 1919 in Amritsar, Punjab, India. Dyer had his squadron block the main exit and gave orders to shoot, first at the people who crowded near the exits in panic, and then at those lying on the ground. After the action he gave no orders to look after the dead and the wounded. In his own words, this act "was not to disperse the meeting but to punish the Indians for disobedience." He thought this was necessary to protect order and save the British empire. Dyer was born in India to British parents and received his early education in India, but from eleven attended Midleton College in County Cork, Ireland, and then briefly studied medicine at the Royal College of Surgeons in Ireland, before deciding on a military career.

Religious engenes, whereas in the case of the latter (passion for justice) it is an unusual strength of ethical engenes. However, it is important to see that the impact of an engene depends on its range of action, and engenes differ: Strife- and Religious engenes are 'long-range', whereas the Family engene is 'short-range', that is, the former appeal to the millions, whereas the latter works only across the family or small circles of friends. Strife engene and Religious engene divide people into "us" and "them," the Strife engene according to ethnicity or race or class, the Religious engene according to religious convictions. Thus, each individual is part of a large community. In contrast, people with passion for justice often find themselves alone or in a small circle of friends. John Brown had 21 followers in the Harpers Ferry attack which cost the lives of 14 people; Adolf Hitler had at least 11.7 million followers (number of people who voted for him in the election of November 1932), and 50 million people died in his war. This is not because Hitler had supernatural power, or was a better commander than John Brown, but because his speeches activated millions of Strife engenes.

Someone with a deficient Moral engene may become a criminal and perhaps kill some people; but someone with an exceptionally strong Strife engene who's Moral engene is also deficient may kill millions. Thus, the fringes of the distributions of Strife- and Religious engenes are fateful because these engenes act across the masses.

III.1.6 What Just Is, Is Not Always Justice[124]

Does trying to understand the inheritable factors mean accepting what is there as normal? Trying to understand the biological roots of behavior is often decried as "positivism" – accepting what is there as a given, rather than trying to change the world. Does the notion of inherited brain engenes imply that we can do nothing about it? Not at all.

Understanding the mechanisms of genocide we will hopefully abandon nationalism and become more suspicious about patriotism.

Knowing about the filthy relationship between Strife and Religious engenes we realize the importance of the state being secular.

Knowing about the common root of authoritarian rule and property protection we will be more reluctant to elect billionaires for president.

---

[124] Phrase borrowed from Amanda Gorman's poem she read at the 2021 inauguration of the U.S. president.

Knowing the role of the frontal lobe in controlling risk taking and responsibility, and knowing that this part of the brain keeps developing until the age of 25, we might consider stopping to recruit young men as cannon fodder, and instead give them more saying in politics and use their idealism and courageous minds for the task of reforming our society.

Knowing about the evolutionary basis of the supremacy ideology, those of us who are American will stop scrutinizing the psyche of mass shooters, but instead put a ban on automatic and semi-automatic weapons (at the federal level, of course). Instead of pursuing the crime of using an automatic weapon, we would criminalize the possession of it. To punish the *intention* of mass murder is difficult, to punish *possession* of an automatic weapon is easy.

Understanding the nature of the role of genders might cure us from the illusion that women and men have equal minds, and that we should just wait for society to become so enlightened as to grant them equal opportunities. No, the prototypes of male and female brains and minds are fundamentally different, and there will not be equal opportunity unless we have laws and institutions that guarantee their equal rights.

The evolution of the role of genders in society explains why women feel they need to watch over sexual morality, even to the extreme of hurting their own cause. In the 2016 presidential election, Hillary Clinton lost critical votes because many women blamed her – not for her own faulty behavior, no – for tolerating sexual misbehavior *of her husband.* Knowing about the peculiar Moral engene, and knowing that it is not going away despite rational insight and election campaigning, one will be less surprised about women's lack of success in elections.

A glaring example of gender-based injustice that springs from this evolutionary Moral engene is the way society treats rape victims. The drive of men to have sex ignoring the woman's consent, or even relishing her non-consent, is a relic of the 'ancient regime'. Before the two-parent family evolved that was the most efficient way for males to procreate their genes. And the counterpart in female behavior was to give in and hold still, the manner that optimizes the chance of insemination leading to pregnancy. In species where females signal their fertile period and males compete with each other for having a chance, that was the optimal way to reproduce. Despite the turn that human evolution took, this ancient heritage is still with us. The corresponding social behavior is rape. When a man uses violence to have sex it is not uncommon that the victimized woman effectively gets paralyzed in response, to her own surprise, "I felt like I wanted to scream or yell or push him. And I don't even know why, but my body just wouldn't react."[125]

In the 'new regime', after the two-parent family genes had won, that ancient behavior has been loaded with taboos and outlawed. The injustice is that the victimized woman, in addition to being traumatized, feels shame and guilt, and this feeling is reinforced by the society. When her female friends find out how she responded during the rape they are appalled, "You didn't do anything? Why didn't you fight? Why didn't you cry for help?" Undoubtedly, this has also been the response of law enforcement officers in countless cases of rape, casting doubt on the credibility of the victim's report.

But understanding our evolutionary pedigree, the occurrence of male sexual violence and the female passive response are not surprising. They are just responses of the standard primate Sex engene.[126] Of course, understanding the evolutionary aspect will not help a victim to get rid of the memory of a traumatic experience, but it will hopefully change how the society reacts.

—

Reflecting upon the above, it seems clear that the evolution of behavioral traits is something we must acknowledge not only for its scientific evidence, but also for its importance for understanding human society. And yet, there are anthropologists who reject sociobiology and evolutionary psychology altogether. They do this because the evolutionary argument has been used to justify social injustice; that is, to justify the persistence of unfair conditions with racist arguments.

Just like Social Darwinism fathered eugenics programs, right-wing politicians, particularly in the U.S., have used the scientific assertion of inheritable traits as a pretext to oppose government spending on social programs, for example programs that would alleviate the existing inequality of education. Programs addressing the obvious and well-documented discrepancies in duration of school attendance and academic achievement between rich and poor are criticized as a waste of tax money because, the argument goes, these

---

[125] Jen Percy, "Paralyzed," New York Times Magazine, Aug 22, 2023. https://www.nytimes.com/2023/08/22/magazine/immobility-rape-trauma-freeze.html
[126] What is surprising is the variety of bogus psychological/evolutionary explanations that have been proposed, such as interpreting the victim's reaction as tonic immobility or as a case of 'freeze reflex' which is a common response in many animal species to avert attention of predators.

discrepancies are simply the result of inherited differences in intelligence. This argument is openly racist, claiming that African Americans, Hispanics, or other Colored people, are less intelligent than Whites. It is clear from what I said under "Whence it came" that this argument is dictated by the Strife engene; it discriminates "us" and "them". Also typical, the argument focusses narrowly on the trait of intelligence whose definition is notoriously problematic (which is why scientists prefer measures that have objective relevance for society, like educational attainment and economic achievement). The narrow focus on intelligence shows that the argument is about competition in society. Lack of education facilitates oppression. The privileged try to keep "them" uneducated and thereby exclude "them" from competing for power and possession, reviving the theme of Social Darwinism, "survival of the fittest."

As the anthropologist Richard Perry points out, the neoliberal emphasis on free markets and deregulation in the U.S. has led to drastic funding reductions for the Head Start preschool program that would assist disadvantaged children, as well as other social assistance programs aimed at providing a minimum support for the poor.[127] Perry blames these calamitous developments on the sciences of sociobiology and evolutionary psychology that he thinks assert "biological determinism," and thus rejects these sciences. He also argues that the term race should be used only in quotes, because it lacks a scientific basis. But no sociobiologist or evolutionary psychologist claims that the genes *determine* our lives, but only that they have some influence. Authors who reject the science ignore that those right-wing politicians who misuse the biological argument don't care a damn about the science; they only care about winning voters, and they know that racist arguments work. Instead of rejecting the science one must reject the faulty claims and reveal the distortions of the scientific evidence (which Perry tries in the remainder of his book).

Many leftists reject the idea of sociobiology because they believe they are defending a good cause; like the tailor in the story I mentioned in the Introduction, who chased away his sons because he believed them to be liars. They reject the science with good intentions. This was a common attitude among intellectuals in the decades after World War II. Having witnessed the horrors of Nazi racism, they thought the ship had veered off course to the right and must

---

[127] Richard J. Perry, "Killer Apes, Naked Apes, & Just Plain Nasty People. The Misuse and Abuse of Science in Political Discourse." Baltimore: Johns Hopkins University Press (2015).

now be steered to the left. And even a little bit too much would be ok because it's for a good cause.

But rejecting the evolutionary roots of human behavior hurts the cause of justice. When policy makers use statistics of test scores (such as average SAT scores or similar) to evaluate the success of educational programs, or for comparing different school systems, the results are misleading. In fact, those test statistics measure the combined effects of education *and* genes. For example, when comparing public schools with private schools, tests will almost certainly sample different genetic pools because public schools must accept children unconditionally, whereas private schools can select. The selection makes a big difference because of the inter-individual variations of genetic code. The genetic make-up of a child is not locked up in a vault but displayed all the time by the child's behavior, one can see the behavioral engenes at work, and the experienced interviewer of a private school will intuitively select 'the best' of the applicants. Thus, the average test scores of public and private schools reflect two populations whose genetic makeups may differ considerably. Thus, the comparison is lopsided. For a valid comparison of the quality of the two types of schools, the genetic makeup of the test subjects must be taken into account. Correlational methods can separate the effects of education and genes, provided the tested subjects are also genotyped. (It sounds unbelievable, but en-masse genotyping has become easy thanks to recent technological progress.) Academic achievement statistics that ignore the influence of biased gene sampling are just one example of many allegedly "objective" evaluations of schools and social programs. No doubt, the evolutionary aspect matters for social justice.[128]

III.2 DEMOCRACY BUILDS ON INHERITED MORAL INTUITION

III.2.1 Political Ethics

Understanding the ambivalence of human evolutionary inheritance, we see the necessity for making decisions about right and wrong, including the option of deciding rationally. Kant noticed that people generally make good moral decisions by common sense, but he argues that we cannot rely on moral intuition because it can easily be corrupted by interest.

---

[128] Kathryn Paige Harden, "The Genetic Lottery: Why DNA Matters for Social Equality." Princeton University Press (2021).

He writes: "One cannot help but admire how common sense is so much better in practical than in theoretical judgments" and, in a rhetorical question, he asks whether philosophers with their theoretical arguments should interfere with people's common sense. But then he says: "It's a wonderful thing about the innocence [of common moral sense], but the bad thing is that she cannot be preserved well and gets easily seduced."[129]

Kant argues that "in his inner, man feels a powerful counterweight against all commandments of duty (that his reason presents him as highly respectable) in his needs and inclinations that he thinks he must satisfy to reach happiness."[130] In short, although people generally have good common sense of what's good and what's bad, that judgment can easily be overpowered by selfish motives. As we have seen looking back at the Weimar republic, even in persons that are revered by their people because of their great merits, like Hindenburg, their heroism may become victim of quite unheroic concerns.

That is why Kant thought we need general principles, and that these could be logically derived from the fact that nature has endowed us with *Vernunft* (reason), in fact, principles that would bind not only us humans, but any reasonable being. Kant here refers to nature as the ultimate source of reason. He did this long before there was a theory of evolution. I think his arguments, translated into the present context, apply well to my analysis of the evolution of ethical engenes. His treatise on ethics boils down to these two assertions:

1. Ethical behavior is not derived from experience and not a matter of belief. It is not arbitrary, but rooted in human nature. In Kant's terms, the basis of moral judgment is metaphysical (not derived from experience and not deduced by rational thinking), it is based on reason/*Vernunft*.

2. We need to choose what is right and wrong. We know what our duty is, and we need to make decisions disregarding our own interests. The criterion of ethical behavior is the good will.

The first point neatly summarizes the section "Ethics" in chapter "Society forming engenes" (I.4.12): the basis of moral judgment is metaphysical because it is rooted in the evolution of the human mind. The second point is the crux of the human condition. There is no ultimate authority that can guide us. We must

---

[129] Immanuel Kant, „Grundlegung zur Metaphysik der Sitten." 2nd Edition. Johann Friedrich Hartknoch (1786), p. 24
[130] Ibid.

follow what we feel is right. However, as Kant cautions, we need principles to preclude our judgments from being corrupted by our interests. And that is why he derived his famous categorical imperative which says, roughly, "You must always act in a way that the principle of your intention could be made a general law for everybody."

I must admit that I cannot really follow Kant's logic of the foundation of the categorical imperative, but it is certainly true, I think, that everybody has the responsibility to decide what is right and wrong. I found it difficult to invoke the categorical imperative as a guide for the decisions we face, but this is a philosophical question I cannot discuss here. The only practical way out that I can see is to rely on those evolutionary engenes that define human dignity to guide us. We listen to our inner voice and decide accordingly. Of course, it is often difficult to hear that voice, not only because, as Kant pointed out, we may get corrupted by the desire to pursue our own happiness, but also because there is not just one inner voice. Our soul is a complex system and even the 'ethical engenes' are several, and they may contradict each other.

But in general people seem to have good moral judgments. Even the Nazi regime had difficulty getting soldiers to carry out mass executions in eastern Europe, and those who refused the order were harshly punished, some ending up in concentration camps. So the regime resorted to filling squadrons with recruits from the occupied countries, having Ukrainians kill Jews, and eventually introduced the gas chamber which bypassed the displeasure of bloodily slaying by reducing the act of killing to turning a valve. Generally people have a robust aversion against doing something they feel is wrong. In the Second World War the Russian army used psychological methods to rid their soldiers of what they called "the inhibitory focus" in the brain ('brain washing'). Perhaps we *can* trust common sense ethical judgments. 'Common' here meaning something that is shared, if not by all, then by a broad majority. This is the time-honored idea of having a jury decide cases in court. So, perhaps we can work around the Kantian problem of personal interests corrupting moral judgments in principle by using the mechanisms of modern democracy. If we decide by voting, we can hope that a majority of people – having the same Moral engenes – will share our own feelings and will arrive at similar judgments. This, of course, was the idea of the founders of our democracy. By electing a legislative we have a good chance that the country is ruled by laws that most of us can agree upon.[131] How the

---

[131] An obvious alternative to electing representatives would be to let people vote directly about each proposed law. This is 'direct democracy' which, to my knowledge, is practiced at national level only in Switzerland.

mechanisms of modern democracy could be used to implement what we feel is right and how mechanisms fail I will discuss in the following.

—

Let us assume we have a catalog of values that we think are 'unalienable human rights,' as there is justice and equality before the law – nobody is above the law –, gender equality, protection of the infirm, freedom of speech, respect for opinions and religious beliefs. Then we want to make these rights the basis of society and protect them against any deviations. This is the political task. Following Kant, we cannot leave this task in the hands of an individual, because even a wise monarch will not be immune to the temptations of selfish motives. Kant's solution was the categorical imperative, a law that he thought must bind all reason-endowed beings and hence everybody ought to accept. But he also had no illusions about human ethical behavior in practice; the philosopher needs to define what acts are ethically good even if nobody would ever act as demanded. If his imperative were followed by everybody (it's a *categorical* imperative), it would establish a moral world, thus overcoming the morally flawed society that would result if everyone individually followed their intuitive moral judgments. But this project appears unrealistic. How can we expect everybody to follow the imperative? Realistically, not even most people will.

Be that as it may, we are searching for pragmatic ways to secure the values we want to establish and save our society from being overwhelmed by forces that we deem evil. We want a world where nobody must fear to be murdered or tortured or starved, but some of the social engenes we inherit make us create inequality and injustice, ignoring the moral laws. Their influence contradicts democracy. The engene that produces chauvinist behavior and strive for autocratic rule, demanding a strong leader and obedient subjects, in millions of people, is a powerful force against the egalitarian idea of society.

But evolution has also endowed us with ethical engenes that produce feelings of compassion and responsibility and sense of justice. That good moral intuition is a virtue of human nature has long been recognized (*das gemeine Vernunfturteil* in Kant's terms; my 2-year-old daughter running outside to warn the birds of the danger of an approaching airplane convinced me that compassion and responsibility are inherited). I argue that moral intuition and sense of justice are faculties that have evolved as part of human society forming engenes, precious achievements of evolution. This insight gives hope. Future generations will have sense of justice and moral values just like our ancestors had. It also opens an unexpected perspective on democracy:

Based on the ethical feelings that are common sense, one can derive moral principles and a human rights catalog that are the basis of a lawful state. The founders of democracies designed institutions that create and protect a social order that honors those ethical feelings and guarantees those rights. I believe there is no reason to conclude, as the historian Joachim Fest did, that democracy contradicts human nature.[132] Given the nature of our inherited ethical engenes, we can secure those values if we base all moral political decisions on a maximum amount of consensus among citizens, because, even if the individual errs, the majority, we can hope, will be right. Because we can trust that humans generally have good moral judgment, we can hope that moral values will prevail in our political system if we base decisions on the choice of a majority. Democracy, one can say, is a rational construct that builds on our inherited ethical engenes. The solution is a society in which laws are made according to the intuitive judgments of many individuals, and institutions ensure that the laws do not conflict with the agreed-upon rights of the individual, and control their enforcement. As far as the judgments of a majority are moral, we can hope that the resulting society is moral. And a welfare state, one can say, is a rational scheme to expand the reach of the Family engene across the entire state. Note that the democratic society is not a society in which a majority rules; it is a society in which a majority establishes laws that conform with the framework of a constitution. Then, what rules are the lawful institutions. Thus, democracy is a way to build a society on inherited moral intuition: feelings of responsibility, compassion, fairness, and sense of justice. As we have seen, these intuitions are not equally strong in all citizens, and whether a majority manifests itself in democratic elections depends on the situation and how well the situation is explained to the citizens.

Considering the evolutionary origin it becomes also clear that the construct of democracy is inherently unstable because humans inherit those contradictory social engenes. For example, the Strife engene demands autocratic rule which contradicts the egalitarian liberal order; it promotes racial discrimination which contradicts sense of justice; it incites violence which contradicts responsibility and compassion. And the Family engene, which tends to be the strongest in a person's near field of society, can breed corruption, wrecking responsible government. The construct may not hold up against these forces. It is important to check if the construct has flaws that may cause it to crumble.

---

[132] „*Zeugen des Jahrhunderts. Roger Willemsen befragt Joachim Fest.*" 60 min. production of the German Television ZDF, First broadcast Feb. 2, 2003. https://www.youtube.com/watch?v=b4KXHBsojGU

III.2.2 Problems With Moral Intuition

The human sense of justice is something miraculous. I called it a precious achievement of evolution. Can we just rely on the moral intuition of our countrymen, as I conjectured, and let the majority decide what is right for the project of democracy? That would be too good to be true. Besides those that support justice there are several other ancient evolutionary engenes that also produce strong moral feelings, and they may corrupt the project of a free and fair society.

One is the Religious engene, which may support some of those goals, but may also generate additional mandates, and even some that conflict with general moral intuition, for example, obedience to religious leaders, mandates concerning the role of genders, etc. And it tends to produce intolerance. That's why modern democracies adopted the principle of separation of church and state.

Another concern, particularly in American democracy, are the 'contentious issues' that produce strong moral feelings and notoriously have big political weight, such as abortion rights, gay rights, and others. It may seem as if the question of abortion rights has so much political weight simply because it is about a fundamental ethical and legal principle, the protection of the unborn life. But other issues that also stir up emotions and carry big political weight are not rooted in fundamental ethical principles. For example, the question of whether the state recognizes the right of two people of the same sex to marry moves millions of voters in the U.S. Those who feel "yes" vote mainly Democrat, those who feel "no" vote Republican. (As of 2019, 75% of Democrats approved same-sex marriage, compared to 44% of Republicans; 15 years earlier, approval had been even lower, 43 and 19%, respectively).[133] As a result, politicians and other people of public life in the "yes" camp gather in the Democratic party, and their public presence fuels emotions against that party in the "no" camp.

Is same-sex marriage a matter of deciding about life and death, as is the question of abortion rights? Or does it violate a fundamental ethical principle? Apparently not. In this case, the emotions are stirred up by moral engenes that evolved to protect the two-parent family (see I.4.6 "Gender and society"). Evolution boosted the importance of sex to cement the bond between woman and man, mother and father of the offspring, because offspring is what counts in evolution. Like in the case of other engenes, it achieved the goal by programming

---

[133] Pew Research Center, poll of 2019, https://www.pewresearch.org/religion/fact-sheet/changing-attitudes-on-gay-marriage/, accessed 7/5/2022.

emotions: one that drives a certain behavior, and another that rewards the behavior with pleasure. And to prevent 'abuse' (behavior practiced just for fun), evolution devised taboos and feelings of guilt. Pleasure should not be wasted.

Protecting the unborn is obviously significant for evolution, and hence the thought of abortion is loaded with an instinctive aversion, abortion harms reproduction. Moreover, evolution also dictates that activity that does not result in reproduction must be suppressed, and of course this holds also for sexual activity (see I.4.12). Taboos, and feelings of guilt when they are violated, are emotional barriers against frivolous usage. The specific actions targeted by these negative emotions correspond to items in the catalog of sins maintained by the Catholic church (and institutions of other religions as well): masturbation, homosexual behavior, extramarital sex. By mental extension, the Catholic church applies the taboo also to contraceptives as they permit sexual pleasure without leading to reproduction. I don't know what punishments the catalog lists for each case, but mothers in Italy threaten their adolescent sons that masturbation will make them blind. Those actions produce feelings of guilt not because they are sinful, but they are declared sinful because they naturally produce feelings of guilt. The "sins" are rationalizations.

Trying to understand this we realize that voters in democratic elections are typically wrong in two ways about those 'contentious issues'.

First, they think that the state needs to endorse certain (religious) standards of sexual behavior and, most importantly, must protect young people against immoral influences. They perceive people who are openly lesbian or gay as a danger. They think young people might learn their sexual preference when they see politicians admitting homosexual orientation, or gay couples kissing on TV. But practice shows that sexual orientation cannot be learned or unlearned. As discussed above, it is based on the individual development of an inherited Sex engene that evolution has strengthened excessively in the human species to create the two-parent family which is the basis of human society. The reason for the variations in sexual orientation is simply the statistical variation in strength and specificity of that engene. There is no reason to expect that sexual orientation can be changed by education. Human nature cannot be 'corrected' by religious intolerance.

Second, they are wrong about the nature of their own feelings. People mistake their personal moral intuition regarding sexual behavior as a response to divine order. Accordingly, the approval rates for same-sex marriage are lowest among evangelical Protestants and highest among not religiously affiliated people (29% versus 79%).[134] But in fact, just as the matter of their concern (variants of sexual orientation) is a product of evolution (creating excessive sex drive), their feelings about it are also rooted in evolution. As explained, evolution has erected taboos to inhibit sexual behaviors that do not lead to reproduction. The resulting moral sentiments often come disguised as religious mandates or fundamental ethical principles.

What can we learn? Imagine two political strategists of a party with a platform of social justice, equal rights, and freedom of religious and sexual orientation. One rejects "biological determinism" but thinks that people's stance towards those contentious issues is a matter of education. This strategist will opt for a campaign that tries to educate people, emphasizing women's right to abortion and the freedom of sexual orientation.

The other strategist believes that there are evolutionary roots of moral judgments. She/he will be cautious not to emphasize abortion rights and same-sex marriage, and rather advise gays and lesbians to keep a low profile because they challenge ancient taboos felt by a majority of people and will turn many voters away, in fact many more voters than what the party might gain among the lesbian/gay constituents. Thus, understanding the evolutionary roots has important practical implications for politics.

There is no question that education matters: overall the opposition to same-sex marriage has dropped considerably between 2004 and 2019. But about *one third* of Americans still opposed it in 2019, and the rift between the parties remained essentially unchanged: 81% of Republicans versus 57% of Democrats being opposed in 2004, and 56% of Republicans versus 25% of Democrats in 2019. The ratio of 56% to 25% means that in a campaign that emphasizes this issue, the Republican party would profit from the instinctive rejection of same-sex marriage twice as much as the Democratic party. It is not good for a party to be identified with a small group like the LGBTQ[135] community. The group deserves recognition as a minority, but should not become emblematic for one of the big political parties. With their ostentatious presence in public they do themselves a disservice, harming a party that supports them. The LGBTQ group also tries to piggy-back on the anti-racist ticket and the Black-lives-matter campaign, which is not fair. (Interestingly, Blacks are less likely to approve same-sex-marriage than Whites.)

---

[134] Ibidem

[135] Acronym for *L*esbian, *G*ay, *B*isexual, *T*ransgender and *Q*ueer.

All this shows that moral intuition can be contaminated by ancient taboos controlling sexual behavior. Not all intuitions are ethical and suitable to support a free and just society. We are born with a number of Moral engenes pulling in different directions, and we must choose at every corner which one to follow. There is no way around responsible conscious decision, which means, we need to understand. We must understand the clash of moral intuitions that heats up the political climate and decides elections. Of course, even with the best education we cannot hope that everybody understands, or even that most people do. But political leaders need to understand. There are plenty of political leaders who know intuitively how to use people's moral intuitions to their advantage. Contentious issues exist because the response of the Moral engene controlling sexual behavior is powerful and fundamentally irrational, producing disgust and hate, which are the motors of intolerance. For our project of democracy we need politicians who understand the complexity of moral intuitions rationally, and make responsible use of their insight.

Why do those 'contentious issues' play such a big role in American politics? Other nations are not split in half about the question of abortion. In fact, nearly all nations have laws that protect women's right to abortion, and the few exceptions are mainly autocratic Muslim states. Do Americans have erratic moral concerns? And does the example of America disprove my conjecture that democracies can rely on the intuition of majorities?

The short answer is No. Polls show that Americans, like people in other countries, overwhelmingly support conditional abortion. The difference is simply that, who rules America is not the majority of voters. Right-wing politicians instrumentalize those 'contentious issues' in their struggle for power. How that is possible I will explain in the next section.

III.2.3 About Elections

The hope for democracy is that moral intuitions that presumably derive from the Family engene and the millions of years when humans lived in bands of hunter/gatherers, that those intuitions will support a free and fair society that protects the individual, and that education of the public and the insight of political leaders will be able to fend off contaminations of moral intuition from the ancient engenes related to reproduction. Recent trends, such as the growing acceptance of same-sex marriage, support that hope. The main threat that remains is the Strife engene which divides society into "us" and "them", produces hate and social injustice, and claims authoritarian rule. Still, I think that compassion, fairness, and justice will prevail in our political system if we base decisions on the choice of a majority. This choice needs to be determined by elections.

Let us now examine the election process in some detail. Modern democracies emphasize equality in the voting process: each adult person has a vote (that this includes women has been widely recognized only recently, and only in some parts of the world).

At the minimum, the voting laws should make sure that the election process produces a reliable result, that is, simply, a result that is not random. By random I mean factors that are accidental and irrelevant regarding the intent of the voters. This is a basic statistical requirement that is free of any political reason. In the voting process, accidental factors include the possibility that some voters who intended to vote did not vote for reasons like they did not have time to go to the polls, they were caught in a traffic jam, they did not feel well, or a child was sick on the voting day, and many other reasons. These are random factors that may not have a systematic effect (like favoring one outcome or another), but they contribute uncertainty. The first requirement for a voting system is that it should minimize the randomness: The variance produced by the will of the voters should be much larger than the variance produced by the random factors. How much, depends on how critical the expected outcome is. For example if the outcome is that one party wins 10,000 votes more than another, then the random variance should be small compared to 10,000; otherwise the result could be a random result, it would have no more significance than throwing dice. When the outcome of a presidential election in a country that has 200 million who can vote depends on a difference of a few thousand vote counts, as it did in the U.S. in the year 2000, this is a clear sign that the election process does not pass this minimum requirement; it is not reliable.

To minimize randomness, the election mechanisms should minimize the ratio of random variance over voter variance. One reason why the election of the U.S. president does not do this is that it ignores the will of about 70% of the voters. This is because the existing election laws of the individual states require that *all* of its electors (each state has a given number) be counted for the party with the most votes in the state (the 'winner-take-all' regime).[136] For example, in a state like Maryland, where the Democratic Party for years has had a majority, all of its 10 electors are counted as Democrat, no matter how many people voted for the Republican party. About 70% of the eligible voters live in such states

---

[136] This is so in 48 of the 50 states. Two states have slightly different rules, but they also award the winning party disproportionately.

where their votes do not count; that is, their voting does not produce any variance. Such a system is technically far from optimal, because the ratio of random variance to voter variance depends on the total number of votes, and using only 30% of the votes unnecessarily increases the randomness of the outcome.

Another requirement, which is the most obvious, is that all eligible voters should count. This requirement is grossly violated in the election of the U.S. president since about 70% of the votes have no influence on the outcome. After the 2016 election, I listened to a discussion on National Public Radio (NPR), where a listener called in asking: "Why is the future of our country, which has 50 states, decided by the voters of only a few swing states[137]?" A very reasonable question, I thought. But the discussants finished her question up in less than 20 seconds: the caller was referred to the discussion of the "popular vote" (the result when counting all votes across the country), and to a website called "nationalpopularvote.com." That was it.

I then looked up what the swing states were;[138] there were eleven; and what the numbers of eligible voters were in these states and in the remaining states including the District of Columbia, and these were 66,868,243 in the swing states and 160,123,145 in the other states. I also looked up the turnout of voters,[139] which was 65.9% in the swing states on average and 58.3% in the other states, which means that in the swing states 44,081,369 people voted, and in the other states 93,346,589 people. One can see that there was quite a difference in voter turnout, 65.9% versus 58.3%, which was obviously caused by the lack of interest in voting of the people in the non-swing states: why should I go voting if my vote doesn't count anyway? Because which states are swingable and which are not is quite predictable, the election campaigns of course concentrated on those 11 states, and there was basically no campaign in the non-swing states, and the candidates did not show up there in person at all. So the lack of interest is understandable. Now, in the hypothetical condition that the votes of all states would have equal importance, it is reasonable to assume that the voter turnout would be as high in all states as it was now in the swing states, namely 65.9%. The number of votes in the non-swing states would then be 105,521,153

---

[137] "Swing states" are the states in which the outcome is notoriously uncertain.

[138]   http://www.politico.com/blogs/swing-states-2016-election/2016/06/what-are-the-swing-states-in-2016-list-224327, accessed 11/17/2016 .

[139]   http://www.electproject.org/home/voter-turnout/voter-turnout-data,   accessed 11/1718/2016

(160,123,145 times 0.659) instead of 93,346,589, a difference of over 12 million.[140]

This simple calculation shows that the problem of the winner-take-all regime is not only that it ignores the popular vote (a problem that the National Popular Vote corporation attempts to fix); it also significantly distorts the popular vote itself by neglecting the will of 12 million people who do not vote out of frustration. It also cripples the campaigns, which means that voters in the non-swing states are being less well informed (if campaigns serve that function at all). Thus, we see that the winner-take-all regime seriously distorts the will of the people in presidential elections by putting the decision in the hands of the small subgroup of voters in the swing states, depriving large numbers of people of the right to participate in the decision.

This is not at all what the founding fathers had in mind when creating the electorate scheme. They wanted the people of each state to elect a certain number of men that they thought would best represent their cause, men that were highly regarded in society because of their merits.[141] Their numbers were in principle to be proportional to the number of inhabitants of each state. But what became the reality is that the electors have no significance at all; almost never does an elector dishonor the mandate given by the state, namely, to vote for the one party that won the majority in his state. No social merits: persons whom the voters don't know and have never seen. The founding fathers did not anticipate that the states would misuse their freedom to choose the way how to instruct their electors. But early on in U.S. history, because the states compete for influence in the presidential elections, they opted for the winner-take-all regime, which maximizes a state's influence.[142,143]

---

[140] Using the data published in May 2017 by the U.S. Census Bureau, Voting and Registration in the Election of November 2016, Table 4a, and using the same calculation, the difference would be 6.597 million. https://www.census.gov/data/tables/time-series/demo/voting-and-registration/p20-580.html, accessed 11/1/2022.

[141] It seems that the founding fathers did not trust the people to elect their president directly. As George Mason of Virginia put it at the Constitutional Convention, "It would be as unnatural to refer the choice of a proper character for a chief Magistrate to the people, as it would to refer a trial of colors to a blind man."

[142] The U.S. Constitution does not mandate the winner-take-all regime but leaves it up to the states to determine how they choose their representatives in the Electoral College and how each representative shall vote.

[143] When Thomas Jefferson, then governor of Virginia, lost the 1796 presidential election to John Adams, he realized that he would have won had Virginia allotted all its electors to

A winner-take-all regime is of course the norm when voters elect one of several candidates, as in the elections of governors and senators and members of the U.S. Congress, where each state elects a governor and two senators, and each of the 435 electoral districts covering the United States elects a person for the House of Representatives. In these elections, independents and candidates of new parties can win a district, senate seat, or governor. This is unlike the presidential election, where the same two parties compete in every state, and the winner-take-all rule is applied over and over again in each of the 50 states, with the result that independent candidates or new parties have virtually no chance to win a majority in the final count of electorates. The winner-take-all regime cements the two-party system.

For the House, the representatives of each of the 435 districts are elected independently from the available candidates, which means a large number of independent decisions, and because the districts are designed to have approximately equal numbers of voters, the proportion of representatives in the House should closely mirror the proportion of voters in the country, that is, the popular vote. The House elections, it seems, live up to the standards of a representative democracy. But in fact there is distortion also in the House elections: The existing laws give the party that wins a majority in a state in one election the right to redefine the districts for the next election (which comes up after two years).[144] Thus, the two-party tradition distorts the outcome of the House elections because the district borders can be redefined after each election, which in most states is done by a committee of the winning party. The winning party takes advantage by redefining the borders of the districts based on the demographics of the two parties' voters, so as to assure that they can win a district by a small but safe margin in the next election. With that strategy, they can win a seat while excluding a maximum number of votes of the opponent

---

his candidacy. In the next election, in 1800, Virginia switched to that rule and he won. He was clearly aware that a proportional regime would be better, but defended the change as a pragmatic necessity: "All agree that an election by districts would be best, if it could be general; but while 10 states choose either by their legislatures or by a general ticket, it is folly & worse than folly for the other 6 not to do it." Later, James Madison tried to make the district method mandatory by constitutional amendment, but did not succeed. Following the election of 1824, the winner-take-all statewide method became the rule. https://fairvote.org/how-the-electoral-college-became-winner-take-all/ (accessed 1/7/2023).

[144] Most states leave the redistricting to a commission which, in some states, is bipartisan. But the legislature controls the redistricting in 43 of the 50 states (as of 2020), that is, in each state, the majority established in the preceding election.

party. It thus maximizes the number of districts the party can win, and it maximizes the number of frustrated voters. Or they shape districts so as to include a maximum number of voters of the opponent party, thus minimizing the number of districts the opponent party can win. Or they can define the districts so that two popular candidates of the opposition must compete in the same district. The practice of redistricting has been called 'gerrymandering', a word created in reaction to a redrawing of Massachusetts Senate election districts under Governor Elbridge Gerry in 1812 that created districts of strange shapes that journalists made fun of, likening one of them to a salamander. That's where the second half of the word 'gerrymandering' comes from. The result of this practice is that over 90% of House members are reelected in each election. The outcome depends to a large extent on the previous gerrymandering instead of the actual will of the people.

The gerrymandering scheme also invites illegal manipulations. A committee can define the districts based on the racial demographics so that the minority voters remain below the 50% margin in as many districts as possible. This scheme has been used deliberately to exclude candidates of the Black minority from winning a district. Indeed, the role of gerrymandering has assumed grotesque importance in American politics. In the summer of 2023, the Supreme Court had to admonish the legislature of the state of Alabama to create at least two districts in which the Black minority would have a chance to win a seat in congress. Until then, the White majority had been able to gerrymander so that Black people, who make up 1/4 of the voters, could only win in one of the 7 districts. (The state subsequently refused to follow the Court's ruling.) What is grotesque is that the Supreme Court feels obliged to meddle with a local commission in manipulating the chances of different racial groups to win seats in congress. The ensuing political discussion focused on the constitutional question of whether the Supreme Court can mandate the legislature of a state. Instead, it should focus on how to do away with gerrymandering. The congressional delegates should be elected to represent the will of the voters, not the skills of a commission in exploiting demographics. In other words, the districts should be fixed.

In both, the presidential election and the election of congressional representatives, the winner-take-all regime and the practice of gerrymandering leave large numbers of voters frustrated and consequently reduces political interest and lowers voter turnout. Why would people go and vote for a presidential candidate knowing that the election result in their state does not influence the outcome? Why would people who are unhappy with the representative of their district go and vote if the chance that they can effect a change is less than 10%? No doubt, the feeling of powerlessness fuels conspiracy theories: the power of the hidden 'deep state'. The deep state is imagination, but the powerlessness is real.

A deeply divided nation?

The most fateful way in which the winner-take-all regime distorts the will of the people is that it implicitly enforces a two-party rule. In principle, there could be three parties in a state, but in practice, given two strong traditional parties, a new third party has virtually no chance to win a majority in any state, let alone the majority of the electorates. So, voters will think twice before they waste their vote on a candidate who has no chance to win. In the U.S. presidential election, this happened in the 2000 election, when the Green Party presented itself as an alternative and won 2.7% of the votes, which, as it turned out, were mainly deviated from the Democrats, thus helping the Republican Party to win the election. You read this right: voters who leaned Democrat helped the Republican candidate to win the presidency.

The voter has only the choice between two packages: Someone who is against abortion is automatically against gun control. It's that absurd: pro-life[145] votes are automatically pro-gun votes because the Pro Life movement and the National Rifle Association both command decisive fractions in the Republican Party: As of 2019, 32% of Republican voters were against abortion under any circumstances, and 69% of Republican voters were against stricter gun control, while in the Democratic Party the corresponding percentages were as low as 14% and 15%.[146] Thus, voters who want to ban abortion completely, vote overwhelmingly Republican (32% to 14%), a party that has a clear mandate to block stricter gun control. And voters who are concerned about social justice and the growing economic inequality pin their hope on the Democratic party, but that party is cozy with finance capitalism which is what creates inequality.

The funneling of all political issues into two bottles has led to a bizarre confusion of terminology: In the U.S., the term 'liberal' is used increasingly by Republicans to denounce the agenda of their Democrat opponents, insinuating that their program aims at *expansion of social welfare*, even *socialism, more state intervention* and *more taxes*. But in the rest of the world, the attribute 'liberal' characterizes parties that fight for free enterprise, *less state intervention, less*

---

[145] Pro Life is the name of the United States anti-abortion movement.
[146] Survey of U.S. adults conducted Sept. 3-15, 2019, Pew Research Center.

welfare spending and *lower taxes*; that is, very much the same goals as those of the Republican party. Thus, what they demonize as 'liberal' is considered the opposite of liberal in the rest of the world; and much of their own agenda (free enterprise, less state intervention, less welfare spending and lower taxes) is in fact liberal. Where does this confusion of terms come from? I think it originates from one single political issue, the fight about abortion rights. 'Liberal' means freedom of choice for women. This issue of course has nothing to do with socialism, taxation, or any economic policies at all. It is just one contentious issue that has a big influence in the elections. This shows how much U.S. citizens are being confused by what are the consequences of a mere technical quirk in the voting mechanism, the winner-take-all regime.

A particularly unfortunate result of the winner-take-all distortion of the voting results is that it reduces all efforts of the two parties to the strife for winning a majority because they realize, whatever their objectives, they can advance them only if they come to power. They have to adjust their declared objectives so as to win the critical percentage of 51% of the votes, or just 50.1%, in as many states as possible: When the public is getting concerned with high crime rates and Republicans are gaining votes because they claim to be the party of law and order, then Democrats feel pushed to show they are also tough on crime, and Democrat-ruled states start to crack down on crime with mass incarcerations. When issues of social justice fail to motivate enough voters (which is in the nature of the social engenes, see above, I.4.11 "Short- and long-range engenes"), Democrats resort to big capital to fund their campaign, which means they need to adjust their program to please big capital. When workers are squeezed by dwindling job opportunities and demagogues blame immigrants for it, a Democrat administration feels pressed to step up prosecution of illegal immigrants, resulting in millions of deportations. Even worse, in the desperate fight to win a majority in the presidential elections, Republicans, after being defeated in 2020, forget their loyalty to the constitution and endanger our democracy altogether.

The result of the two parties adjusting their agendas and priorities is that the pattern of elections invariably shows a tight race with either party receiving about 50 percent of the votes in a number of states. And that is the reason why the outcome of an election is hard to predict, as political augurs know; even the best algorithms fail in predicting which party will prevail in the swing states. Five times in history a candidate won the presidency against the majority of votes, most recently in the 2000 and 2016 elections, and another four times the winning margin was smaller than one percent, notably in John F. Kennedy's election 1960 (49.7% for Kennedy, 49.5% for Nixon). While the people have the illusion of actually electing the president, the election process is essentially a roulette. Perhaps some Americans appreciate the random character of the presidential election, accepting the outcome as a trial by ordeal. In God we trust.

Especially in recent decades it seemed that America was plagued by the two parties bitterly fighting for power. Does this mean that America is a "deeply divided" country, as recent comments will have it? Is it even becoming "ungovernable"? I would hope not. Of course, there are some contentious issues that polarize voters, like abortion rights, but as the above polls show, 14% of the Democratic voters are *also against* abortion under any circumstances; and some 30% of Republican voters are *not against* stricter gun control. What appears like an epic struggle for winning the sympathy of the voters is nothing but the effect of the winner-take-all regime that forces both parties to fight about the 50 percent margin in a dozen critical states.

The two parties position themselves on the Left and the Right, but the political reality shows that the wishes of the people cannot be lined up along the Left-Right axis; people have a multi-dimensional variety of political positions. The struggle against gun violence is not in line with the struggle for equal rights for women, and neither of them aligns with the Left-Right axis. Also concern about the environment and the planet is not a question of Left and Right. Those are movements in different dimensions. And people's priorities are changing, which is good, because new political tasks come up and the urgency of tasks changes over time. It is not good that all goals and priorities of the voters are squeezed into the two-party corset. Clearly, if 'conservative' means destruction of our planet, then there is a need for a *real* conservative party. And if 'socialist' is equivalent to 'liberal' (in the sense used by religiously minded people), then there is a need for a *real* socialist party and a *real* liberal party. The right to promote one's opinion by founding a political party is a fundamental condition of freedom in a democracy.

Perils of a two-party system

Coming back to the theoretical underpinning of democratic elections which, I argue, is the notion that people have ethical engenes in common. Genetically coded mechanisms guide the development of ethical behavior when we grow up and guarantee the continuity of our values across generations. But the strengths of these engenes differ between individuals, and therefore we can only trust that political decisions are ethical if they are based on the judgments of many people, a solid majority. Now we can see that the two-party system creates a problem.

As elections in Western countries in the last decades have shown, a substantial fraction of people are strongly motivated by the Strife engene and therefore tend to have authoritarian, xenophobic and racist views (see Table 3 under II.4 "Growth of xenophobic nationalism"). Although the vast majority of these people respect the rules of law, some of them are fanatic and reject the democratic order; and because these are highly active, they exert a strong influence.

Remember what happened to the Weimar Republic when two extreme factions in the parliament, the Nazis on the right and the Communists on the left, rejected the democratic order and aimed at dismantling the republic. The result was that, when these factions grew stronger, at some point, the coalition of parties supporting the republic lost the majority and from then on were unable to form a legitimate government, and the parliament could no longer pass laws. In this deadlock situation, the constitution gave the president (which according to the constitution was mainly a symbolic authority) the privilege to name the chancellor, and allowed the chancellor to govern by decrees instead of laws. That is how Hitler and the Nazi party came to power without ever controlling a majority in parliament.

The problem with the two-party system in the U.S. is that the Right extremists find themselves exclusively in one party, the Republican Party, and, although a small fraction nationwide, they constitute a substantial fraction in the Party. Assuming, for example, that Right extremists make up 5 percent of the voters nationwide and their sympathizers perhaps 25 percent,[147] for the Party that would be about 50 percent. Thus, they could have a solid majority in many states and take control of the Republican caucus and the nomination of the presidential candidate. A minor proportion of voters nationwide assumes a decisive role in the party. And because the presidential election, being decided by a few swing states, is essentially a roulette, there is a 50% chance that this candidate will become the president of the United States.

A flawed design of representative democracy can give a minority undue power in controlling the fate of a nation. In the case of the Weimar Republic, a

---

[147] Recent elections in various European countries have shown that nationalist-xenophobic parties are supported by about 15% of the voters on average. A recent study in the U.S. has found that some 20 percent of white Americans now have "strong levels of group consciousness," meaning they "feel a sense of discontent over the status of their group," see A. Jardina, "White Identity Politics." (Cambridge Studies in Public Opinion and Political Psychology), Cambridge University Press (2019).

Party that represented only 33% of the voters of the nation was propelled to power because of the presence of another party, the Communists, that took up 17% of the votes, so that together they reached 50% and could thus disable the parliament. In the U.S., a right-wing faction that may represent only a quarter of the voters can be propelled to power because of the presence of another Party (the Democrats) that takes up about 50% of the votes.[148] In the Weimar Republic, it happened, because the Communist Party could not enter a coalition with any other party. In the U.S., it can happen because there are only two parties.

When I wrote these lines in May 2020 during a COVID-19-related extended vacation in the Bolivian mountains, my concerns about the stability of the American democracy seemed theoretical and overly pessimistic, even presumptuous. How could this exemplary democracy be endangered by the right-wing faction of a party, however aggressive and militant? Would the institutions that have proved reliable bulwarks of the democracy for over two hundred years not guarantee stability? Unfortunately, the dramatic events following the presidential elections of November 2020 have made it clear that the danger is real. The two-party system can endanger even the venerable democracy of the United States. The narrow winning margins in swing states gave rise to wild claims of voter fraud and "stolen elections", leading to the unfortunate storming of the Capitol by a violent mob trying to overturn the election result. And, even worse, in the following, the losing Republican Party almost entirely abandoned its role in politics, concentrating instead on the goal of winning the next election by tweaking the voting process, producing hundreds of new laws in the Republican controlled states to restrict and impede the voting in the hope to reduce selectively the turnout of voters for the opponent party. These desperate attempts include not only means of voter suppression, but also, in case that might not suffice, establishing their own party officials to oversee the voting process and the vote counting, with the obvious goal of manipulating the vote counts post festum. (Remember, when Hitler called for new elections after becoming chancellor in 1933, he had his storm troopers stand guard in front of the election locales to "oversee" the voting.)

In healthy democracies that use a proportional representation of voters rather than the winner-take-all regime, such manipulations are unheard of (except in pseudo-democratic dictatorship countries). Imagine a party that tries to tweak the election result by manipulations like voter suppression. Suppose it is able to

---

[148] To be more accurate, the Democrats generally receive more votes than the Republicans, but, because of the peculiar assignment of electorates that favors the Southern states both parties win about equal fractions of the electoral college on average.

suppress X votes of an opponent party that would normally get a total N_{tot}. Then, the effect of that manipulation would be to reduce the share of the opponent party by X/N_{tot}, a percentage that is generally small (it might flip one seat in parliament at best) compared to what a party can achieve by efficient campaigning. So, for that small advantage no party in a healthy democracy would go down the shameful path of vote manipulation. The incentive to do so comes from a condition in the United States that rewards a tiny winning margin in a state with its entire chunk of the electoral college. In Pennsylvania in 2020, for example, out of the 6.9 million cast votes, 80,555 – a mere 1.2% – decided to which party its 19 electorates were assigned. Narrow winning margins of course appear just by the law of random variation in some of the 50 states. Thus, the two-party system, which is a mere technical consequence of the winner-take-all regime, can turn into a threat to the American democracy. In contrast, proportional representation generally leads to coalitions, fomenting compromise which is the essence of politics.

What might seem a minor technicality, the winner-take-all regime, has wide reaching consequences for U.S. citizens, and also the rest of the world, given how much the U.S. weighs on international politics. A viable democracy rests on the quality of the individual votes. If the voters feel they are not represented by any of the extant parties, and if large contingents of voters are frustrated and do not vote, then the elections do not reflect the values of the people. What we perceive as our values is not arbitrary; they are deeply rooted in human nature. But human individuals are not stereotyped; individual people can embrace different values. Only when these are adequately represented, and political decisions rely on consensus or the judgment of a solid majority, can we hope that the true human values will prevail. It's a hope, but the only hope we have. It means we cannot afford to squander millions of votes. The impact of the elections must honor the intention and judgment of the people. We cannot accept that they reflect random variations or the goals of a fanatic minority, or that the tallying of votes is manipulated by political rivalry and short-sighted interests. In particular, it means that the U.S., who pride themselves as the pioneers and defenders of democracy in the world, must amend their election rules.

An argument that is frequently raised in favor of the institution of the electoral college is that it preserves the federal character of the constitution, because the number of electors is not strictly proportional to the number of inhabitants of each state but gives smaller states relatively more weight. However, this is not an argument for the winner-take-all regime. It is easy to preserve the relative weights of the states while letting each state allot its electors in proportion to the votes. For example, if 66% of Marylanders voted Democrat and 32% Republican and 2% for other candidates, then seven of the ten electors would count for the Democratic candidate and 3 for the Republican candidate (to be more accurate, 6.6 for the Democrat, 3.2 for the Republican, and 0.2 for the others). Clearly, the Republican voters would then feel less frustrated than under the winner-take-all regime where their votes do not count at all. Thus, if we want, we can keep the traditional numbers of electors per state so that people in smaller states have a relatively greater influence (or whatever the goal had been). The important point is to give parties and presidential candidates a proportional representation in each state. Thus, there is no reason to adhere to the winner-take-all regime to maintain the traditional weights of the states in the federation. We can have both, the traditional weights and a proportional representation of candidates and parties.

Nothing positive can be said about the winner-take-all regime. As long as the tradition was that the individual electors could freely decide for whom to vote, a state breaking with that tradition could increase its influence relative to the other states by ordering its electors to vote all for one candidate. But since all states are doing the same the winner-take-all regime has no point. It only distorts the election, giving a few 'swing states' (which are accidental) the privilege to decide for the entire country and making the outcome of elections erratic.

The evolutionary perspective is relevant. If the election scheme is carefully designed, the result will have continuity, because the individual moral judgments are, and will be, grounded in the ethical engenes, which will remain substantially the same in the foreseeable future. The moral basis of our democracies will last for hundreds or thousands of years – provided the democratic institutions last.

So much about number one, the decision. We need to choose what is right and wrong. Next, we must see that we have institutions that guarantee a lawful state according to the constitution. This is number two, the institutions.

III.2.4 Preserving the Lawful State

Understanding how easily a political leader, and even a legitimate government, can exploit the discontent of people to mobilize the power of hate of the Strife engene, we come to appreciate the division of powers in a democracy, specifically the fundamental importance of the judiciary and the legislative being independent of the executive. The suspension of civil rights and the muting of the parliament by the government of the Weimar Republic opened the door for

Hitler, the Nazi terror, and the initiation of a war that would cost 50 million people their lives.

Indeed, the rule of law is the most important condition for a society that supports human dignity. Dictators have always tried to bend the law by installing judges and manipulating courts. The Nazi party began to replace judges and attorneys as soon as they came to power, resulting in a nightmare of lawlessness.

There is also a danger today that courts become politicized. When the U.S. Supreme Court decides who is the legitimate president after an election, as it did in 2000, or when it declares that a constitutional right that was upheld for 50 years from now on no longer exists, like a woman's right to abortion, it is clear that these decisions reflect the personal political and moral convictions of a few judges but do not honor the will of the people. When courts make decisions that ought to be made by the legislature it means that the lawful state is compromised.

Fateful role of the police

The end of the Weimar Republic also gives us another warning: the importance of the police being loyal to the constitution. In the days of the crisis with growing radicalization and street demonstrations by Communists and Nazis, it became clear that the police force was anything but loyal to the constitution; it was already subverted by Nazis.

From the above discussion of the roots of the political Right and Left, we can understand that the police were in a dilemma; not only then, but in general. Police represents authority, law and order, the authority of the state. In general their main occupation is to protect safety and private property. Protecting authority, law, order, and property are the archetypal functions of the Strife engene. In the political spectrum these functions are claimed by the Right. The Left is generally more anti-authoritarian and anti-conservative. While the leftists proclaim free love, conservatives are appalled by that and see themselves as the guardians of moral laws; where 'moral', as we saw above, applies primarily to women, translating into oppression of women's rights. In this dilemma, the police naturally side with the Right. They must be Right, else they would be wrong. However, the Right agenda tends to violate basic human rights that are agreed upon by modern democracies, like gender equality and freedom from religious patronizing. It endangers even equality before the law because rich people can afford better lawyers. Even in today's Germany with its bad experience, crimes of Right-extreme terrorists killing perceived immigrants were neglected or covered up for decades, and only recently the government recognized that part of the police has obviously been blind on the right eye. Because of that natural dilemma, a democratic society must take special care to create a police force that is loyal to its values.

After what we said above about the nature and function of the police, this seems a task like the quadrature of the circle; but it is feasible. Indeed, the Swiss have come close to the ideal. Having grown up in Germany, I was surprised, well, amazed, by how the Swiss police, and state officials in general, perform their jobs like any other citizens, correct and polite, without the kind of aloof and threatening attitude that we are used to in Germany and the U.S. (Switzerland might not be the only country to have achieved that; I know only those three countries sufficiently well). Perhaps the attitude of the police is a function of the political polarization of a country and the general political maturity of its citizens, the former having a negative influence, the latter a positive.

Needless to say that similar care should be taken in procuring teachers for public schools, although in the education system the task is easier because the candidates have better education and teachers are naturally motivated for teaching. Here we don't face a basic dilemma like that of the police job. Interestingly, public school teachers in Switzerland are paid well and have the secure status of government officials; they are not hired and laid off according to changing demands and fluctuating budgets. It's a privileged position, and consequently the quality of teachers is high.

Police and the racial divide

In the case of the police, the situation is aggravated if there is a racial divide. In a country like the U.S. in which many Whites depreciate the African American minority, the chance is high that White police officers treat members of the minority unfairly, with the result that the latter will hate the police and defy its authority. In this case, the police will feel their authority challenged and be tempted to use force, defending not only the authority of the state, but also the dominance they feel entitled to as Whites. In the extreme, they will violently act out their racist prejudice and hate. It also happens, tragically, that Black officers abuse their authority against Black citizens presuming their inferiority. The situation is complicated because Black people in the U.S. are not just a minority like any other, but are generally descendants of slaves; their ancestors were not immigrants, but the victims of a horrible injustice committed by the ancestors of the White ethnicity. And then there is the broken promise after the civil war to give each family of former slaves 40 acres of land. White officers will tend to suppress the notion of these historical facts in their mind, because the possibility that the Black minority could demand vindication of the historical crime is an unpleasant thought, and that suppression will produce additional aggression.

Behavior in critical situations is not rational, and the two coercive forces of the Strife engene, one claiming racial supremacy and the other obedience to the authority, is hard to control by the ethical engenes. That is why law enforcement in America is in a very difficult situation, and it is actually remarkable that in the overwhelming majority of instances the police are fair and correct. The terrible exceptions of violence and vigilantism show, what we have seen again and again, that behavioral engenes, and specifically the ethical engenes, are expressed to different degrees in the individuals; there is a distribution: in most police officers, the ethical engenes are in control despite the difficult situation; the problem lies in the fringes of the distribution.

Recognizing the importance of the attitude of the police in critical situations, in addition to the regular challenges of the job, it is clear that a society must pay special attention to this institution. The dilemma explained above, and knowing its evolutionary roots, mandate not only the best education and training for police officers, but also that the state be able to screen the candidates to exclude extreme authoritarian-leaning and potentially uncontrolled individuals. Thus, the salary should not only be adequate for the known challenges officers face; it should be sufficiently high to attract enough candidates so the government can select. To make the screening discrete, a two-stage selection scheme could be adopted: first, candidates are selected according to the scores of a screening test (which are not disclosed to the candidate), and from those with passing scores a fraction is then selected by lottery. Psychologists have clever ways of designing tests that subjects cannot fake based on knowing the aim of a test,[149] and the lottery adds a true random effect that underscores the fairness of the scheme. An important part of course is education and instruction according to the goal of serving a fair society. A reorganization of the police force like this must be implemented from top to bottom of the command hierarchy. A well-formed police force will gain recognition by the public, which will add prestige to the job that is often lacking in countries in which the police is in a desolate state. Needless to say, one can select among candidates only if the salaries are attractive, requiring additional funding for police departments, rather than defunding as some critics demand.

---

[149] M R Banaji, "Implicit attitudes can be measured." In H. L. Roediger, III , J. S. Nairne , I. Neath , & A. Surprenant (Eds.), The nature of remembering: Essays in honor of Robert G. Crowder (pp. 117-150). Washington, DC: American Psychological Association (2001).

The point is, again, that the behavioral engenes that form a personality are expressed to different degrees in each person, and education and training have only a limited effect. Ignoring this leads to failure after failure, and every time a person dies in the hands of police the enraged public calls the officer a murderer and demands harsh punishment. Brutal action with deadly outcome is not necessarily murder. How could the prosecution ever prove that the death of the victim was intended? The court will not deliver the expected harsh sentence, leaving the public frustrated. Punishment offor excessive violence does not correct for the basic mistake of having recruited the wrong persons for the police job. Harsh punishment would enrage all the police officers who are doing their job correctly and would make future recruiting more difficult. In all likelihood the prospect of harsh punishment would not dissuade officers against using excessive force because behavior in critical situations is guided by compulsive engenes, and police behavior is no exception. The threat of harsh punishment will not change the behavior of someone who cannot control the force of the Strife engene claiming obedience to authority and asserting racial supremacy. The behavior is the response of that engene, it is not under rational control. Excessive demands for punishment are also irrational, a product of the ethical engenes: harsh punishment serves to satisfy the thirst for justice of the enraged people but does not solve the problem of having the occasional wrong person on the job.

Consider the present practice of recruiting. The following information is from the USA Today Classifieds Blog "8 Requirements to Become a Police Officer."[150] It first lists some basic requirements like minimum age and clean record, and mentions a psychological evaluation: "This determines if you have any emotional or mental conditions that could interfere with your duties." This reflects the standard belief that people are either normal, or have mental conditions, and those need to be excluded. Some college credits are also required, and a written entrance exam will test the candidate's reasoning and problem-solving abilities. Many academies value clarity of writing (e.g., being able to file incident reports). Important of course is the physical examination: "Police officers need to be in top physical condition in order to carry out their duties." Accepted candidates will receive "12-14 weeks of training, where they will learn about civil rights and law at both the state and federal levels" and will "also learn about accident investigation and traffic control, learn about security cameras, a basic understanding of how to use a computer." And: "Of course,

---

[150]   https://classifieds.usatoday.com/blog/careers/8-requirements-become-police-officer/, accessed 6/10/2020

you'll go through extensive firearms and self-defense training. You'll also learn about first-aid and emergency response to an extensive degree." – A lot to learn in 12-14 weeks! Finally, the last point, "Principled Conduct," gives a vague description of the difficulties, "The job itself requires officers to not only enforce the law. It also entails that they carry themselves in an ethical manner. As a cop, you'll interact with a wide range of people on a daily basis. You'll encounter people from a variety of racial, social, and religious backgrounds. It's your job to act objectively while still in accordance with the law. This demands a great deal of patience and respect" etc. And the ad concludes, "Becoming a police officer is not easy. But after all the blood, sweat, and tears, earning your police badge will feel dignifying."

What kind of persons will this ad attract? Obviously men (and women?) in top physical condition who like extensive firearms and self-defense training, and who look forward to wearing the "dignifying police badge." Similar as in the recruiting of Navy Seals, this ad appeals to the pride of candidates and lures them with the promise of status and self-fulfillment, a cheap trick that saves the state salaries for a job that is inherently difficult and dangerous.

In 12-14 weeks of training which covers firearms, self-defense, first aid emergency response, new technologies and more, how much time will there be to impart knowledge in laws and ethical conduct? Given the general difficulty of enforcing the law, and the additional problem of representing the authority of the state in a society with a racial divide, thus little training seems ridiculous. If one lures young men with the promise of extensive weapons training, the dignifying police badge, and the prospect of representing the authority of the state, how can one expect the result to be officers that respect the constitutional values when dealing with young men of a racial minority who hate the police and defy its authority?

Knowing about the existence of innate behavioral engenes like those that claim racial supremacy and demand obedience to authority, and their control by the ethical engenes, and understanding how the strengths of these engenes vary across people, it is clear that the solution must be selection during recruitment. After the recent death of George Floyd under the heavy knee of a police officer a chorus of publications of institutions and societies seeking to position themselves favorably in the dispute called this new incident of police violence "a reminder of the persistent systemic racism in the U.S. and elsewhere." I think it is rather a reminder of the wrong way we have designed the institution of law enforcement, and we may not have to wait until the persistent systemic racism in the world goes away to fix that problem.

The present practice of recruiting police officers is not going to weed out racists and individuals that are all too eager to use force and apply the firearms entrusted to them. Rather, it will enrich the sample of police recruits with young men who love a job that gives them the authority to do so. Assuming that people who sympathize with ethnocentric, xenophobic, and racist ideologies make up about 15 percent of the entire population, as recent election results in Western countries suggest (Table 3), the percentage of such people among the police is probably higher than that, perhaps as high as 50%. In contrast, by using the appropriate selection scheme, one might be able to reduce it to a level that will make the police an institution the country can be proud of.

Of course I do not doubt that authoritarian mindset and a prerogative for racial supremacy are to a large extent the product of education and environment. Sons learn from their fathers. The point is, there is *also* a genetic disposition, and that disposition *varies across people*. Improving the candidate selection scheme is important whether the variation comes from family tradition or genetic makeup. The difference is that, if those negative traits were entirely a matter of tradition, we would expect that with good education they would gradually disappear, and society would become less and less racist over time. But if there is a genetic component, as I argue in this essay, this expectation will be thwarted; as new brains are born those traits will always reappear. Thus, what may seem like an academic subtlety has consequences of historic importance.

III.2.5 More About Elections

As pointed out, the basic task of a modern democracy must be to have people use their intuitive judgment to choose, within the frame of the constitution, what is right and wrong. This needs to be done by voting. In most countries people can vote from the age of 18 and can be elected for office from the age of 25. There seems to be a consensus that the opinions of people under the age of 18 are worthless; supposedly they are not able to make good decisions, and in fact need to be excluded because their votes might dangerously contaminate the result. This apparent consensus may have originated from a general mistrust against popular voting of the founding fathers of modern democracies, since they also excluded women, and, in the case of the election of the president of the U.S., they opted for the scheme of the electoral college which was meant to entrust the actual decision to a small group of men that were elected by the people of each state. Thus, the people would elect the men of their trust, and those wise men would then elect the president. It seems clear that the foundation of the American democracy was influenced by engenes of patriarchal hierarchical order.

Why not include young people?

I do not agree with the view that young people are unable to judge what is best for society. As high school teachers can attest, teenagers are quite intelligent. They might be short of attention span and interest in academic stuff, but their intellects are as good as those of adults. And young people in my view have excellent moral judgment, probably better than adults. Admittedly, they are still learning about the world, but their learning about the common cause could be much accelerated if they would share responsibility. And for the society it would be a boon to include more young people in the political decision making. Their fresh minds and idealism would compensate for shortage of knowledge (if there is any). Considering all this, it seems reasonable to lower the voting age to 15, or even lower. Obviously, this does not mean that society transfers the rule of power to teenagers; they would still constitute only a small percentage of the voters.

What happens around age 25

It is interesting to consider the biological basis of social behavior. Responsible behavior is related to the frontal lobe, which matures, as brain scientists have found, only around the age of 25; it takes that long until the pattern of connections assumes its final state. Insurance companies know that young men are more likely to take risks and consequently charge male drivers under the age of 25 higher premiums for liability insurance. One might take the insight of brain scientists as a fact, the development of the brain takes that long; until the age of 25 the brain is still immature (at least in men, it seems). But why does it take that long, whereas the body and other brain functions mature 5-10 years earlier?

In human evolution, the introduction of the two-parent family required that fathers take their share of responsibility for the family, which they were not doing before. This was a big innovation. Instead of just the mothers raising the kids, there were now two adults pulling together, and the two could divide the labor and specialize. Raising the babies of course remained the domain of the mother, but as the kids grew older, they would depend more on food provided by the hunting father, and they would need his protection against the dangers of nature as well as in the society where he could secure them a place in the hierarchy.

Around the age of 25 young men become fathers and the growing burden of responsibility for a family means a big change. Before, they seek adventures, explore their surrounds and quarrel with rivals. Human society needs warriors, and warriors must take risks. Thus, evolution has programmed a mental change to take place around the age of 25, from adventure-seeking risk-taking behavior to more reasonable responsible behavior, and from outward oriented to domestically focused actions, from the freedom of the lonely to the duties of procuring resources for the offspring, from revolutionary to conservative.

Also, as one can easily see in our society, once people have family, they are getting more concerned about *their* wellbeing than that of the public. Men are getting stressed to procure the resources, focus on their career and produce income – which is going to be taxed by the public. In short, 25 is the age when men become more conservative. This was quite obvious in the 1968-generation students whose minds were socially innovative and revolutionary until they entered the age of 'maturity' and took positions in companies, gradually ascending to more and more responsible levels. As CEOs, they forgot their youthful dreams altogether. In women the frontal cortex apparently matures earlier, around age 20, and their behavior is naturally more responsible early on, but women also get stressed when raising children while having to produce income at the same time, or attending to a career. This produces a similar change in behavior as in men, from idealistic to realistic, away from public and towards private concerns. The attitude of people might change again many years later when retirement takes away the stress, when they become grandfathers and grandmothers and begin to care about the world for their grandchildren.

As the development of the brain shows, the change from revolutionary to conservative behavior is biological, most likely programmed when evolution created the two-parent family which may have occurred millions of years ago; it is not merely a product of civilization. With the present age limit of 18 years, democratic elections mainly admit voters from the upper part of the age pyramid, which means that the vast majority of votes comes from people who are most concerned and stressed about their own lives and want to reduce any burdens imposed by the public, be they rightful or not. Adding young voters would reduce the prevalence of the mature generation that is overly concerned with their personal interests.

Why not give privilege to young people?

Another healthy modification of the election process would be to weight voters differently. It might be heresy to depart from the principle that each vote counts equally, which most people now regard as a fundamental law of democracy (although not so long ago it was accepted that women votes were weighted zero). But given the mental change around age 25 as described above and the corresponding shift of interest from public to private wellbeing, society should give young people the privilege of weighting their votes higher than those of older people. As it is now, the only privilege society gives to young men (and increasingly also to young women) is the privilege of being the first to die for their country. Weighting the votes according to the age of the voters would actually not violate the principle of equality because across life it would give every person the same degree of influence in politics, only that it would change with age. In the same vein, one might also consider giving older people increased weight in view of their greater experience and wisdom.

Should women rule the world?

In the same vein, should women not be given more weight than men? In section "Gender and society" I pointed out how female and male characters differ and how that difference manifests itself already at a young age. The contrast highlights a quality of women that Rilke praised in his poetry. And regarding politics, I have heard women sigh, "all would be better if women ruled the world." It is certainly true that men are generally more aggressive and more violent than women, and a lack of the compassion engene, which is common in men, is naturally rare in women because of their motherly disposition. Also, looking at the history of female leaders it seems that women are less likely to be obsessed with power.

But history also shows that their evolutionary endowment is not above all suspicion. Women enthusiastically applauded Hitler, more so than men, and the obviously autocratic and racist candidate in the 2016 U.S. presidential election got more votes from women than men. As already pointed out, when people in post-war Germany, years after the Nazi terror had been abolished, were asked how they judged the men who attempted to assassinate Hitler and were executed for it, the polls showed that most people still viewed them as traitors, and women more so than men. And recent studies in the U.S. found that among Whites, the proportion of people who think that White identity is important is higher among women than men.[151] While these accounts indicate a disposition toward obedience rather than thirst for power, both traits are children of the Strife engene, and the racist attitude proves that lineage. Thus, although less aggressive and more compassionate, women are no less under the power of the Strife engene

---

[151] Ashley Jardina, "White Identity Politics." Cambridge Studies in Public Opinion and Political Psychology. Cambridge: Cambridge University Press (2019). See also Seyward Darby, "Sisters in Hate. American Women on the Front Lines of White Nationalism." Little, Brown & Company (2020).

which boosts ethnic feelings and makes people attracted to men of power and eager to embrace autocratic rule.

And looking at the history of women in power we see an indication that the force of the Religious engene supporting the Strife engene might be stronger in women, which can be fateful. Examples are Queen Isabella the Catholic, who incited the Spanish inquisition, the merciless persecution of Jews and Muslims and anybody suspected to be unfaithful to the Catholic religion; and the recent case of Aung San Suu Kyi, prime minister of Myanmar and recipient of the Nobel Peace Prize, who showed that even a person that had been thoroughly exposed to the Western code of human values seemed to give preference to her ethnic-religious identity. When confronted with the genocide and expulsion of the Muslim minority by aggressive Buddhists, her ethnic-religious bond appeared to be stronger than her moral feelings.

Still, women have only rarely won leadership roles, and only recently, in the second half of the 20th century have their odds become more favorable. And when a woman did ascend to power, it happened perhaps because she had rather more male qualities letting her prevail against resistance, and in the end may not have been as free to rule as she intended. In recent decades, women in politics have generally proven to be efficient, more responsible and of higher moral quality than men. Thus, the leadership qualities of women might be quite different from the qualities of women as voters shown by the statistics mentioned above. The role of their evolutionary endowment is ambiguous, and regarding women in power, the jury is still out.

III.3 UTOPIAS AND ILLUSIONS

I believe that a few simple changes to the voting system in the wealthy countries could change the world. This may never happen, given that the country that is now the wealthiest, the United States, is unlikely to change its election laws substantially, because the constitution gives each state the right to determine how to use its allotted electors, and the winner-take-all regime maximizes a state's influence on the outcome of the presidential election. Still, there is hope; we need utopian dreams.

Most of us want a world where nobody has to fear for their life, for being tortured or starved. Most people I know expect, or hope, that progress in Enlightenment and education will get us there some time. In contrast, my utopia is based on an analysis of human nature, a realistic picture of the evolutionary engenes that all humans inherit. I think to expect that Enlightenment and education will rid us of the problems of aggressive nationalism, racism and social inequality is an illusion.

And religion? Is there any hope that Christianity will make the world better? The history of the colonization and Christianization of Latin America is not encouraging. Today, Christianity is the largest religion with 2.4 billion followers who think they are followers of Jesus Christ. When Jesus said "I am the Way, the Truth and the Life"[152] he said Way, not House, but the Christian Churches build the biggest houses in the world.

We cannot ignore the human biological heritage. Homo sapiens is the lone survivor of a long list of hominids; lone survivor for good reasons. Our last companion was the Neanderthal whose traces show that they were contemporaries of Homo sapiens, even living in the same regions. Homo sapiens wiped them out, either by force or by starvation. Both species competed for hunting grounds, caves, water, and other natural resources. Paleontologists and historians often point to climate change as the cause of the disappearance of the other hominids. Climate changes occur all the time, but ecological marginalization by competition comes first, and then a climate change finishes the job. It happens today when Amazonian indigenous ethnicities are pushed farther and farther into what's left of the virgin forest, until a drought or other natural cause finally wipes them out by starvation. It is a pattern that probably repeated itself many times since Homo erectus emerged. This is how the Strife engene evolved to its present strength, and no education or Enlightenment will make it go away.

The reason for hope are ethical engenes producing compassion, responsibility, honesty, and sense of fairness. They are strong in most people because they derive from the Family engene which is stronger than any other social engene in the near range. Strife and Religious engenes are only powerful because they have long-range forces; they can create "us" and "them" categories across entire populations. If one could only design the democratic institutions so that those long-range engenes cannot overwhelm the Family engene, a stable and fair society might be possible. One necessary condition is that laws are made according to the will of the majority. That's what elections are supposed to do. Elections can impart the Family engene with a wide range. Its range should also be extended more generally to all political decisions, and to have continuity between elections. With modern means of communication it should not be

---

[152] More lyric in German: „*Ich bin der Weg, die Wahrheit und das Leben.*" Comparing this with the reality makes me cry.

difficult to motivate people; marketing experts achieve it all the time when raising funds for non-profits by showing pictures of children in need on TV. Why not have referendums nationwide like Switzerland, where people vote several times per year?

Exploring how evolution may have laid the foundations of the human mind I have discussed many details – which seems unavoidable since the human mind is complex. My discussion is one attempt to understand where its peculiar traits come from. In this last chapter I will summarize what seem to me the most important points.

Understanding the evolutionary basis of the human mind is difficult and the scientific insight is scarce and often counterintuitive. Simply the thought of connecting mental processes to the genes makes people shake their heads in disbelief. How can something as complex as the human mind have evolved by evolution? Does the variety of human mental abilities not disprove the hypothesis that they have a genetic code?

The Evolutionary Basis of the Human Mind

To understand, we need to appreciate two important aspects of Darwinian evolution: the enormous expanse of time over which the genomes of the species have formed, and the variation of the genome of each species across its population at any point in time.

(1) During the unfathomably deep history of life on the planet unimaginable numbers of new features were created by mutations and continually tested by natural selection. This gigantic factory of mutation-and-selection explains the evolution of technically highly sophisticated organs such as eyes, nervous systems and brains, including the human brain. On the tree of evolution, the homo genus branched off from apes millions of years ago, the most recent branching being that from the chimpanzee line 6 million years ago. Bipedal hands-free running, hunting, and meat-eating creatures that science classifies as humans have existed for 2 million years, a short time compared to the ape branching points, but still enough time to accumulate significant mutations. Most of this took place in Africa, but about half a million years ago (and perhaps earlier) the first Homo species migrated out of Africa, populating Eurasia.

Curiously, our ancestors were not among those early emigrants; Homo sapiens appeared out of Africa only much later.

(2) The other important aspect is the variation. Variation produced by mutations is of course the basis of evolution; variation is innovation. But it also means that at any point in time the genome of a species varies across the population. In today's human population no two brains have the same genetic code, except for the rare occasions of identical twins, and even these brains develop differently because of variable gene expression and variable influences of environment and education. Genetic code does not mean stereotyped minds. The result of this inherent variability is that each of the behavioral engenes (as I call the inheritable behavioral programs) develops differently in different individuals, and part of this variation is innate, and most of what is innate is inherited. Whether it is language skill or mother love or religious intolerance, if we measured the strength of the underlying engene we would find a distribution across people; most are average, but some are far from the average. In a few individuals we would find the engene to be extremely strong, in others weak or absent altogether. A small defect of a certain gene, and its bearers cannot learn a language. Alteration of some other gene makes its bearers unable to recognize faces. Likewise, there can be defects in the genetic basis of the ethical engenes. Of course, one's upbringing can enhance or reduce the strength of an engene, but only so much. This roulette of variation, I argue, inevitably produces people who are possessed by an excessively strong drive to power and have no moral concerns. Looking at recent history we can see such individuals who became instruments in monumental breakdowns of human civilization. Some had good education and were liked in their family, but that did not change their mental disposition to commit horrible crimes because their judgments of good and evil, by nature, were conditional on ethnicity or race; and that could not be influenced by upbringing and education. If the Compassion engene is defective, I doubt that education can repair it.

Part I of this book is devoted to the question of the evolutionary origin of the engenes; why some have detrimental effects, and why these evolved at all. These questions led us to examine the principles of Darwinian evolution and to correct the common misunderstanding that its goal is to improve fitness for survival, whereas in fact evolution does not have a goal. Mutations are random and nature selects the genes that make individuals efficient in procreating a line of offspring, that is, producing offspring that are again able to produce offspring. It's nothing else, evolution is fundamentally open ended.

We also saw that the process of evolution inevitably includes what I call 'reflexive evolution', evolution of genetic code that merely improves spreading itself across the species instead of improving its fitness, and can even reduce fitness. Many inheritable patterns of behavior improve the chance of the agent to procreate her/his genes; not only behaviors that improve fitness and benefit the species, such as skills in foraging and brood care, but also skills in competing with rivals that do not provide any other benefits besides giving their genes a reproductive advantage. The advantage is relative to the genes of the rivals. One can easily see that instances of reflexive evolution must be widespread; it is inherent in the principles of evolution. Overall, reflexive and regular evolution must reach a balance, simply because only regular evolution improves the fitness of a species, reflexive evolution is merely an adornment.

Reflexive evolution is particularly strong in social species because a society provides many opportunities to compete. Consequently, many features of human society bear its signature. Several faculties have been proposed as defining the human species, such as the ability to make tools, the use of fire, and language, but I argue that the single most powerful trait that made Homo erectus and ultimately Homo sapiens conquer the world is society. Society gives the individual shelter, protection, and insurance. And society rewards. I don't see any other species in the mammalian animal kingdom whose existence depends so much on society as the human. As E.O. Wilson pointed out, in this sense humans resemble ants and bees.

And as human society formed over the eons, a number of social engenes with peculiar characteristics evolved, like a Brood-care engene that remains functional throughout life, and a continuously active Sex engene. Among the most remarkable innovations are engenes shaped by reflexive evolution. Because engenes are behavioral machines that consist of three components – a motivational mechanism that creates desire, an effector mechanism that initiates and controls action, and a reward mechanism that instills pleasure and satisfaction upon its completion – engenes control not only the behavior but also set the stage for activities of the mind, and hence human culture. Reflexive evolution developed and enhanced engenes with strong perceptual and emotional components because these are valued by society. While the ancient engenes served to procure nourishment and shelter and to secure offspring, the new engenes (based on reflexive evolution) provided pleasure and entertainment and other produces that the society rewards, including individual attractiveness and its corresponding sensitivity, behaviors of self-aggrandization and self-sacrifice. While the ancient engenes strengthened the species, the new engenes differentiated within the species. Thus, engenes produced and modified by reflexive evolution are at the root of a diverse range of human activities, from economic to political to cultural.

Considering the enormous time span of evolution makes us realize that much of what forms our society and determines our culture has roots that go back millions of years. Curiously, when sociologists talk about "evolution of culture" they usually refer to the historical past, or sometimes as far back as the Neolithic revolution. But that is a different concept of evolution that has nothing to do with the evolution we talk about here. "Evolution of culture", as they describe it, relies on tradition, and tradition is short lived (unless it is coded in writing). Great civilizations were completely forgotten after a few hundred years. The memory of human tradition does not last long, as the silent monuments of Tiwanaku and Chichén Itzá attest, whereas genetic code lasts almost forever. But gene mutations trickle at a constant rate, that is, the frequency of mutations per individual and generation is roughly constant, and, because the number of generations during the Neolithic is less than one percent of the number of generations since Homo erectus emerged, only a tiny fraction of what the mutation-and-selection process achieved since then likely comes from the Neolithic. Thus, what distinguishes us from Australopithecus was nearly all created during the Paleolithic.

Now, to understand the society that evolution created, I argue, we must look at the variation of those engenes across the population. The random process of mutations and other factors produce variability in the strength of any of those engenes, meaning that each has a bell-shaped statistical distribution that has its fringes: small proportions of individuals in which an engene is either overly strong or exceptionally weak. It is important to see that this is normal, an inevitable consequence of the laws of evolution. At this point, I think, a large part of the public is misled, adhering to the concept of normal versus pathologic, the idea that there are well-defined limits of what is normal, and that, what's outside the normal range, must be treated separately. For example, it is often argued that psychologists should be able to diagnose the pathologic in people who act out in mass-shootings. With the same expectation, the American government delegated a highly qualified psychologist to the Nuremberg trial to analyze the psyches of the Nazi leaders that were tried. This was certainly appropriate and gave important insights, but it did not, as far as I know, reveal anything peculiar in the 10 Nazi leaders that were found guilty of committing the most horrible crimes, except that most had above average IQ and above average self-esteem and no feelings of guilt or regret. That is, they were in the fringes of distributions with respect to a number of those engenes; presumably high regarding the Strife engene, and low regarding the Compassion and other ethical engenes.

Once we realize that people who are able to commit the most horrific crimes against humanity can be apparently normal persons in society, loving family fathers, well educated and cultured people, we need to understand how this is possible. The paradox, in the words of Hannah Arendt, is the banality of evil. To commit a monstrosity one does not have to be a monster. The resolution of the paradox is the presence of those very engenes in the population and their dual nature that creates leaders and followers, a drive to power on one side and loyalty and obedience on the other; sense of mission versus yearning for spiritual experience; extreme greed versus patient servility. The mutual excitation of the engenes in leader and followers produces the demonic power.

DEMOCRACY IN PERIL

Understanding that human social behavior has evolutionary roots makes us realize that education and environment have only limited influence on the progress of society. Every time a child is born it comes with that inheritance, and education and influence of civilization must start their work from scratch. We cannot merely wait for the progress of civilization to solve the problems of human society, such as genocide, exploitation, poverty, and injustice. Having grown up in a lawful, democratic state we may not see that some of those social engenes contradict our democracy. Engenes that produce chauvinist behavior and strife for autocratic rule, demanding a strong leader and obedient subjects in millions of people, are a powerful force against the egalitarian idea of society. We cannot ignore this.

But evolution has also endowed us with ethical engenes that produce feelings of compassion and responsibility and sense of justice. Democracy, we can say, is a rational construct that builds on those engenes. Based on the ethical feelings that are common sense, one can derive moral principles and a human rights catalog that are the basis of a lawful state. To establish a democracy then requires the design of institutions that create and protect a social order that honors those ethical feelings and guarantees those rights. I argue that moral intuition and sense of justice are faculties that have evolved as part of human society forming engenes. This insight gives hope. Future generations will have sense of justice and moral values just like our ancestors had. It also opens an unexpected perspective on democracy. Because we can trust that humans generally have good moral judgment, we can hope that moral values will prevail in our political system if we base decisions on the choice of a majority.

The edifice of democracy rests on the pillars of its institutions. But it is inherently unstable because humans inherit those contradictory social engenes. The Strife engene demands autocratic rule which contradicts the egalitarian liberal order; it promotes racial discrimination which contradicts sense of justice; it incites violence which contradicts responsibility and compassion. The pillars of the edifice may not hold up against these forces; they can have flaws that cause the edifice to crumble. I have recounted historical examples showing how flaws in the constitution can help an aggressive minority to abolish the lawful state. In the Weimar Republic, the polarization between extreme left and extreme right paralyzed the parliament, helping the Nazi party to seize power without being legitimized by a majority of votes of the people. In the U.S., the two-party system allows an aggressive racist minority to control one of the parties, pushing their presidential candidate through in the primaries, and, since the general election is essentially a roulette, to seize power and compromise the lawful state.

In my discussion of the Nazi regime and Hitler I concluded that it would be wrong to see Hitler as the demon that caused the disaster of the Second World War and the Holocaust. What was demonic was the power of the Strife engene present in millions of people. Hitler was a normal person except that he had a strong drive to leadership and strong racial sentiments and no moral issues, qualities that, in a population of millions, are shared by many. Like other historical figures, Hitler used the opportunity of an economic crisis to excite the people's Strife engene which brought him millions of followers, and he took advantage of a weakness of the democratic institutions to grab power. It is important *not* to understand this as the work of the unusual demagogic power of one man, or the result of a unique historical constellation. Hitlers are everywhere, and economic and political crises occur all the time, and the Strife engene is still with us. And democratic institutions, unfortunately, still have weaknesses today. It can happen again. This conclusion makes me uneasy, and that is why I wrote this book.

AFTERWORD

Reflecting upon the purpose of my writing, I come back to what I said in the beginning, a plea for a rational understanding of human nature. Not because "rational" is superior, but because only rationally we can understand the cohabitation of feeling and reasoning in the human mind.

Indeed, human behavior is to a large extent intuitive, motivated by mechanisms that are grounded in evolutionary heritage. Only occasionally people use rational thinking, such as when they consider the price of something they want to buy, or when they think about the future consequences of an intended action. That is, people use rational thinking once in a while to supplement their intentions that are themselves irrational. I do not exempt myself from this assessment. If I decided to be philanthropic and spent my money according to the principle of justice, I would still give in to the drive of the 'Family engene' and give preference to my children and grandchildren. Every marketing expert knows that people's decisions are irrational. It is key to manipulating the behavior of the consumer. Not the individual but the millions.

Still, when it comes to understanding the human mind, we hesitate to trust rational insight. It is hard to accept that the historical facts recounted under "What it did" could be rooted in human nature, could be "normal" in the sense of evolution. So, time and again we reject the rational insight and rather believe that the horrible was an unfortunate exception, that the masses were seduced by a vile leader, that they accepted cruelty and lawlessness unknowingly, or unwillingly, that the reason for the behavior of a mass murderer must be a childhood trauma, et cetera. We find it easier to accept historical accounts of the events or psychological 'explanations', rather than accepting the truth that those behaviors are natural, the result of ancient behavioral modules that are still present in today's people.

Exercising rational insight does not mean that we should repress the irrational. On the contrary, we must understand it because it is the core of our nature. 'Engenes' move our behavior throughout the day, day in and day out. They give us values and desires that motivate us to act. Rational understanding

267

is often decried as cold and austere, or as contradicting our deeply felt beliefs and values. Some might fear that theorizing about the roots of emotions would interfere with their emotions. But understanding the evolutionary origin of love makes love no less powerful, and thinking about the origin of shame does not make shame go away.

Many will object to the implication that religiousness has evolutionary roots. It is not meant to interfere with anybody's beliefs, but simply to open the reader's eyes to the origins of human social behavior. Appreciating the evolutionary ground of religion makes us see the danger looming when the power of religion is subjugated by the Strife engene, the most fateful product of human evolution that creates the categories of "us" and "them", breeding bigotry and evil nationalism.

Also regarding democratic elections it is important to see that most people vote by their gut feelings. Their decisions are largely emotional, not rational. But democracy *is* a rational construct, a building that protects our rights and values. We live in that building, and we must protect it. We must not allow voters to damage the building. Voting enables democracy because most voters have good intuitions and sense of justice, but the democratic institutions must not be up to voting.

In particular, a political leader who intends to unhinge the lawful state should not be allowed to run for president or other public office. When German voters helped Hitler to power despite his previous insurrection attempt and his declared intent to unhinge the constitution, it could happen because the Weimar constitution did not have a clause to prevent it; something like the 'Disqualification Clause' in the Fourteenth Amendment of the Constitution of the United States. Unfortunately, when a political party concerned about the upcoming election warns "Democracy is on the ballot" they seem to have forgotten that clause. The democratic institutions must not be subjected to the irrational forces of an election. This is particularly important in the U.S. where the outcome of the general elections is erratic because it depends on a small percentage of 'swing voters' in a handful of 'swing states', not the entire country. If the democratic institutions need to be adjusted, it must be by amending the constitution, which requires experts pondering the principles and technicalities of democracy. Any repair must again be a rational construct. Entrusting the fate of our democracy to the ballot shows a dangerous misunderstanding. Why is the Clause not applied to a potential candidate in 2024 who disqualified himself when instigating the insurrection of January 6, 2021? Allowing this candidate to be on the ballot means gambling with democracy.

Picture Credits

Plate 1. Louvre Museum. Photograph Wikimedia Commons, licensed by Creative Commons Attribution-Share Alike 2.0 Generic.

Plate 2. Reproduced from

https://it.wikipedia.org/wiki/Callicebus_donacophilus.

Photography (A) Grendelkhan, (B) Lea Maimone.

Plate 3. Reproduced, with permission, from: Das Goldene Wilhelm Busch Album, Fackelträger Verlag, Hannover, 1959.

Plate 4. © 2023 Artists Rights Society (ARS), New York / VG Bild-Kunst, Bonn.

Book cover by the author, based on cave painting in Carricola, Spain. Photo Norbert Hentges.

Acknowledgments

I want to thank my dear friends who commented on earlier versions of my manuscript: Edwin Gould who, after reading the Introduction, said the best critique I would get if I asked the critics of E.O. Wilson's "Sociobiology" (an advice that I did not heed); Barbara Leons, Ken Nakayama, Ernst Niebur, Lothar Spillmann, Magda von der Heydt-Coca, and Gerald Westheimer. Special thanks to Lothar, Ken, and Ernst for their critique and detailed comments. I am also grateful to Philipp Kaufmann and for pointing out important books to read and to Tsela Döbeli for discussion.

As to the origins of my thinking, I want to acknowledge the German education system which in my time was free, from elementary school to graduation from university. The public schools were good – private schools were thought to be for problem children. At the Max-Planck Gymnasium in Göttingen instruction in physics was excellent. But I was most impressed by a biology teacher, Manfred Büttner, who introduced me to Alexander Oparin's "The Origin of Life", Grey Walter's cybernetic tortoises, and I. M. Bochenski's "Die zeitgenössischen Denkmethoden" ("The Methods of Contemporary Thought"). At the university I was free to study what I liked as long as I passed the exams required by the physics curriculum, with the result that it took me six years

269

instead of the regular five to get my degree. I sat in on many courses just for fun, like "The Origin of Man," read by Gerhard Heberer, professor of zoology and anthropology at the University of Göttingen, courses on formal logic, the foundation of the number concept, depth psychology, and graphology. I loved Herbert Schober's course on physiological optics at the University of Munich which enticed me to embark on vision research.

About the Author

Joachim Rüdiger von der Heydt is a professor emeritus of the Johns Hopkins University. He is recognized for his contributions towards understanding the neural processes underlying visual perception, subjective contours, and figure-ground organization (published under the name Rüdiger von der Heydt). He is the recipient of the 1986 Alfred Vogt Preis of the Swiss Ophthalmological Society and the 1993 Golden Brain Award of the Minerva Foundation, Berkeley, California.

Detailed Table Of Contents